Environmental Injustice in the United States

Environmental Injustice in the United States

Myths and Realities

James P. Lester
Colorado State University

David W. Allen
Colorado State University

Kelly M. Hill
former policy specialist, National Conference of State Legislatures

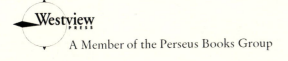
A Member of the Perseus Books Group

Copyright © 2001 by Westview Press, A Member of the Perseus Books Group

Published in 2001 in the United States of America by Westview Press, 5500 Central Avenue, Boulder, Colorado 80301-2877, and in the United Kingdom by Westview Press, 12 Hid's Copse Road, Cumnor Hill, Oxford OX2 9JJ

Visit us on the World Wide Web at www.westviewpress.com

Library of Congress Cataloging-in-Publication Data
Lester, James P., 1944–2000
    Environmental injustice in the United States: Myths and realities. / James P. Lester, David W. Allen, and Kelly M. Hill.
        p.   cm.
    Includes bibliographical references and index.
    ISBN 0-8133-3819-0
    1. Environmental justice—United States   2. Environmental justice—Political aspects—United States.   3. Social justice.   I. Allen, David W.   II. Hill, Kelly M. (Kelly Marie)
III. Title.

GE180 .L47   2000
363.7'05'793—dc21   00-043787

The paper used in this publication meets the requirements of the American National Standard for Permanence of Paper for Printed Library Materials Z39.48-1984.

10   9   8   7   6   5   4   3   2

Dedications

As former Prime Minister Margaret Thatcher once said, "Truth is too precious to become the slave of fashion." I dedicate this book to those students of mine who have an inquiring mind and the ability to question conventional thinking about public policy issues.

James P. Lester

I dedicate this book to my father, W. R. Allen, now deceased, and my brother, Robert J. Allen, for their infinite patience and encouragement through the years. Part of this book belongs to Beverly Blair Cook, Cornelius Cotter, and James Gibson—all of whom taught me my trade yet remain blameless for what I did with the lessons. I would also like to thank John Albright, Manfred J. Enssle, and Thomas Knight, who, collectively, listened to the story of the project more times than anyone has a right to expect. Finally, this book is for W. B. Yeats, Dylan Thomas, and Lawrence Ferlinghetti—simply because you cannot read quantitative literature all the time and remain sane.

David W. Allen

Dedicated to the memory of Weldon K. Hill—my grandfather, my mentor, my friend.

Kelly M. Hill

In memorium
James P. Lester, 1944–2000

Contents

Figures and Tables

Figures

ix

Tables

Preface and Acknowledgments

The expression "environmental racism" is defined as "race-based discrimination in environmental policymaking; race-based differential enforcement of environmental rules and regulations; the intentional targeting of minority communities for toxic waste disposal and transfer and for the siting of polluting industries; and the exclusion of people of color from public and private boards and commissions, regulatory bodies, and environmental non-profit organizations" (Collin, 1993).

Although the issue of environmental racism has existed at least as long as the environmental movement itself, it received serious attention only in the 1990s. Indeed, African Americans in Louisiana and Mississippi contend that state decisions involving hazardous waste treatment plants have had the effect of unfairly exposing them to more toxic pollutants than is the case for white citizens. They assert that the state's permit procedures, which are supported by federal money, are partly to blame. These claims caused Bill Clinton's administration to agree to investigate complaints that Louisiana and Mississippi were violating the civil rights of African Americans by permitting industrial pollution in their neighborhoods at a rate far greater than is the case for white neighborhoods. Specifically, the federal Office of Civil Rights, located within the U.S. Environmental Protection Agency (EPA), notified the two states in question in October 1993 that it had opened an investigation under the 1964 Civil Rights Act, which bars discrimination in federally funded programs.

In contrast to the argument that prompted an investigation under the 1964 Civil Rights Act, others argue that state officials are not deliberately steering pollution toward black communities. Rather, factors other than racism—such as the cost of land, population density, and geological conditions—have dictated the location of such noxious facilities. At any rate, in 1992 EPA established the new Office of Environmental Equity to address issues associated with environmental racism, and on February 11, 1994, President Clinton issued Executive Order No. 12898, requiring federal agencies to avoid inflicting disproportionate environmental harms on minorities and the poor.

Despite growing interest in this thesis, until the mid-1990s there had been limited systematic research—whether at the state, county, city, or neighborhood (i.e., census tract or ZIP code) levels—that examined the idea of environmental injustice. Most empirical work has focused on the disparities in environmental quality caused by the siting of industrial and waste disposal facilities in black and Hispanic communities. However, much of the current literature does not pay sufficient attention to the distinctive social, economic, and political forces that affect these siting decisions; neither does it rely upon a rigorous assessment of the unique effects of each of these variables on environmental quality outcomes. Such an analysis is essential in order to understand the race- and class-based equity issues associated with environmental policy. Thus, the fundamental purpose of this book is to provide systematic insight into the social, economic, and political dynamics of environmental decisionmaking and the impacts of those decisions on minority and poor communities.

During a five-year project such as this, one incurs many debts. The idea for this book began in a graduate seminar, "The Politics of Growth and the Environment," taught by James Lester in 1992.

David Allen joined the project in 1994 with a grant from the College of Liberal Arts at Colorado State University in Fort Collins. This grant enabled us to hire a research assistant and to begin the process of collecting data and reading existing work on the topic; Kelly Hill was very helpful in this regard. In addition, she also prepared much of Chapters 2 and 3.

The Western Political Science Association (WPSA), through its annual meetings in 1994, 1995, and 1996, provided an outlet for presenting preliminary research results. We are grateful to Professor Debra Salazar of Western Washington University for organizing a panel on environmental justice at the 1994 WPSA meetings and including us on that panel. Professor Sheldon Kamieniecki of the University of Southern California allowed us to organize another panel at the 1995 annual meeting, and Professor Jane Bayes of California State University–Northridge also provided much support through her role as program chair for a similar opportunity at the 1996 meeting. The WPSA meetings in spring 1999 allowed us to present our complete findings and to discuss and compare our results with other environmental policy scholars, such as Christopher Foreman (of the Brookings Institution) and Evan Ringquist (of Florida State University). We are especially grateful to Professor Ringquist for sharing his results with us and for challenging our findings on several instances. Finally, we are very grateful for the support and encouragement we received from Loren Crabtree (provost) and Wayne Peak (chair of the political science department) at Colorado State University. Any errors or omissions in this book are the responsibility of the authors.

We must admit that at the outset of this project in 1994 we were skeptical of many of the *strident* claims regarding environmental injustice. However, our analyses (as well as our findings) over the past five years have caused us to reconsider our original positions.

James P. Lester
David W. Allen
Kelly M. Hill

I

Introduction
The Nature of the Problem

An emerging body of literature, collected under the genres of environmental racism or environmental equity, argues that unbalanced proportions of environmental hazards are located in black, Hispanic, and poor communities (see, e.g., Mohai and Bryant, 1992; Bullard, 1990a, 1993a; Capek, 1993; Jordan, 1980; Szasz, 1994; United Church of Christ, 1987). Sometimes the expression "environmental justice" is used in connection with this issue. This term, broadly defined, gives rise to at least two testable propositions: the environmental racism hypothesis, which maintains that unbalanced proportions of environmental hazards may be located in minority communities; and the environmental classism hypothesis, which focuses on whether the same problem affects poorer communities more so than affluent ones. Both hypotheses are important and, to a large extent, because of the environmental racism hypothesis, the topic of environmental justice has been called the "civil rights movement of the 1990s." Moreover, the growth of the environmental justice movement in the United States surprised even seasoned policymakers by its speed and the magnitude of its impact on national policy (Cutter, 1995; Goldman, 1992; Grossman, 1991).

A brief review of the history of this movement is instructive insofar as it illustrates how this issue rapidly arrived on governmental agendas. One of the first reports to document the correlation between toxic risk and income was the Council on Environmental Quality's (CEQ) 1971 annual report to the president. The CEQ report acknowledged that income disparities adversely affected the ability of the urban poor to elevate the quality of their environment. Environmental justice became a nationally recognized issue in 1982, when a protest in Warren County, North Carolina, resulted in a request for the U.S. General Accounting Office (GAO) to study hazardous waste landfill siting in EPA Region 4. The GAO study found that three of four commercial hazardous waste facilities were in predominately African American communities and that the fourth was in a low-income community (U.S. General Accounting Office, 1983). This was followed by the United Church of Christ Commission for Racial Justice study, which found that race, not income, was the major factor that was significantly related with residence near a hazardous waste site (United Church of Christ, 1987).

In the early 1990s, the environmental justice movement began to significantly affect national policy. Two major environmental justice conferences were held during 1990–1991. An outcome of these conferences was the formation of the Michigan Coalition—a group of social scientists, civil rights leaders, and environmentalists interested in making environmental justice a national policy issue. In response to concerns of the Michigan Coalition and of the U.S. Congressional Black Caucus (CBC), the EPA formed the Environmental Equity Workgroup, whose findings were reported in a two-volume report (U.S. Environmental Protection Agency, 1992a, 1992b). Shortly thereafter, in November 1992, the Office of Environmental Equity was established within the Environmental Protection Agency, and in February 1994 President Clinton signed Executive Order No. 12898, which requires every federal agency to achieve the principle of environmental justice by addressing and ameliorating the human health and environmental effects of the agency's programs, policies, and activities on minority and low-income populations in the United States (Bullard, 1994a; Cushman, 1993, 1994). In addition, during late 1994 and early 1995, EPA produced a draft proposal for an "environmental justice plan," and several bills have been introduced in Congress to deal with the issues associated with environmental justice.[1]

Why Study Environmental Justice?

There are at least three reasons for studying environmental justice. First, the conventional logic is that environmental injustice is a fact of life. Both conventional logic and popular opinion seem to assume that communities of color and the poor are adversely affected by exposure to toxic hazards. This view is reflected in the media, in popular magazines, and among many students of environmental politics and policy. Yet such assumptions may be unwarranted or misplaced to some extent. For example, class—more so than racial classification—may be highly correlated with exposure to toxic hazards. Other factors, such as the location of manufacturing plants, may have caused low-income individuals or persons of color to relocate near the source of jobs.

Second, there is still a lack of systematic research (i.e., multilevel analysis) that seeks to understand the relationships among such variables as race, class, political mobilization, and exposure to toxic hazards at various levels. Thus, while research conducted during the mid- to late-1990s is relatively sophisticated, it is still limited in many ways. We discuss the nature of these limitations in Chapters 2 and 4.

Finally, we need to study environmental justice in order to provide a sound basis for policy design. One of our working assumptions in this book is that public policies should be designed on the basis of a competent and informed understanding of the relationships between race, income, politics, and exposure to toxic risks rather than solely on the basis of pressure politics from activist groups. The precondition of a competent understanding of relevant aspects of a societal problem thus allows design of policies that reach to the heart of a problem instead of merely raising false expectations that environmental harms will be ameliorated.

Thus, the primary purpose of this book is to systematically examine a fundamental question: When other explanations are held constant, does race, income, or political mobilization matter with regard to the distribution of environmental hazards such that we can impute discrimination in the level of environmental protection?

Examining the Environmental Justice Thesis: Conceptual Issues

In developing a model to guide our analysis, we followed the steps suggested by W.T. Morris (1970). Specifically, we surveyed the extant literature in order to piece together multiple explanations about the distribution of toxic hazards. This literature suggests four broad categories of factors that affect the distribution of hazards as well as their presumed effects.

Race and Ethnicity Factors

A growing body of literature demonstrates relationships between toxic facilities and African American and Hispanic communities (Mohai and Bryant, 1992; Bullard, 1983, 1993a; Bullard and Wright, 1992; Grossman, 1991; Jordan, 1980; Kazis and Grossman, 1983; United Church of Christ, 1987; U.S. General Accounting Office, 1983); that is, we find statements that, based on case studies of southern U.S. locations, contend that "black communities, because of their economic and political vulnerability, have been routinely targeted for the siting of noxious facilities, locally unwanted land uses, and environmental hazards" (Bullard, 1990a: xiv). Although most of the case-study evidence is based on locations in the South, one author argues that "it is clear that environmental inequities, social injustice, and racism (individual and institutional) are not limited to the southern United States" (Bullard, 1990a: xv). Indeed, research that studies Michigan (West, 1992), Detroit (Mohai and Bryant, 1992), Los Angeles (Burke, 1993), New Jersey (Greenberg, 1993, 1994), a broad range of counties (Hird, 1993), and the fifty individual states (Lester, Allen, and Lauer, 1994) would tend to support this proposition of nonregionality.

Thus, there is a body of evidence from both pre- and post-1992 research to support the ecoracism thesis; that is, race has been found to be either a statistically significant predictor (e.g., Burke, 1993; Gelobter, 1987, 1992; Harrison, 1975; Lavelle and Coyle, 1992; West, 1992; Zimmerman, 1993) or the most important predictor (e.g., Lester, Allen, and Lauer, 1994; Mohai and Bryant, 1992; United Church of Christ, 1987; Zimmerman, 1993) of exposure to environmental harms.

According to the predominant trend in the research, there should be a relationship between the percentage of the population that is black or of Hispanic origin and the location of noxious facilities in the United States.

Class Factors

There is also an economic dimension to the environmental injustice thesis, that is, because of economic vulnerability, the poor have been targeted for environmentally hazardous facilities (Bullard, 1990a: xiv). In other words, because the poor tend to reside in areas where the land is cheap—possibly caused by the presence of existing industry—new industries select these areas for the location of noxious facilities. Further, according to a 1983 study by the GAO, there was a strong relationship between the siting of hazardous waste landfills and the class status of the four surrounding communities (U.S. General Accounting Office, 1983). The GAO study revealed that one-fourth of the population in the communities under study had incomes below the poverty level. Finally, many studies have demonstrated that combined economic and racial inequities are associated with the presence of environmental hazards (e.g., Anderton, et al., 1994; Asch and Seneca, 1978; Berry, 1977; Bullard, 1983; Freeman, 1972; Gelobter, 1987; Greenberg, 1993; Hird, 1993; Kruvant, 1975; Lavelle and Coyle, 1994; Mohai and Bryant, 1992; United Church of Christ, 1987; U.S. General Accounting Office, 1983; Zimmerman, 1994), and some studies have indicated that class status alone predicts the existence of environmental harms (e.g., Asch and Seneca, 1978; Burch, 1976; Cutter, 1994; Hird, 1993; Kruvant, 1975; U.S. Council on Environmental Quality, 1971). Thus, in part, it is argued that class status is related to the risks posed by the location of toxic waste facilities and exposure to other noxious facilities.

Political Mobilization

It is also argued that black, Hispanic, and poorer communities have had few advocates and lobbyists at the national level and within the mainstream environmental movement. Thus, there is a potential relationship, it is argued, between the powerlessness of these groups and the siting of noxious facilities (Bullard, 1990a: 6–7). Only a few previous studies (Allen, 2001; Allen, Lester, and Hill, 1995; Crews-Meyer, 1994; Hird, 1993; Lester and Hill, 1995; Lester and Allen, 1996; Lester, Allen, and Lauer, 1994; Ringquist, 1995) have examined the relationship between political mobilization and exposure to toxic hazards.

Exogenous Factors

Although a general articulation of the environmental injustice thesis has focused on the relationship among race, class, and political mobilization as predictors of environmental hazards, other factors have begun to emerge in the literature, either by direct inclusion or by implication. In order to be inclusive, this research collects rival explanations under a single heading: exogenous explanations. Under this rubric, we refer to variables that have been included or implied in extant research but do not fall within any of the three traditional variants (race, class, political mobilization) of environmental justice. These exogenous variables include pollution severity, public opinion (partisanship and ideology), political culture, fiscal capacity, legislative professionalism, and organized interests. We explore the rationale behind the inclusion of each of these exogenous variables in Chapter 4.

Based on the race, class, political mobilization, and exogenous factors, the following general hypothesis is posited for testing: When all other explanations are held constant, the greater the ethnicity, the lower the level of social class, and the lower the degree of political mobilization, the greater the severity of exposure to adverse environmental quality outcomes.

Examining the Environmental Justice Thesis: Methodological Issues

There is also a set of methodological issues that has affected the study of environmental justice. To systematically examine the environmental injustice thesis, it should be probed within the context of multilevel analysis, multiple dependent variables, and across time. Figure 1.1 illustrates the complexity involved in an examination of the environmental injustice thesis.

Previous research on this topic has tended to examine this subject at a single level of analysis (e.g., the county) or within the context of a single dependent variable (e.g., hazardous waste sites), both of which are based on a single point in time. In this book we examine the question at three levels of analysis, including the contiguous forty-eight states, where we employ seven measures of environmental harms, 2,080 U.S. counties for which TRI

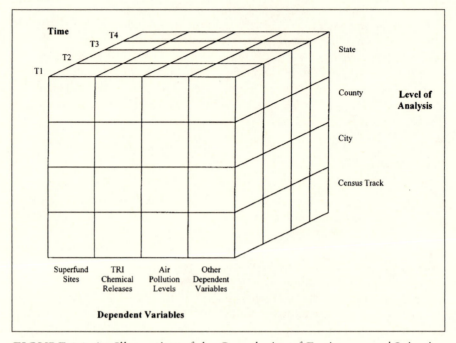

FIGURE 1.1 An Illustration of the Complexity of Environmental Injustice Analysis

(Toxic Release Inventory) data were available, and 410–414 U.S. cities over 50,000 population for which TRI data were available. We examine the relationships of several categories of explanatory variables to these environmental hazards.

The Plan of the Book

This book is intended to fulfill four primary purposes: First, we review the extant literature on environmental justice; second, we critique this literature from conceptual as well as methodological standpoints; third, we present empirical data on the nature of environmental threats at several different levels of analysis; and fourth, we draw conclusions and provide recommendations for policymakers. The book is organized into three parts. Part 1 discusses the origins of the environmental justice movement, outlines the patterns of research in environmental justice, and presents some unanswered questions in environmental justice research. Specifically, Chapter 2 reviews the evidence on environmental injustice from the earliest studies in the 1970s to the most recent studies in the late 1990s. Chapter 3 discusses how the issue of environmental justice arrived on the governmental agenda, using the framework suggested by John Kingdon (1995); Chapter 4 presents the model that guides our research in Chapters 5–7. Part 2 includes our empirical work that tests our hypotheses. Specifically, Chapters 5–7 analyze the relationships between race, class, political mobilization, and exposure to environmental hazards in U.S. states, counties, and cities when all other explanations are held constant. Chapter 8 recaps the conclusions from the empirical analyses contained in Chapters 5–7. Finally, Part 3 focuses on the development of a rational, equitable, and efficient policy to ameliorate environmental injustice. Specifically, Chapter 9 places the Chapter 8 conclusions against the backdrop of existing policies for mitigating environmental injustice in the United States. Then, Chapter 10 discusses several varieties of policies that might be designed to ameliorate environmental injustice and concludes with several specific recommendations for policymakers who are concerned with achieving environmental justice.

Notes

1. For example, in 1992, Representative John Lewis introduced the Environmental Justice Act (H.R. 5236); Senator Paul Wellstone introduced the Public Health Equity Act (S. 1841) in 1994; and Representative John Dingell introduced the Environmental Insurance Resolution and Equity Act (H.R. 228) in 1995.

2

Environmental Injustice Research: Reviewing the Evidence

The literature on environmental justice has been organized by some authors (Allen, Lester, and Hill, 1995; Cutter, 1994) under four headings, including: early descriptive literature (primarily case studies); normative and/or prescriptive studies; reviews and critiques of existing work; and data-based, quantitative studies. What follows is a review and critique of this literature.[1]

Early Descriptive Literature

This literature outlines the environmental justice movement's origins and also illustrates, primarily through case studies, a relationship between environmental disparities of various types, communities of color, and/or low-income communities. The earliest pieces focused on a dispute in Afton, North Carolina, over the siting of a soil dump contaminated with polychlorinated biphenyls (PCBs) in a largely African American community. Afton's population was more than 84 percent African American at the time; Afton is in Warren County, which in turn had the highest percentage of African Americans in North Carolina and was one of the state's poorest (Beasley, 1990a, 1990b; Bullard 1990a, 1990b, 1993a, 1994a; Carroll, 1991; Colquette and Robertson, 1991; Coyle, 1992; Geiser and Waneck, 1983; Hurley, 1988; MacLean, 1993; Maraniss and Weisskopf, 1987; Meyer, 1992; Spears, 1993; White, 1992). Other cases studies of Texarkana, Arkansas, Los Angeles, Detroit, St. Louis, Boston, and Buffalo also serve to exemplify environmental injustice as it applies to minorites (Attah, 1992; Boerner and Lambert, 1995; Burke, 1993; Jetter, 1993; Krieg, 1995, 1998; Lee, 1993; Mann, 1991; Szasz, et al., 1992). Questions have also been raised regarding inequitable siting of lo-

cally unwanted land uses (LULUs) in Latino and Native American communities (Angel, 1992; Beasley, 1990a, 1990b; Geddicks, 1993; Goldman, 1992;
Ong and Blumenberg, 1993; Ramirez, 1992; Russell, 1989; Satchell, 1992;
Schneider, 1994; Siler, 1991; Small, 1994). Latino claims regarding environmental inequities stress the need for examining the western and southwestern United States, which have large resident Hispanic ethnic communities
(Martinez, 1992; Southwest Organizing Project, 1983). In a different fashion, Native American claims about environmental inequities focus on extant
legal relationships—idiosyncratic to the junction between Native Americans and federal and state governments—as the root causes of environmental injustice (Geddicks, 1994). Further, other Native American claims are
more in the traditional realm of land use and takings (Angel, 1992; Beasley,
1990a; Geddicks, 1993; Ramirez, 1992).

Claims of environmental injustice are not confined to incidences of communities of color. Low-income communities in general have also been discussed in descriptive studies of inequitable LULU sitings (Beasley, 1990a,
1990b; Burch, 1976; Camia, 1993; Clean Sites, Inc., 1990; Davies, 1972; Freeman, 1972; Goldman, 1992; Gottlieb, 1992; Gould, 1986; Handy, 1977;
Kazis and Grossman, 1983; Truax, 1990; WIN News, 1992).

Other concerns raised by these studies focus on the health problems arising from toxic threats (Brown and Masterson-Allen, 1994; Grossman, 1991;
Rees, 1992; West, 1992). Responses to these toxic threats most often occur
after some type of health problem is noted in the community and attributed
to the existence of a site (Brion, 1988; Bullard, 1990a; Cable and Benson,
1993; Environmental Health Coalition, 1993; Fruedenberg and Pastor, 1992;
Glickman and Hersh, 1995; Inhaber, 1992; Moses, et al., 1993; Najem, et al.,
1985; Rios, Poje, and Detels, 1993; Sexton and Anderson, 1993; Thomas,
Noel, and Kodamanchaly, 1999; White, 1992). This literature maintains that
the adverse health problems attributed to various LULUs have a profound
effect on families. As a result, women have risen to the forefront of the
movement's community efforts (Chiro, 1992; Easton, 1992; Tailman, 1994;
WIN News, 1992). In addition to the health-concerns studies, the literature
investigates the proposition that people of color are more likely to be exposed to environmental hazards in the workplace (Edwards, 1992; Gottlieb,
1992; Hair, 1993; Lampe, 1992).[2]

Normative and Prescriptive Studies

Normative and prescriptive studies stress means to ameliorate a disproportionate, race- and/or class-based distribution of environmental hazards. For
example, one strand in this literature provides guidance to grassroots organizations by explaining how they can achieve environmental justice within
the current political system (Bruce, 1993; Bullard and Wright, 1992; Cama-

cho, 1998; Taso, 1992). Another strand reviews the history of litigation directed at countering environmental racism and injustice and reveals reliance on civil rights suits brought under section 1983 of the Civil Rights Act (42 U.S.C. 1983) and the equal protection clause of the Fourteenth Amendment. In relatively early legal actions, with the burden of proof resting with the affected community, discriminatory intent was difficult to establish because of inadequate historical data—although some federal lawsuits did bring remediation in some circumstances (Austin and Shills, 1991; Brown, 1992; Chase, 1992; Cole, 1992a, 1992b; Coleman, 1993; Collin, 1992; Colopy, 1994; Colquette and Robertson, 1991; Dubin, 1993; Godsil, 1991; Jones, 1993a, 1993b; Lazarus, 1993). The early lack of uniform results in federal court led some authors to recommend using state and local laws and procedures for remedying inequities (Cole, 1992a, 1992b; Keeva, 1994; Lyskowsi, 1994; Mitchell, 1993; Reich, 1992). However, more recent developments involving Title 6 of the Civil Rights Act of 1964, expanded action under interim guidelines by the EPA Office of Civil Rights, and a grant of certiorari by the U.S. Supreme Court in *Chester Residents Concerned for Quality of Living v. Seif* (132 F2d 925 [3d Cir 1997], cert. granted June 8, 1998 [97–1620]) may result in a new precedent that will allow environmental justice concerns to become a more permanent fact of EPA enforcement and compliance action (Chamber, 1998).

Another strand examines prevention, instead of amelioration, of environmental injustice (Bullard, 1994a, 1994b, 1994c). Some recommend that risk assessment during the siting process would allow officials to determine whether people of color and the poor would be disproportionately affected by potential risks, including assessment to ensure that environmental inequities do not result from a high concentration of sites, rather than from one particular site (Goldman, 1991; Harding and Holdren, 1993). This seems to be a current strategy of the EPA carried out under Title 6 of the Civil Rights Act of 1964 and a set of interim guidelines issued by EPA (Chamber, 1998). Prevention through proactive policymaking has also been advocated in other literature (Chase, 1992; Collin, 1992; Jones, 1993a, 1993b; Kraft and Scheberle, 1995; National Conference of State Legislatures, 1995; Ward, 1994).

Review and Critiques of the Literature

Extant critiques range from the examination of methods employed by existing empirical studies (Bowman, 1996; Cutter, 1995; Kamieniecki and Steckenrider, 1996; Mohai and Bryant, 1992) to criticisms of the movement's stakeholders and suggested policy solutions.[3]

Along methodological lines, critiques argue that sample selection is a crucial consideration; in particular, samples should include areas with and without environmental harms so that findings are not biased toward conclusions of environmental injustice (Boerner and Lambert, 1995; Gelobter, 1992; Waters, 1993). However, some also note that the sociohistorical contexts of these different areas must also be considered (Krieg, 1995, 1998). Moreover, S. Cutter (1995) argues that extant findings tend to depend on a mix of four conditions: the time frame of the analysis; the nature of the environmental threat studied; the groups included in the analysis (e.g., global measures of percent minority versus only African Americans and Hispanics versus other ethnic groups); and the level of the analysis employed (states, counties, cities, Standard Metropolitan Statistical Areas (SMSAs), or ZIP codes)—and that all these conditions should be considered when designing studies to assess evidence for or against environmental injustice.

Nonmethodological critiques assert that people of color and the poor have been excluded from the traditional environmental movement, including the fact that persons of color and the poor were not represented in leadership positions or on established committees or national mainstream environmental groups. The perception of elitism by people of color about the traditional environmental movement extended into the late 1990s, when several grassroots organizations publicly criticized the ten largest national environmental organizations for failing to represent minority concerns as legitimate environmental issues (Hahn-Baker, 1994; Lewis, 1992; MacLachlan, 1992; Rees, 1992; Sierra Club, 1993).

Further, as environmental justice garnered national attention with the establishment of the EPA's Office of Environmental Equity, critics began to question the effectiveness of the Environmental Equity Office and the seriousness of its efforts on behalf of minorities (Collin, 1992; Lavelle, 1992a; Mohai, 1993); others examined congressional hearings on environmental justice legislation (Lavelle, 1992a, 1992b, 1993).

Quantitative Studies

Quantitative studies tend to focus on either process or equity outcomes. The process studies look at causal mechanisms of inequity by examining the political mobilization of communities with regard to siting decisions. Some of these studies suggest that often minorities and the poor are politically inactive until a LULU becomes a problem in the community (Collin, 1992; Taylor, 1989). This may be due, in part, to either concerted industry efforts to place LULUs in areas where individuals lack the resources to oppose the siting decision, or as a result of so-called environmental blackmail (Kazis and Grossman, 1983).[4] Other studies reveal that race-based inequities occur not only in the process of siting decisions but also in connection with the enforcement of environmental laws (Cole, 1992a, 1992b, 1994; Colquette and Robertson, 1991; Lavelle and Coyle, 1992). However, most recent research indicates—insofar as U.S. district court decisions are concerned—that discrimination in enforcement decisions may be absent (Ringquist, 1998: 1162).

Outcome equity studies, like our book, look at the spatial-temporal distribution of environmental problems in relation to communities of color and the poor and have generated the majority of the quantitative literature on the subject. These studies divide into two general categories: market dynamics; and cross-sectional correlates/multiple determinants of environmental harms.

Market dynamic studies account for the volatile U.S. housing market. This literature first determines an area's demographic composition prior to becoming a LULU host. After establishing this baseline, the research determines if minorities and the poor suffer disproportionate exposure to real and potential environmental hazards because of inequitable siting decisions or due to other circumstances, such as housing discrimination or the location of jobs, which causes individuals to move into such environmentally undesirable areas (Hurley, 1988). Although the literature addressing this issue is considerably underdeveloped in comparison to other literature on environmental justice, studies that examine market dynamics report mixed results.[5]

Quantitative outcome equity studies, which have produced the majority of the quantitative environmental justice studies, test whether persons of color and the poor are disproportionately exposed to environmental harms in terms of either correlation or regression analysis using a cross-sectional design. Under these conditions, a positive relationship between race and risk is said to establish race-based environmental injustice. In contrast, a negative relationship between social class and environmental hazards is said to establish class-based environmental injustice. The studies in this area have been classified into pre- and post-1992 time periods (Allen, Lester, and Hill, 1995; Mohai and Bryant, 1992). Pre-1992 studies generally determined that race (either in the presence or absence of a control for social class) was associated with higher rates of exposure to environmental hazards for a variety of geographic areas, such as regions, counties, SMSAs, or ZIP codes, and for a variety of environmental harms, such as air pollution, solid waste, pesticides, hazardous waste, and toxins (Asch and Seneca, 1978; Attah, 1992; Berry, 1977; Bullard, 1983, 1990a; Burch, 1976; Clean Sites, Inc., 1990; Colquette and Robertson, 1991; Costner and Thornton, 1990; Davies, 1972; Dorfman, 1979; Fitton, 1992; Freeman, 1972; Gelobter, 1987; Gianessi and Peskin, 1980; Gianessi, Peskin, and Wolfe, 1979; Gould, 1986; Kohlhase, 1991; Kruvant, 1975; Lavelle and Coyle, 1992; Mohai and Bryant, 1992; United Church of Christ, 1987; U.S. Council on Environmental Quality, 1971; West, 1992; White, 1992). Some pre-1992 research did point to the environmental racism hypothesis as the predominant explanation for the frequency, distribution, and/or severity of environmental hazards; that is, among these cited studies in which a determination about the relative importance of race and class was provided, race was the most important predictor of risk in six cases (Freeman, 1972; Gelobter, 1987; Gianessi, Peskin, and Wolfe, 1979; Mohai and Bryant, 1992; United Church of Christ, 1987; West, 1992).

Post-1992 research continued the inquiry (Adeola, 1994; Allen, 2001; Allen, Lester, and Hill, 1995; Anderton, et al., 1994a, 1994b; Arora and Carson, 1999; Been, 1994, 1995; Boer, et al., 1997; Boerner and Lambert, 1995; Bowen, et al., 1995; Bowman and Crews-Meyer, 1995, 1997; Burke, 1993; Crews-Meyer, 1994; Cutter, 1994; Downey, 1998; Greenberg, 1993, 1994; Hamilton, 1993, 1995; Hird, 1993, 1994; Hird and Reese, 1998; Holm, 1994; Krieg, 1995, 1998; Lester and Allen, 1996; Lester, Allen, and Lauer, 1994; Mitchell, Thomas, and Cutter, 1999; Perlin, et al., 1995; Polloch and Vittas, 1995; Ringquist, 1995, 1996, 1997, 1998; Shaikh, 1995; Shaikh and Loomis, 1998; Stretesky and Hogan, 1998; Stretesky and Lynch, 1999; Szasz, et al., 1992; Yandle and Burton, 1996; Zimmerman, 1993, 1994). Some of this research points to additional explanations for environmental hazards, such as industry and manufacturing, political mobilization, population density, severity of the communities' overall environmental crisis, and transportation grids (Adeola, 1994; Allen, 2001; Allen, Lester, and Hill, 1995; Anderton, et al., 1994a; Bowman and Crews-Meyer, 1995, 1997; Burke, 1993; Hird, 1993, 1994; Hird and Reese, 1998; Holm, 1994; Lester, Allen, and Lauer, 1994; Lester and Allen, 1996; Mitchell, Thomas, and Cutter, 1999; Perlin, et al., 1995; Polloch and Vittas, 1995; Ringquist, 1995, 1996, 1997). Even with ancillary explanations, a set of basic conclusions remains constant. First, post-1992 research that analyzes only race and class correlations of environmental risk found that race is the most important predictor of risk. Second, post-1992 research that includes a battery of additional explanations finds that race and class still constitute a set of statistically significant predictors of risk; however, they are not consistently the most important predictors.[6] Given these findings, there are a number of conceptual and methodological issues that warrant additional consideration.

Major Conceptual Issues

A central conceptual issue focuses on defining what is meant by "environmental justice." First, there is the conceptual problem of rigorously defining exactly what we mean by the term itself. What exactly constitutes environmental racism? If full information is available about the environmental risks associated with the location, yet the minority community either does not take advantage of this knowledge—or simply chooses to ignore it—then does a condition of environmental racism exist? The countervailing response to this scenario would ask whether the decision by minorities to locate in environmentally undesirable areas is corrupted by such items as redlining, whereby persons of color, regardless of environmental hazards, are restricted in their choice of housing locations due to housing discrimination. Second, these statements could also be asked about low-income individuals, that is, regardless of the level of information about environmental hazards, low-income individuals and families may find that their choices of location are constrained by issues of affordable housing, notwithstanding issues of proximity to environmental dangers.

A second definition of "environmental racism," and the one we employ in our research, stems from cross-sectional outcome equity studies. This definition is based on the assumption that if environmental injustice exists then a statistically significant positive relationship should be evident between some measure of race and some measure of an environmental harm when all other explanations are held constant. Additionally, environmental injustice can be assumed to exist in the presence of a significant negative relationship between social class and environment harms when all other explanations are held constant. To use these definitions, two issues must be addressed: the definition of "race" and the conceptual model that is employed, that is, what controls will be imposed on the relationship between risk, race, and class?

Definition of "Race"

The definition of "race," given the limitations of existing data, tends to be fixed by major U.S. census categories: African American, Native American, Hispanic, and Asian American. Some research combines these categories into a "percent minority" variable. We think this strategy is flawed. Combining all four census categories into a global percent minority measure presents two problems. First, the census classifies Hispanics as being of any race, including black. Combining all four census categories into a global percent minority measure therefore creates an overcount and, in some cases, leads to population figures in excess of 100 percent. Second, and perhaps more important, comprehensive percent minority variables create a situation wherein it is not possible to determine if one minority group, subsumed within the comprehensive measure, is experiencing either more or less environmental injustice—or none at all.

Some research solves this problem by using, as individualized measures, all four racial/ethnic census categories. Although this strategy improves on the combined measure, it still presents problems. Including the four separate measures in an equation analyzing a restrictive sample may lead to problems associated with multicollinearity. Furthermore, this strategy does not account for the overcount problem associated with the Hispanic population. Our solution was to focus on two racial classifications: African American and Hispanic. We assessed the environmental racism hypothesis independently for each group.

The decision to focus on these communities of color was not an arbitrary decision. First, both groups were included in a seminal study of the subject (United Church of Christ, 1987). Thus, our research provides a point of comparison to that earlier work. Second, African Americans have been the object of pernicious and long-term discrimination in a variety of other settings (Mrydal, 1944). Thus, we can ascertain whether this group is similarly situated with regard to environmental hazards. Third, we focus on Hispanics because this group constitutes, according to census projections, the fastest growing ethnic group in the United States. It makes sense to assess whether this segment of the population is bearing a disproportionate share of environmental risks.[7]

The Conceptual Model

Most conceptual models are too limited in that they tend of take the forms noted in Equations 2.1–2.3.[8]

Eq. 1: $Y_{environmental\ harm} = a + b_1 Race$
Eq. 2: $Y_{environmental\ harm} = a - b_1 Class$
Eq. 3: $Y_{environmental\ harm} = a + b_1 Race - b_2 Class$

(Adeola, 1994; Anderton, et al., 1994a, 1994b; Asch and Seneca, 1978; Attah, 1992; Been, 1994: Berry, 1977; Boerner and Lambert, 1995; Bullard, 1983, 1990a; Burch, 1976; Clean Sites, Inc., 1990; Colquette and Robertson, 1991; Costner and Thornton, 1990; Davies, 1972; Dorfman, 1979; Fitton, 1992; Freeman, 1972; Gelobter, 1987, 1992; Gianessi and Peskin, 1980; Gia-nessi, Peskin, and Wolfe, 1979; Gould, 1986; Greenberg, 1993, 1994; Handy, 1977; Holm, 1994; Kohlhase, 1991; Krieg, 1995, 1998; Lavelle and Coyle, 1992; Mohai and Bryant, 1992; Shaikh, 1995; Shaikh and Loomis, 1998; Szasz, et al., 1992; United Church of Christ, 1987; U.S. Council on Environmental Quality, 1971; U.S. General Accounting Office, 1983; West, 1992; Zimmerman, 1993, 1994; Zupan, 1973).

At a minimum, these models fail to take into account the concerns about political mobilization advanced by the so-called process equity strand in the literature.[9] As a consequence, a minimalist conceptual model would take the following form:

Eq. 4: $Y_{environmental\ harm} = a + b_1 Race - b_2 Class - b_3 Political\ Mobilization$

Even though the minimalist model in Equation 2.4 is an improvement on Equations 2.1–2.3, it is still much too constricted. The environmental politics literature would suggest that additional measures (pollution potential or severity, public opinion—partisanship, ideology, and political culture—fiscal capacity, legislative professionalism, and organized interests) affect pollution levels. The justification for this pool of additional measures is set forth in Chapter 4. Thus, at a minimum, a properly specific model would require the addition of these functionally relevant variables. Thus, we use a model as specified below in Equation 2.5:

Eq. 5: $Y_{environmental\ harm} = a + b_1 Race - b_2 Class - b_3 Political\ Mobilization +/- b_n X_n +/- I_n X_n$

Where X_n = additional variables from the general environmental politics literature;
and $I_n X_n$ = an exhaustive set of two way interactive terms constructed from the pool of independent variables.

Methodological Issues

There are at least six serious methodological flaws inherent in the extant research on environmental injustice. First, there is the problem that some early evidence supporting the environmental injustice thesis is based on case studies. Case studies are a valuable first step in any research agenda, but they are limited in that one cannot generalize beyond the case under study; just because incidences of the problem are found in the city of Houston, one cannot extend this finding to other cities in Texas or elsewhere in the United States.

Additionally, there is the problem about what geographic areas are selected for study. This problem contains at least two dimensions. First, some literature focuses on SMSAs or ZIP code areas (see, e.g., Anderton, et al., 1994a; Attah, 1992; Been, 1994; Boerner and Lambert, 1995; Bowman and Crews-Meyer, 1995, 1997; Gould, 1986; Hamilton, 1995; Mohai and Bryant, 1992; Ringquist, 1995, 1996, 1997; Shaikh, 1995; Shaikh and Loomis, 1998; Szasz, et al., 1992; United Church of Christ, 1987). Although this strategy does establish proximity to a hazard, it does entail a flaw with regard to policymaking. The units capable of designing or implementing policy solutions below the federal level are state, county, and city governments. There are no ZIP code, census tract, or SMSA policy generating/implementing structures. Thus, it makes sense to study geopolitical entities that will have to oversee the elimination of environmental injustice—namely, states, counties, and cities.

The selection of geopolitical entities involves another problem. Research based on states (e.g., Lester, Allen, and Lauer, 1994), counties (e.g., Allen, 2001; Hird, 1993, 1994; Hird and Reese, 1998), and cities (e.g., Greenberg, 1994; Lester and Allen, 1996) are likely to contain aggregation errors that can mask exposure patterns (Kamieniecki and Steckenrider, 1996). We recognize that our use of state, county, and city data may contain aggregation bias. However, by being able to compare across all three geopolitical entities, we can potentially lay claim to a commonality of results. Additionally, we want to point out that with any analysis a trade-off exists between aggregation problems (variation within the regions of analysis) and the availability of data (the finer the resolution, the lower the availability of region-specific data). The geopolitical units selected for our analysis are large enough to include the effects of hazards yet small enough to record significant socioeconomic variation,[10] and they can generate sufficient data sources to operationalize and test the model in Equation 2.5.

Third, most of the existing research has examined too few environmental threats; in other words, these studies have utilized too few dependent variables. Just because there is evidence of a relationship between toxic exposure of a single type (e.g., Superfund sites) and minority populations or the poor, that finding says nothing about the multitude of other kinds of toxic exposures and minority populations and the poor, such as water pollution and air pollution of varying types.

By the same token, the available research has been limited by the number of independent variables used in the analyses. Most environmental injustice research used models based on Equations 2.1–2.3. Many other measures besides race, class, and mobilization—as suggested by the environmental politics literature—could have been used as independent variables. We discuss these variables in Chapter 4.

Finally, most of the previous research has been limited to a single unit of analysis (e.g., state, county, city, ZIP code, SMSA), when what is needed is multiple analyses at several different levels. Finding evidence of environmental injustice at the county level says nothing about the relationship between toxic exposures, race, class, and mobilization at other levels of analysis, such as states and cities.

Given the conceptual and methodological problems in existing literature, the question arises as to how, without substantial scientific proof of the existence of race- or class-based inequities, did environmental justice surface onto the public agenda as a major public policy issue during the early 1990s? Moreover, why did the Clinton administration decide to vigorously pursue this issue when previous administrations (from Richard Nixon to George Bush) looked upon this issue as one that needed additional research before policies were put into place? Chapter 3 is devoted to those questions.

Notes

1. Before proceeding, however, two points need to be made. First, the race dimension inherent in the environmental justice literature has, according to some, turned this issue into the civil rights movement of the 1990s. As such, existing literature reflects a heavy emphasis on the connection between persons of color and environmental harms. However, environmental injustice also contains a class dimension; that is, an additional hypothesis asserts that low-income individuals and communi-

ties are affected by a disproportionate share of environmental problems. Thus, while the reviewed literature does reflect the emphasis on race, comments regarding social class also need to be woven into the skein of relationships that add up to environmental injustice.

Our second point is organizational in nature. As with any four-part classification schema of the literature, there is going to be some overlap between items referenced in each category. In order to make it easier for the reader to follow the comments of the review, we have attempted to minimize the repetition of articles in each section of the review.

2. In the area of health-and-safety case studies, establishing a nexus between a LULU and health problems is difficult in that national health statistics, collected mainly by the Centers for Disease Control, does not categorize health findings along the lines of race. Therefore, a historical examination of rates of disease, such as cancer, in conjunction with race-based inequities in LULU distribution patterns was not possible. This compounds the difficulties of providing evidence for the existence of systematic environmental injustice (Johnston, Williams, and Harris, 1993; Lewis, Keating, and Russell, 1992).

3. Reviews include interviews with movement leaders (Almedia, 1994; Camia, 1993; Multinational Monitor, 1992; Truax, 1990) and brief summations of the history of environmental injustice (Allen, Lester, and Hill, 1995; Cutter, 1995; Doyle, 1994; Greenberg, 1993; Lester, Allen, and Lauer, 1994; Zimmerman, 1994).

4. Environmental blackmail occurs when a community, in desperate need of economic growth, is presented with an opportunity to host a LULU without being fully aware of the associated risks.

5. A brief comparison of two studies exemplifies this point. Been's (1994) reanalysis of the GAO (1987) four-site data and Bullard's (1983) seven-site data determine the increase/decrease in minority population before/after siting. Although Been found no evidence of market dynamics in the GAO data, she did find evidence of market dynamics in Bullard's Houston data. However, in the latter instance Been notes that she had to combine SMSAs because of redistricting and because some of the sites in question fell at SMSA boundaries. Been also notes that there is some evidence that the necessary combination of SMSAs is correlated with increases in minority population. Additionally, Been was unable to compare the market dynamics of SMSAs with sites to SMSAs without sites. Thus, no conclusion can be drawn as to whether population changes in the areas studied by Been were greater or less than the shifts in minority populations in SMSAs where there were no LULUs. A more recent study of Denver, Colorado, addressed the comparison issue (Shaikh and Loomis, 1998). The authors compared ZIP code areas with stationary air pollution sites to areas without such sites. The authors found that the minority population increases within ZIP codes with LULUs, but this population increase was not statistically different from similar minority population increases in ZIP codes without LULUs. Anderton, et al. (1994a, 1994b) report results similar to Shaikh and Loomis (1998) for treatment, storage, and disposal facilities. See also Kohlhase (1991).

6. Some post-1992 research reports the absence of clear race-risk relations for *some* environmental harms (Allen, Lester, and Hill, 1995; Greenberg, 1993; Shaikh, 1995; Shaikh and Loomis, 1998; Yandle and Burton, 1996). Cutter (1994) reports that there was a relationship between "racially mixed" neighborhoods and the harm she

studied. Hird (1993, 1994) reports a race-risk nexus between the percentage of non-white population and the distribution of NPL sites but finds no relationship between race and the speed of NPL cleanup.

7. We do not mean to imply that environmental injustice is absent for Native Americans or Asian Americans. These groups were excluded from our study for several reasons. The distribution of Native Americans, coupled with their distinct legal situation within the United States, does not make them a good study subject given our method of data analysis—ordinary least squares regression. Other research designs would be more effective for assessing the race-risk nexus for this ethnic classification. Further, the distribution of Asian Americans throughout our samples would have lead to statistical problems that we could not overcome. These groups are deserving of study, and we encourage other researchers to undertake this task.

8. Equations 2.1–2.3 mean that most of the literature deals with only *two* concepts—race and class. The articles may have *many* measures of race and several measures of class. However, the two concepts that are dealt with—regardless of the number of measures employed—are still only race and social class. As such, the notation is designed to reflect the conceptual nature of the analysis, not the number of types or variables that may have been employed.

9. It should be noted that some of the extant literature has made allowances for this indicator in the conceptual model (Allen, 2001; Allen, Lester, and Hill, 1995; Crews-Meyer, 1994; Hamilton, 1995; Hird, 1993, 1994; Hird and Reese, 1998; Lester, Allen, and Lauer, 1994; Lester and Allen, 1996; Ringquist, 1995, 1966, 1997).

10. Hird (1993: 323, n. 1) advances a similar argument to justify his study of environmental injustice at the county level. We feel that we are on safe ground by employing a similar justification.

3

Environmental Justice:
Getting on the Public Agenda

Agenda-setting is characterized by the appearance of problems and issues that grab the policy spotlight for brief moments while solutions are found or interest diminishes and they fade into obscurity. Some of these issues also continuously reemerge for consideration among government decisionmakers, and the associated problems, which may not have been satisfactorily addressed by government policies on the initial iteration, often return to the agenda redefined and thus amiable to solution. The environmental justice movement highlights this agenda-setting process.

Questions regarding the inequitable distribution of the nation's pollutants and their potential adverse health effects among certain segments of the population have been debated since the early 1970s. Since that time, there has been increased recognition of the phenomenon, as well as a redefinition of the debate as the concept matured. The problem has been defined by three distinct interpretations: environmental equity, environmental racism, and environmental justice. "Environmental equity" refers to the idea that potential pollution sources, such as LULUs, and their related health effects should not be disproportionately distributed among specific segments of the population, namely, the poor and minorities. "Environmental racism" is a broader label used for any policy, practice, or directive that differentially affects the environment of individuals, groups, or communities based on race. More recently, the expression "environmental justice" has been coined to encompass the concepts of environmental equity and environmental racism, with the assertion that environmental justice can be achieved only when all individuals, regardless of race or socioeconomic status, are equally protected from environmental harms and their related adverse health effects. Environmental justice advocates state that the overriding goal of the movement is the creation of a society wherein no racial or ethnic group or social class disproportionately bears the risks associated with pollution. In such a society, pollution would be eliminated at its source. These definitions of the problem have framed the debate since around 1970.

The Model and Methods of Analysis

In order to carry out a complete examination of environmental justice and its movement in the policy arena, J.W. Kingdon's (1984, 1995) agenda-setting model is employed. Using this model, we will examine the problem, policy, and political streams of the environmental justice movement and analyze the "coupling" of these streams in order to determine which factors were present to allow the issue to reach the decisionmaking agenda. This model is outlined in Figure 3.1, and the following paragraphs provide a narrative description of model components

In the *problem stream*, an issue appears by definition rather than by condition. It is not enough for a phenomenon or a crisis situation to simply occur. It is only when the condition is defined as a problem with a potential solution that it may begin moving toward a place on the policy agenda. If a solution is not available, there is no reason for the issue to be addressed. When a problem eventually gains national attention, alternative solutions may be offered, and entrepreneurs—defined as individuals who are willing to invest their resources (time, energy, reputation, and sometimes money) in the hope of future return—begin to emerge during this stream in their attempt to define the issue in a particular light and offer potential solutions that reach specific goals.

According to the Kingdon framework, it is during the *policy stream* that issues move onto the governmental agenda. In this stream, government officials who can publicly act upon potential solutions become aware of problems and make an attempt toward instituting solutions. As a result, the problem moves to the decisionmaking agenda, and policy communities begin to emerge. These communities comprise individuals both within and outside of government who have an interest in seeing the problem solved. Oftentimes, entrepreneurs will serve to organize these communities. The more closely knit these communities are, the more likely they are to push for cohesive policies to address the problem. When several policy communities are focused on an issue, the problem may lose its place on the agenda due to lack of consensus over the solution. In this instance, the problem may be redefined, outside of the government realm, and brought back at a later time.

There are several elements that a problem and its solution must meet in order to viably remain in the policy stream. These include: technical feasibility, value acceptability within the policy community, tolerable costs of implementing solutions, anticipated public acquiescence, and a reasonable

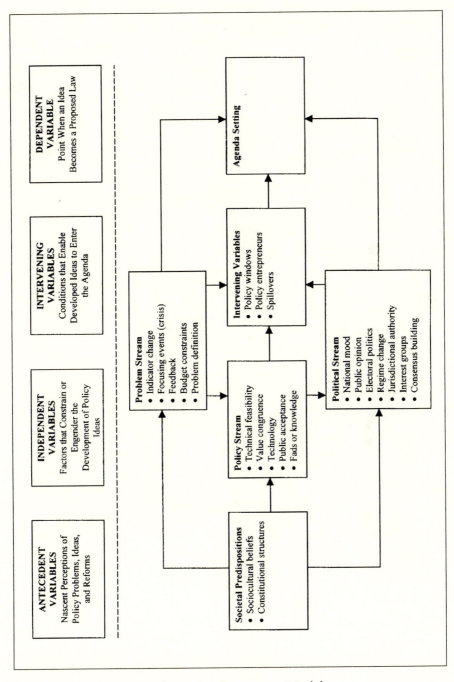

FIGURE 3.1   The Agenda-Setting Process—a Model

chance for public receptivity. If an issue does not meet these conditions, it may not succeed in the policy stream (Kingdon, 1984, 1995).

Problems find solutions on the decision agenda when policy windows open. Windows, in essence, are an opportunity for action—the right time and place. Entrepreneurs are continuously looking for this chance to push the issue forward on the agenda. In most situations, a window will be open when the problem and policy stream come together, or couple.

Electoral, partisan, and interest- and pressure-group factors affect the way issues finally get onto the policy agenda. This is known as the *political stream*. There are three areas of influence to be aware of when analyzing this stream. National mood or public opinion can cause a window to open; social movements and their entrepreneurs can influence national mood; but a "crisis" is more likely to capture public attention and force open a window.

An analysis of the environmental justice movement will allow for a complete discussion of Kingdon's agenda-setting model, because it illustrates the movement of an issue through all three streams (problem, policy, political) on several occasions.[1]

The dependent variable of the Kingdon model is the point when an idea for solving a problem actually becomes a proposed law. However, before an issue receives widespread public policy attention, antecedent variables come into play to garner attention for the issue and move it through the problem stream. Through various defining events and the adoption of the issue by policy communities, a potential solution to the problem is outlined. The independent variables to consider in the agenda-setting model are factors that constrain or engender the development of policy ideas.

Intervening variables are the final set of variables that need to be considered in the agenda-setting model. Intervening variables are conditions that enable developed ideas to enter the policy agenda. These conditions can vary according to each situation and issue. In most circumstances, it is necessary for the issue to be well defined in the problem stream and to have the support of a policy community and policy entrepreneurs before the windows of opportunity will open. Entrepreneurs attempt to be aware of the intervening variables that will allow them to move the issue onto the agenda.

During an examination of the agenda-setting process of the environmental justice movement, these four variables will be taken into account. The variables can be seen during all three phases of the model; and although they may overlap at times, each serves a distinct role in the promotion of the issue.

The Problem Stream

Within the problem stream an issue's definition begins to solidify as events highlighting the problem take place and entrepreneurs begin to outline pos-

sible solutions. As a result, the issue may gain the attention of national policymakers and move toward taking a place on the public agenda.

Although it was not labeled as such, early stages of the environmental justice movement have origins in two events in 1967 and 1968. These events
provided the backdrop for what was later to become a larger movement for
environmental equality. In 1967, Houston was the site of a demonstration to
protest the siting of a city-owned garbage dump in a largely African American community. Part of the concern arose because an eight-year-old girl had
accessed the dump, fallen, and drowned. The unsafe conditions of the dump,
both in terms of security and health concerns, added to a larger feeling of inequality against which the community was fighting. This protest, coinciding
with one over the treatment of African American students in a local junior
high school, culminated in a violent clash with Houston police and the ar-
rest of several hundred student protesters. The second event, although more
strongly based in the struggle for civil rights, emerged from a 1968 protest in
Memphis in which Martin Luther King Jr. tried to assist Memphis garbage
workers in their protest against unequal pay and unsafe working conditions.
King's assassination during this visit was a galvanizing event for the civil
rights movement, and as a result any environmental justice message was
overshadowed (Bullard, 1994c). It was not until 1971 that the issue of the inequitable distribution of environmental burdens among minority and low-
income individuals surfaced again.

Inequities Recognized

In 1970, President Richard Nixon established the Council on Environmental
Quality's as part of the National Environmental Policy Act. The purpose of
the CEQ was to provide an annual report on the state of the environment in
the United States. The annual report was to examine the underlying causes of
environmental problems in the United States and include recommendations
on the best methods for achieving the president's national environmental
goals. The second annual report of the CEQ (August 1971) devoted a whole
chapter to the examination of the environmental quality of inner cities.

This weaving of environmental, social, and economic concerns is an ele-
mental component of the modern environmental justice movement. These
environmental concerns for the inner city include: inadequate housing, high
crime rates, poor health, unsanitary conditions, inadequate education and
recreation, and drug addiction.

Although all of the concerns in the CEQ report needed to be addressed in
order to improve the living conditions within cities, several appear to be
more closely tied to issues of equality and fairness. This debate did not go
unnoticed in the CEQ report. Upon interviewing several individuals from
inner-city organizations from places like Cleveland, Boston, Detroit, and

Los Angeles, the CEQ report discovered a gap between the inner city and traditional environmental movements. Inner-city organizations expressed concern over whether their environmental issues would be lost in the shadows of the national environmental movement's policy agenda.

Although the environmental equity concerns of the inner city were nationally recognized in the CEQ report, they failed to enter the national decisionmaking agenda. Several factors may have contributed to the issue fading from national prominence. First, the mainstream environmental movement had several events around which to coalesce its agenda-setting strategies. For instance, in 1970 the first national Earth Day celebration, sponsored in part by Senator Gaylord Nelson, sealed the place of the mainstream environmental movement on the policy agenda. From this stemmed NEPA, the Clean Air Act, and the Clean Water Act, a wide-ranging set of legislation that opened new avenues of influence for mainstream groups and entrepreneurs. The entrepreneurs who were once on the outside of the policymaking loop now were among the insiders' group (Baer and Bositis, 1993) that had a stake in maintaining the issue networks (Heclo, 1979) that developed around environmental concerns. The legitimizing of mainstream environmental groups through policy influence did, in fact, keep inner-city environmental issues off of the public environmental policy agenda. Second, because mainstream environmental issues primarily focused on preservation, conservation, and aesthetics, they did not demand a change of the whole political-social system itself, only change within the system. Therefore, these issues were easier for public officials to address with acceptable solutions.

Yet environmental equity did not disappear completely from the problem stream. It continued to be explored in academic circles during the 1970s. Indeed, several studies found a significant relationship between race and the hazards present in the region studied (Asch and Seneca, 1978; Berry, 1977; Burch, 1976; Davies, 1972; Dorfman, 1979; Kruvant, 1975).

As the studies began to accumulate in favor of the environmental justice hypothesis, several events began to garner attention for the movement. A 1979 class-action lawsuit regarding hazardous waste against the city of Houston, the state of Texas, and Houston-headquartered Brown Ferris Industries (BFI)—*Bean v. Southwestern Waste Management Corporation*—brought the issue of environmental equity back into public light. The difference this time was that the issue was redefined to reflect racist intent, alleged to be the impetus behind the disproportionate distribution of environmental hazards. Such inequities were now being labeled as "environmental racism."[2]

Early discussions of environmental disparities focused on disproportionate distributions among minorities and low-income communities. It therefore became an issue of inequities among several populations, and the *Bean* case signaled a shift in the way the issue was to be interpreted. However, it was not

until 1982 that strong ties were established between the struggle for environmental equity and civil rights in minority communities. It was during this
year that Benjamin Chavis—then the head of the Southern Christian Leadership Conference, later the head of the National Association for the Advancement of Colored People (NAACP)—coined the expression "environmental
racism" to describe the inequitable distribution of environmental risks:

> Environmental racism is racial discrimination in environmental policymaking.
> It is racial discrimination in the enforcement of regulations and laws. It is racial
> discrimination in the deliberate targeting of communities of color for toxic
> waste disposal and the siting of polluting industries. It is racial discrimination
> in the official sanctioning of the life-threatening presence of poisons and pollu-
> tants in communities of color. And, it is racial discrimination in the history of
> excluding people of color from the mainstream environmental groups, decision
> making boards, commissions, and regulatory bodies. (quoted in Bullard,
> 1993b)

A formal melding of the civil rights movement and its earlier, inner-city
environmental movement finally occurred during an October 1982 disposal
facility siting dispute in Warren County, North Carolina. Citizens of Warren County joined with national civil rights activists and political leaders to
protest the siting of a PCB-contaminated soil dump site in the town of
Afton. The population of the proposed site was more than 84 percent
African American at the time; Warren County had the highest percentage of
African Americans in the state (65 percent) and was one of the poorest
counties in North Carolina (1980 per capita income was $5,000; Geiser and
Waneck, 1983).

The protest was the final step in a series of actions that local citizens took
to see their concerns about the landfill addressed. In reaction to the siting
decision, a grassroots group—Warren County Citizens Concerned about
PCBs—was formed. After examining the siting decision for some time,
group members began to think that economic interests were more of a moti-
vating source behind the siting considerations than was overall citizen safety
(Geiser and Waneck, 1983). When group members perceived that their concerns were being ignored, they began to organize a display of civil disobedi-
ence reminiscent of earlier civil rights and environmental protests. More
than 500 individuals were arrested while attempting to bodily block the
roads to the landfill.

Even though the landfill was eventually sited in Afton, the national attention that resulted proved invaluable to establishing environmental racism as
a legitimate national problem. The recognition was due, in part, to the national leaders present at the protest, including Leon White of the United
Church of Christ's Commission for Racial Justice and Joseph Lowery, Ben

Chavis, and Fred Taylor of the Southern Christian Leadership Conference. The organizations they represented had a long history of providing guidance throughout the civil rights movement and into present-day equality controversies. In addition, District of Columbia delegate Walter Fauntroy of the Congressional Black Caucus attended the protest and subsequently moved environmental justice into the policy stream by commissioning a 1983 GAO study of the distribution of hazardous waste landfill siting in EPA Region 4 (in the South) (U.S. General Accounting Office, 1983).

The Problem Stream Diminishes

Although the 1983 GAO report failed to move environmental justice onto the decisionmaking agenda, the issue did not disappear completely. Academicians continued to study the inequitable distribution of environmental risks in search for an underlying causality. These studies were both qualitative and quantitative, however most were studies of single cases (Asch and Seneca, 1978; Berry, 1977; Bullard, 1983; Burch, 1976; Davies, 1972; Dorfman, 1979; Freeman, 1972; Gelobter, 1987; Gianessi and Peskin, 1980; Gianessi, Peskin, and Wolfe, 1979; Gould, 1986; Kruvant, 1975; United Church of Christ, 1987).Although several scholars continued to examine the environmental racism problem from a normative perspective, a landmark quantitative study emerged in 1987 from the United Church of Christ's Commission on Racial Justice. This study, *Toxic Wastes and Race: A National Report on the Racial and Socio-Economic Characteristics of Communities with Hazardous Waste Sites*, is constantly referred to by proponents of environmental justice as proof of that environmental inequities are racially motivated (United Church of Christ, 1987).[3] Although the study itself was faulted on methodological grounds (Anderton, 1996), the criticism did not diminish its influence on state and federal public policy. Indeed, it is repeatedly cited as justification for the need for environmental justice legislation (e.g., Camacho, 1998).

Grassroots Environmental Justice

Although the problem stream appeared to diminish during the 1980s, the fight for environmental justice only strengthened at the grassroots level. For example, the Southwest Network for Environmental and Economic Justice (SNEEJ) was trying to build a network among environmental justice organizations throughout the U.S. Southwest by making the critical link between environmental and social-economic concerns (Almedia, 1994). The grassroots organizations affiliated with SNEEJ almost exclusively comprised persons of color. SNEEJ was not opposed to working with mainstream groups, however its essential position is that relationships should be inclusive in nature, unlike the exclusionary practices of the past (Almedia, 1994). Indeed, grassroots activity by environmental justice organizations during the 1980s helped to establish the problem as more than a branch of the civil rights movement. However, since the organizations were usually communities of color as well as low-income communities, their struggles tended to reinforce the idea that the problem was one of environmental racism, not simply inequity (Bullard, 1993a, 1994a; Mitchell, 1993).

The Business Perspective

Throughout most of the early environmental justice movement, business and industry maintained that inequitable distribution of environmental hazards was unintentional. Inequities, if they existed, were simply a coincidence based on the fact that circumstances, such as cheap land for factories and zoning codes, were the impetus for siting decisions. Industry asserted that they were good neighbors abiding by the most stringent environmental requirements of federal, state, and local governments. However, in the late 1980s the environmental justice movement was further legitimized on the national stage when business and industry recognized that the issue—even though the actual proof of the problem was not universal—was pressing enough, at least from a public relations standpoint, to begin addressing the issue proactively. For example, in 1989 Dow Chemical Company embarked on an effort to protect a community near its plant in Morrisonville, Louisiana. In order to provide a greenbelt around its facility, Dow offered to buy all of the land and buildings in Morrisonville, a low-income, African American community. The program was available to all residents who rented or owned property in Morrisonville before May 16, 1989.[4]

Although efforts by Dow constituted a step toward improving relations with a facility's host community, the program was affected by a degree of controversy. Some viewed it as example of environmental blackmail. Others viewed it simply as a Band-Aid covering the deeper problem of the systematic polluting of communities. Despite some of these objections, more than 99 percent of the community accepted the offer. This marked one of the first in a longer series of efforts by business and industry to open the lines of communication with affected communities in order to address environmental concerns before they develop into a larger, adversarial confrontation (Hill, 1996).

The Contemporary Period:
"Environmental Justice" Defined

Beginning in 1990, two events served to define the problem of inequitable distribution of environmental hazards in broader terms of environmental justice. The first of these events occurred as a result of a 1990 conference—the Conference on Race and the Incidence of Environmental Hazards sponsored by the University of Michigan's School of Natural Resources—wherein scholarly involvement in the environmental justice movement took a political turn. At this conference, papers outlining the inequities in a variety of minority communities were presented as evidence of a greater problem of intentional disproportionate distribution of environmental hazards. Among those in attendance were academicians who had devoted considerable energy to exposing the environmental racism phenomenon, as well as civil rights activists; representatives from various levels of government were also represented (Mohai and Bryant, 1992).

The purpose of the conference was twofold. First, through the presentation of evidence supporting environmental justice claims, the members of the so-called Michigan Coalition wanted to increase scholarly interest in the subject in the hope that greater empirical evidence would surface in support of the movement. The scholar-activists also hoped to bring the issue onto the public policy agenda. As part of this effort, some members of the Michigan Coalition sent out a memo requesting a meeting with Louis Sullivan, who was secretary of the U.S. Department of Health and Human Services (HHS), EPA Administrator William K. Reilly, and the chair of the Council on Environmental Quality, Michael R. Deland. The memo stated that coalition members wanted to discuss the agencies' involvement in the following:

> Undertaking research towards understanding the environmental risks faced by minority and low-income communities;
>
> Initiating projects to enhance risk communication targeted to minority and low-income population groups;
>
> Requiring, on a demonstration basis, that racial and socioeconomic equity considerations be included in Regulatory Impact Assessments;
>
> Ensuring that a racial and socioeconomic dimension is overlaid on present and future geographic studies of environmental risk;
>
> Enhancing the ability of historically black colleges and universities and other minority institutions to participate and contribute to the development of environmental equity;
>
> Appointing special assistants for environmental equity at decision making levels within agencies and;
>
> Developing a policy statement on environmental equity. (quoted in Bryant and Mohai, 1992)

Copies of the memo were sent to all of the state governors, members of the CBC, and several state legislators. Meetings that followed the issuance of this memo served as a catalyst to move environmental justice into the policy stream.

The second event occurred in October 1991, when several of the entrepreneurs from the Michigan Coalition extended their efforts toward assisting proto–environmental justice grassroots organizations by serving as advisers to the First National People of Color Environmental Leadership Summit. The United Church of Christ, led by Benjamin Chavis, served as the primary organizer for this conference, which attracted more than 500 activists. The conference reinforced the national importance of the movement, expanded its scope beyond merely an antitoxics campaign, and redefined it as a concern of environmental justice. The importance of this redefinition is that it made the issue an inclusive one, the underlying purpose being to protect the health of every community. Conference attendees made a conscious decision not to create a national environmental justice organization out of the meeting.[5] As part of their efforts to address the environmental issues facing communities of color, conference delegates adopted seventeen "Principles of Environmental Justice" (Bullard, 1994a). The principles, set forth as a resolution that was adopted on October 24, 1991, are as follows:

Principles of Environmental Justice

WE THE PEOPLE OF COLOR, gathered together at this multinational People of Color Environmental Leadership Summit, to begin to build a national and international movement of all peoples of color to fight the destruction and taking of our lands and communities, do hereby re-establish our spiritual interdependence to the sacredness of our Mother Earth; to respect and celebrate each of our cultures, languages and beliefs about the natural world and our roles in healing ourselves; to insure environmental justice; to promote economic alternatives which would contribute to the development of environmentally safe livelihoods; and, to secure our political, economic and cultural liberation that has been denied for over 500 years of colonization and oppression, resulting in the poisoning of our communities and land and the genocide of our peoples, do affirm and adopt these Principles of Environmental Justice:

1. Environmental justice affirms the sacredness of Mother Earth, ecological unity and the interdependence of all species, and the right to be free from ecological destruction.
2. Environmental justice demands that public policy be based on mutual respect and justice for all peoples, free from any form of discrimination or bias.
3. Environmental justice mandates the right to ethical, balanced and responsible uses of land and renewable resources in the interest of a sustainable planet for humans and other living things.
4. Environmental justice calls for universal protection from nuclear testing, extraction, production and disposal of toxic/hazardous wastes and poisons

and nuclear testing that threaten the fundamental right to clean air, land, water and food.

5. Environmental justice affirms the fundamental right to political, economic, cultural and environmental self-determination of all peoples.

6. Environmental justice demands the cessation of the production of all toxins, hazardous wastes, and radioactive materials, and that all past and current producers be held strictly accountable to the people for detoxification and the containment at the point of production.

7. Environmental justice demands the right to participate as equal partners at every level of decision-making including needs assessment, planning, implementation, enforcement and evaluation.

8. Environmental justice affirms the right of all workers to a safe and healthy work environment, without being forced to choose between an unsafe livelihood and unemployment. It also affirms the right of those who work at home to be free from environmental hazards.

9. Environmental justice protects the right of victims of environmental injustice to receive full compensation and reparations for damages as well as quality health care.

10. Environmental justice considers governmental acts of environmental injustice a violation of international law, the Universal Declaration on Human Rights, and the United Nations Convention on Genocide.

11. Environmental justice must recognize a special legal and natural relationship of Native Peoples to the U.S. government through treaties, agreements, compacts, and covenants affirming sovereignty and self-determination.

12. Environmental justice affirms the need for urban and rural ecological policies to clean up and rebuild our cities and rural areas in balance with nature, honoring the cultural integrity of all our communities, and providing fair access for all to the full range of resources.

13. Environmental justice calls for the strict enforcement of principles of informed consent, and a halt to the testing of experimental reproductive and medical procedures and vaccinations on people of color.

14, Environmental justice opposes the destructive operations of multi-national corporations.

15, Environmental justice opposes military occupation, repression and exploitation of lands, peoples and cultures, and other life forms.

16. Environmental justice calls for the education of present and future generations which emphasizes social and environmental issues, based on our experience and an appreciation of our diverse cultural perspectives.

17. Environmental justice requires that we, as individuals, make personal and consumer choices to consume as little of Mother Earth's resources and to provide as little waste as possible; and make the conscious decision to challenge and reprioritize our lifestyles to insure the health of the natural world for present and future generations.

The activists took these principles, along with a renewed sense of vigor for their cause, back to their respective organizations. Networks were established among the various groups, and a nationwide push for environmental justice began with full force.

The Problem Stream Summarized

Following the conferences, the environmental justice problem found itself on the policy agenda for the third time in as many decades. What had started as a 1970s issue of inner-city environmental concerns about the disproportionate distribution of environmental hazards among low-income communities transformed into allegations of intentional environmental racism. Although this definition of the problem prevailed throughout the 1980s, the issue did not make progress in the policy stream for a variety of reasons, most of them due to the Reagan administration's positions on traditional environmentalism and the civil rights movement. However, grassroots struggles for environmental health and safety in communities and workplaces kept the issue alive at local and state levels. In the 1990s, the issue was redefined again, this time as one of a right to live and work in an environmentally safe environment. This right was known as "environmental justice."

By the early 1990s, environmental justice had moved from the systemic agenda onto the institutional agenda. Therefore, it is now pertinent to address how the movement made its way through the policy stream, identify the entrepreneurs who helped to define its relevance, and discuss the windows that opened and how the problem and policy streams were coupled in order to allow decisions to be rendered.

Environmental Justice Enters the Policy Stream

In the policy stream, an issue moves from being a problem that has the potential to be solved through government resolution to one where those in positions of authority have fully recognized it and are prepared to act (Kingdon, 1984, 1995). In the case of environmental justice, the issue was redefined several times by conscious efforts and crises events. The policy entrepreneurs who joined the movement in the late 1970s and early 1980s were charged with leading it through these periods and finding opportunities—or open windows—through which they could maneuver the problem onto the public policy agenda.

Although the issues set forth in the 1971 CEQ report were not comprehensively addressed by a specific piece of legislation, the document essentially laid out the tenets of the modern environmental justice movement. It expanded the definition of the "environment" to include anthropocentric concerns such as housing, high crime rates, and poor health, to name a few.

It should come as no surprise, then, that legislation was not introduced to specifically address these concerns. Aside from the turmoil of Watergate that plagued the Nixon administration, inner-city environmental concerns did not meet the criteria for agenda survival necessary to stay viable within the policy stream, that is, because inner-city environmental problems can be caused by a myriad of sources that produce myriad cumulative effects, solutions to inner-city environmental problems were not, at the time, technically feasible as a whole. Furthermore, because the environmental and civil rights movements were not working together to address these issues, it was even more difficult for inner-city environmental concerns to be legitimized. Indeed, during this period the "environment" was perceived as pristine wilderness, not a dilapidated tenement. Thus, the basis of support needed to move the issue onto the policy agenda did not exist among the activist communities. If a policy community, such as the civil rights and environmental communities, cannot prioritize a problem, then they will not devote the effort needed to convince officials that the issue must be addressed. It can be argued that these costs of solving inner-city problems laid forth in the CEQ study far outweighed the benefits (U.S. Council on Environmental Quality, 1971). Effectively addressing inner-city environmental concerns called for a fundamental change in the value structure of society. Such drastic change is difficult enough with full public support; it is next to impossible without the strong backing of policy communities. Since there was no reasonable chance for receptivity for such a policy agenda, no action was taken to solve the problem by policymakers and entrepreneurs. Therefore, environmental justice moved back into the problem stream. By the 1980s, it began to resurface through defining crisis events such as the Warren County landfill protest.

The events in Warren County served dual purposes for the environmental justice movement. First, several individuals who would become the leading entrepreneurs pushing environmental justice onto the policy agenda participated in the protest, most notably Chavis and environmental justice scholar Robert Bullard. Second, and more important, the Warren County protest was the crisis event that served to place environmental justice in the policy stream for the first time since 1971. In sum, after attending this protest, District of Columbia delegate Fauntroy, as a member of the House Subcommittee on Commerce, Transportation, and Tourism in the Committee on Energy and Commerce, commissioned a GAO study of EPA Region 4.[6] The study was done to determine the correlation between the location of hazardous waste landfills and the racial and economic statuses of surrounding communities. Even though the 1983 GAO study found that three of the four hazardous waste facilities examined were in African American communities, the issue of environmental justice largely disappeared from the national policy agenda.

Coupling the Problem and Policy Streams

In the 1990s, windows of opportunity opened to allow the problem stream of environmental justice to couple with the policy stream. This resulted in the problem being addressed and further legitimized through agency initiatives, legislation, and executive orders.

For example, the University of Michigan's 1990 conference on race and the incidence of environmental hazards served as a policy launching pad for environmental justice. The Michigan Coalition appealed to members of the CBC to organize a forum at its annual Legislative Weekend in order to discuss the issue. U.S. Representatives Ronald V. Dellums (D.–California), Edolphus Towns (D.–New York), John Conyers Jr. (D.–Michigan), and John Lewis (D.–Georgia) agreed to sponsor it. The forum resulted in several CBC members sending a letter to EPA Administrator Reilly asking that he respond to the Michigan Coalition's request that the agency adopt an initiative to examine environmental justice issues (Dellums, 1992).

Within this time frame, the 1991 National People of Color Environmental Leadership Summit brought grassroots activists into the national spotlight. After the summit many of the leaders continued their national presence by providing testimony at various congressional committee and subcommittee hearings. The early actions of this growing policy community resulted in EPA's recognition of environmental justice concerns and the development of the Environmental Equity Workgroup within the agency (Hill, 1996:60–61).

The Environmental Equity Workgroup

The Environmental Equity Workgroup, comprising a cross-section of forty EPA staff members, was assigned the task of evaluating evidence that minority and poor communities bear a higher burden of environmental risk. In February 1992, it published findings and submitted them to Administrator Riley in a report entitled *Environmental Equity: Reducing the Risk for All Communities* (U.S. Environmental Protection Agency, 1992a).

The workgroup findings can be summarized into the following categories:

- there was a general lack of data concerning adverse environmental health effects by race and income; even though data was lacking, it was possible to observe disproportionate exposure to pollutants by socioeconomic status and race;
- there was a problem with the lack of health data categorized by race and income levels in that the lack of this data precluded any examination of expo-

sure to multiple levels of exposure to environmental risks—therefore, there was no way to account for the synergistic effects of multiple paths of exposure;

- that much opportunity existed for the EPA to improve communication efforts with affected communities;
- that all EPA regional offices had differing approaches toward environmental equity issues and that national environmental equity training should take place within the agency in order to broaden the agency's ability to address equity issues effectively;
- that Native American nations and communities, in addition to having a unique relationship with the federal government, often lack the infrastructure necessary to address environmental justice issues effectively. (Hill, 1996:60–61)

As a result of these findings, the EPA issued several environmental justice recommendations for future action. Among those not already mentioned were: establish and maintain information that provides an objective basis for assessing risks based on race and income; incorporate environmental equity into the risk assessment process; identify and target opportunities to reduce high concentrations of risk among various populations; selectively assess and consider the distribution of projected risk reduction in major agency initiatives and rulemaking; and establish mechanisms to ensure that environmental equity concerns are incorporated in the agency's long-term planning and operations (Hill, 1996:62).

Regardless of any action taken to achieve these ends, this report is a milestone in the coupling of the problem and policy streams of the environmental justice movement. It marks the first official recognition of the issue by the executive administration, as well as a commitment to address it. Part of this commitment was fulfilled with the establishment of the EPA's Environmental Equity Office (since renamed the Environmental Justice Office) and the National Environmental Justice Advisory Council (NEJAC) in 1992. NEJAC members represent all of the stakeholders in the environmental justice movement—community activists, academic interests, Native American communities, and business and industry.

Environmental Justice and Legislative Initiatives, 1992–1995

During 1992–1995, several legislative initiatives took place. On February 25, 1992, the House Subcommittee on Health and the Environment discussed the impacts of lead poisoning on low-income and minority communities. This hearing provided environmental justice entrepreneurs with a forum to present the issue to Congress and solicit support for future legislation.[7]

Also, during the 102nd and 103rd sessions of Congress, additional legislation was introduced. This proposed legislation is summarized in Figure 3.2.

In terms of placing environmental justice onto the policy agenda, the most influential efforts at the subcommittee were those of Benjamin Chavis. On behalf of the United Church of Christ's Commission for Racial Justice, he submitted a proposal for an Environmental Justice Act of 1992. The legislation he proposed included defining the top 100 environmental high-impact areas (EHIAs, i.e., counties in the United States; in some cases, regions and cities could be substituted). Future siting of polluting facilities in these areas would be limited. In addition, the HHS secretary would make community grants available to EHIAs to allow affected communities to obtain technical assistance in responding to the public participation afforded by the proposed legislation.

Several environmental justice activists, at both the national and grassroots levels, and members of the business community shared their views at other hearings. Leading the activists, Benjamin Chavis, then director of the NAACP, testified before the House Subcommittee on Transportation and Hazardous Material on November 18, 1993; he spoke to the need for specific environmental justice legislation rather than simply allowing the issue to be addressed through the reauthorization of existing statutes.[8] According to Chavis, only specific legislation would allow the federal government to account for the cumulative effects of pollution on minority and low-income communities. Chavis also used the opportunity to label the issue as one of racism and to criticize the Clinton administration for not including environmental justice concerns—particularly the cumulative effects of pollution—in the national health care debate. At the same hearings, along with offering support for pending legislation, Robert Bullard suggested a four-prong strategy for addressing environmental justice. This included the enforcement of existing laws and regulations, an executive order on environmental justice, new federal legislative initiatives, and state and local legislative initiatives.[9]

Other entrepreneurs entered the discussion of environmental justice during the November hearing. For example, Deejohn Ferris, of the Lawyers' Committee for Civil Rights Under Law, supported several bills (H.R. 1924, H.R. 1925, and H.R. 2105) as "planks of the environmental justice platform" and offered further policy suggestions. Ferris, as the program director for her organization's Environmental Justice Project, outlined several steps the federal government should take in doing a comprehensive evaluation of EHIAs, including examining multiple exposure pathways and looking at cumulative exposures; and assessing the health and environmental effects of pollution on various populations. Ferris also called for the federal government to create an interagency council to address the issues internally. From the testimony of these activists, it is clear that the inner-city environmental concerns of the early movement still served as the movement's basis.

FIGURE 3.2 Summary of Recommended or Introduced Environmental Justice Legislation, 102nd and 103rd Congresses

Item	Title	Contents
Testimony at Hearing, February 25, 1992	Environmental Justice Act of 1992[1]	Placed into the record at committee hearings as the recommended form for legislation. Define top 100 EHIA counties (in some cases regions or cities could be substituted). Future pollution siting in EHIA areas to be limited. Secretary of Health and Human Services makes community grants available to EHIAs to obtain technical assistance in responding to public participation afforded by the act.
HR5326 S2806	Environmental Equity Act of 1992	Contained a majority of the recommended provisions of the Environmental Justice Act of 1992.
HR3800	Amended Comprehensive Environmental Response, Compensation, and Liability Act of 1980	Proposal that included many of the environmental justice movement's points of contention with reauthorization of Superfund.
HR1924[2]	Environmental Equal Rights Act of 1993	Proposed amendment to Solid Waste Disposal Act to allow petitions to be submitted to prevent certain waste facilities from being constructed in environmentally damaged communities. An "environmentally damaged community" is one within two miles of the borders of the solid or hazardous waste facility.
HR1925	Environmental Equity Information Act of 1993	Proposed amendment to Comprehensive Environmental Response, Compensation, and Liability Act of 1980 to require collection and maintenance of health data on the race, age, gender, ethnic origin, income, and education level of persons living in communities adjacent to toxic substance contamination.
HR2105[3]	Environmental Equity Act of 1992	Reintroduced Environmental Justice Act of 1992 and included provisions to assure nondiscriminatory compliance with all environmental health and safety laws. Assured equal protection of public health. Provided for collection of health data as originally proposed in HR 1925.
S1834[4]	Superfund Reform Act of 1994	Proposed amendments—based on different positions of environmental justice activists.

NOTES:
[1] Introduced in testimony on February 25, 1992, as part of Reverend Benjamin Chavis's testimony before Subcommittee on Health and the Environment.
[2] HR1924, 1925, and 2105 were brought up for discussion on November 18, 1993, at the House Subcommittee on Transportation and Hazardous Materials Hearings (Hill, 1996: 65).
[3] Recommends assembly of data needed to assess long term health problems and to establish scientific basis for claims of race/income/environmental health risk nexus.
[4] Remarks by Florence Robinson of the North Baton Rouge Environmental Association in favor of retaining retroactive liability clause versus remarks by Benjamin Chavis on behalf of the Alliance for Superfund Action Partnership favoring a business-tax type mechanism. No actual legislation proposed by environmental justice entrepreneurs.

The November 1993 House hearings also gave the business community the opportunity to share its concerns. Charles McDermott, director of government affairs for WMX Technologies, Inc.—provider of several environmental services, including solid and hazardous waste landfills—discussed his company's stance on the pending legislation. Although supporting H.R. 1925 and H.R. 2105, he said WMX could not support H.R. 1924 for several reasons. First, it unfairly singled out waste facilities as the purveyors of environmental risk, when, as mentioned throughout the hearing, health problems in affected communities are usually cumulative in nature. Second, he noted that operating permits could be denied after construction was completed, resulting in large financial burdens for the company. Finally, he said that a participatory siting process was already in place but that it could be improved within its current context without further legislation.

The involvement of the business community in the environmental justice debate signaled the maturity of the movement and its legitimate place in the policy stream. During the early stages of the environmental justice movement, business was Goliath to the grassroots David. This is not to say that a confrontational relationship no longer exists. However, as an issue enters the policy stream it will not go very far if policy communities are fragmented and demand alternative solutions to the problem. The business community obviously recognized that this was an issue that needed to be addressed proactively, regardless of the actual proof of its occurrence. Therefore, business interests in 1993 may have been attempting to work within issue networks in order to have a say in the early stages of policy formation. Additionally, business disapproval of various pieces of legislation may also signal the early stages of development of another policy community that will offer alternative solutions to the problem. In the future, these alternatives may signal yet another redefinition of the problem. But for the time being it appeared that the business community, while looking after its own interests, understood the political importance of giving credence to the concerns being outlined by the environmental justice movement.

Environmental justice also became an issue during the June 28, 1994, hearings before the Senate Committee on Environment and Public Works on the reauthorization of the Comprehensive Environmental Response, Compensation, and Liability Act of 1980 (CERCLA, also known as Superfund).[10] Saying that environmental justice concerns have been largely ignored, Chavis presented an eight-point plan that outlined what areas of CERCLA needed to be improved upon: (1) public health must be the focus; (2) adequate funding must be provided; (3) site prioritization must be based on public health risks; (4) remedies must be effective; (5) the litigious liability financing system must be replaced; (6) the public must be an active, empowered participant in the process; (7) tough liability must be maintained prospectively; and (8) communities harmed by toxic disposal must be helped to recover.

These points were developed through a cooperative effort between the NAACP and the Alliance for a Superfund Action Partnership (ASAP). ASAP's membership includes national and multinational corporations, local government leaders, and some grassroots organizations.

Presidential Environmental Justice Actions

During the Bush administration, the environmental justice movement found a niche within EPA. In response to the Michigan Coalition and CBC members, the EPA began studying the issue and, in 1992, established the Office of Environmental Equity (now the Environmental Justice Office) and the National Environmental Justice Advisory Council. However, it was not until the Clinton administration that environmental justice assumed a high priority as a policy concern within the executive branch. In fact, two leading policy entrepreneurs of the movement, Chavis and Bullard, served on the natural resources and environment transition team. As part of this effort, they helped prepare a briefing document for the new EPA administrator, Carole Browner (Bullard, 1994b).

In addition, Vice President Al Gore was a leading proponent of environmental justice legislation during his last term in the U.S. Senate. This concern followed him to the White House. Such recognition within the executive branch culminated with the signing of the Executive Order on Environmental Justice (No. 12898) on February 11, 1994. The executive order prioritized the achievement of environmental justice as an integral part of every agency mission. Each agency was charged with developing a strategy for achieving environmental justice. The strategies were to accomplish the following: promote enforcement of health and environmental statutes in minority and low-income areas; ensure greater public participation; improve research and data collection of health and environmental information in affected communities; and identify differential patterns of consumption of natural resources among minority and low-income populations. The latter refers to the adverse health effects experienced by some minority communities (namely, Native Americans) due to a higher consumption rate than that used to establish safety standards. In compliance with the order, the Departments of Defense, Health and Human Services, Housing and Urban Development, Labor, Agriculture, Transportation, Justice, Interior, Commerce, and Energy, the Nuclear Regulatory Commission, the National Aeronautics and Space Administration, and the EPA submitted their final strategies to the president in mid-1995.

Through this order, the movement's main issues of contention were finally recognized within the decision agenda of the policy stream. The EPA was designated as the lead federal agency for carrying out the administration's environmental justice agenda. As part of this effort, Administrator

Browner was appointed chair of the Interagency Working Group on Environmental Justice, created by the order. The working group's task is to provide guidance to federal agencies on the implementation of the executive order and assist in coordinating the research and data collection required. The Interagency Working Group also serves as a clearinghouse for each agency during the development of its environmental justice plan.[11]

There are two problems with Executive Order No. 12898 that may jeopardize the future of environmental justice in the policy stream. The first is the nature of an executive order itself; any order can be rescinded by the next president (a real possibility only if the Democrats lose the White House in 2000). Moreover, without sustained congressional action on environmental justice, the order's policy future remains uncertain. Along these same lines, the order is meant only to improve the internal management of the executive branch; it is not an enforceable statute. If an agency chooses to ignore it upon occasion, it would be extremely difficult to address the situation through litigation. However, the presidential memorandum issued with the order emphasizes that Title 6 of the Civil Rights Act of 1964 provides an opportunity for federal agencies to address environmental hazards in minority and low-income communities. This title may be used by affected communities to ensure agency action as well. Title 6 prohibits discrimination on the basis of race, color, and national origin in all federally assisted programs. These regulations apply not only to intentional discrimination but also to policies and practices that have a discriminatory effect.

The Policy Stream Summarized

Although the problem and policy streams of the environmental justice movement have coupled in the 1990s, its future on the national policy agenda remains uncertain. Congress has yet to pass legislation specific to environmental justice despite several attempts from 1992 to 1996. Perhaps reauthorization of Superfund may cause some of the health and public participation issues addressed in other federal statutes to come to the fore. Even though the policy formation process is slow at the national level, states have begun to examine environmental justice and its implications within their borders. We discuss some of these state actions in Chapter 9.

If the problem fades from the national policy agenda, it may nevertheless reemerge at a later date, although this seems unlikely given that it has already undergone three distinct redefinitions. In order to fully summarize the phenomenon, then, it is necessary to look at the political stream that has played a part in both the problem and policy streams. The interaction that occurs between the key players in the movement, leaders of other policy communities, and government officials really sets the stage for policymaking as well as the future of the movement as a whole.

Therefore, we now turn toward the political stream for a more in-depth examination of its role in the agenda-setting process of environmental justice.

The Political Stream

Although it is within the problem and policy streams that an issue is defined and subsequently followed with action by federal decisionmakers, the political stream makes the coupling of all the streams possible.

Political factors that affect the decisionmaking agenda are electoral, partisan, and interest-group pressures. Through the political stream, policy communities are established, and potential solutions to the problem are offered to government officials. The political stream offers entrepreneurs the opportunity to build consensus in order to move the agenda forward. Aggressive entrepreneurs take advantage of this stream to promote the solutions they (and their interest groups) want to see implemented through the windows of opportunity opening in the policy stream (Kingdon, 1984; 1995).

In this section, the political stream will be explored in relation to the three defining periods of the environmental justice movement. It was during the third phase of the movement that the problem, policy, and political streams coalesced and made way for government action.

The general mood of the country during Richard Nixon's terms in office was one of social change. Myriad social movements were politically legitimized as their entrepreneurs played a role in legislative actions during this period. An issue area where some of the greatest strides were made was in environmental policy. NEPA (1969) was one of many pieces of legislation to highlight the significance of environmental concerns on the policy agenda. Although publicized in the 1971 CEQ annual report, several political factors led to the disappearance of inner-city environmental concerns (or environmental justice concerns, as they became known).

The main reason was the upheaval in the federal government caused by Watergate. President Gerald Ford was forced to contend with a public consumed by the scandal, and he had little time to consider any emerging problem streams. Even though inner-city environmental problems were still occurring, there were not any crisis situations to force the issue with policymakers. While environmental issues remained under consideration, the concerns being addressed were within the realm of the traditional environmental movement. Since traditional environmental organizations had already begun establishing themselves as a policy community with a stake in decisionmaking, it is not unusual that they would continue to promote the concerns that brought them bargaining power in the first place. Accordingly, the political situation was not ripe for new issues. In addition, under the Carter administration a new crisis emerged when the Organization of

Petroleum Exporting Countries's oil embargo brought energy issues to the forefront. Government attention was immediate because every car-owning American was directly affected at the gas pump.

It was not only the mainstream environmental organizations that did not have time to address inner-city environmental issues; civil rights groups could not afford to pave the way for new problem streams. Despite several gains during the 1960s, civil rights groups were still struggling to implement programs and ensure that African Americans would become equal throughout society, which included political decisionmaking. Thus, the policy communities at this time were too preoccupied with maintaining their positions in the policy stream to risk losing it to an issue that had not yet captured public attention.

Crises Stimulate the Reemergence of the Political Stream

In 1982, the political stream was once again flowing in favor of the environmental justice agenda. The Warren County protest marked the first time national policy entrepreneurs acted to promote the issue onto the public agenda. Although protests over the siting of such a dump site may be more reminiscent of traditional environmental protests (such as those of the antinuclear movement), circumstances surrounding the location of this dump opened the way for a series of civil rights–based claims of environmental racism.

Civil rights leaders used their existing policy community, which included members of the CBC, to move the issue into the policy stream. Following the Warren County protest, District of Columbia delegate Fauntroy commissioned the GAO study to examine the distribution of hazardous waste landfill siting in EPA Region 4. Even though this study did not lead to any immediate policy action, it later served as the cornerstone for future policy developments.

One reason for the lack of immediate action may be that the issue had become more narrowly defined in terms of race and region. Labeling the phenomenon as one of environmental racism caused it to be viewed as a minority concern and, as such, only one of several civil rights issues to be addressed. The issue encompasses a greater right to protection from environmental risk and adverse health effects, but labeling it in the context of racism served to polarize support for a solution. In addition, environmental racism and justice were being looked at as a regional issue rather than one of national concern. The movement's redefining events in the 1980s occurred in the South, as did the GAO study of inequitable siting. Thus, even though the issue was nationally recognized, it did not appear to be a problem of such magnitude that it warranted action by national policymakers.

The political stream of environmental justice was further slowed by the Reagan administration (1981–1989) as social policy was subjected to challenges like deregulation and decentralization. As a result, both environmental and civil rights organizations found themselves mobilizing around traditional themes in order to preserve their places on the policy agenda. This polarization caused environmental justice to once again be moved from the public agenda.

Confrontation Within the Movement

Even though it appeared that the window of opportunity had closed at the national level in the late 1980s and early 1990s, the issue did not disappear completely. Grassroots organizations continued their efforts at state and local levels. As the mood of the country began to shift favorably toward accepting environmental justice on the policy agenda, a political struggle emerged between national-level entrepreneurs and their counterparts at local and regional levels.

On March 15, 1990, a letter was sent from members of Louisiana's Gulf Coast Tenant Leadership Development Project and the Southwest Organizing Project to the so-called Big 10 national environmental organizations.[12] The letter was meant to call attention to the fact that low-income and minority communities are severely underrepresented in these organizations, which profess to include all communities in their environmental struggles (Hill, 1996:82).

Three points of contention were outlined in the letter. First, the point was made that some, not all, of the mainstream organizations accepted funds from the same corporations that were "killing" the affected communities of the environmental justice movement. Second, the compositions of the staff and board members of the mainstream organizations were questioned. Several of the organizations had people of color on the board or in staff positions, but environmental justice activists felt these were token positions rather than evidence of a sincere attempt to incorporate the concerns of these communities into decisionmaking processes (Sierra Club, 1993).[13]

The third point outlined in the letter questioned for whom the national organizations acted. Environmental justice advocates asked if the Big 10 were representing all Americans, or all people, as is the case with international organizations, and why they had not involved persons of color and the poor at the start of their campaigns. According to some grassroots activists, much of the environmental policy bargaining that had taken place resulted in granting polluters concessions in low-income or minority communities in exchange for maintaining protection in more traditional realms (such as wilderness preservation; Hill, 1996:84).

After the accusations of environmental racism were aired, many of the Big 10 organizations offered a series of examples of how they had involved communities of color in their environmental protection efforts. This was met with little acceptance on the part of the grassroots organizations. To illustrate the lack of concern for affected communities among the Big 10, environmental justice activists pointed to the "Blueprint for the Environment," a document submitted to the Bush administration that contained 750 recommendations from eighteen environmental organizations. Among the recommendations were proposals for every cabinet department except two—the Department of Housing and Urban Development and the Department of Labor. Grassroots activists said this showed the lack of concern for minority and low-income communities, because recommendations could have easily been made in areas such as lead poisoning, energy conservation, and workplace safety (Sierra Club, 1993). Since the letter, many of these organizations have made valid attempts to place environmental justice concerns on their agendas.

Disagreement among grassroots and national environmental justice organizations have not been kept behind closed doors. During an April 12, 1994, hearing on the Superfund Reform Act of 1994 (S. 1834) before the Senate Subcommittee on Superfund, Recycling, and Solid Waste Management, the national and grassroots environmental movements split over the issue of liability. Florence Robinson of the North Baton Rouge Environmental Association spoke on behalf of the Keystone Commission (see Dellums, 1992) in favor of retaining Superfund's retroactive liability clause, better known as "polluter pays."[14] It is reasoned that this clause causes corporations to be responsible for their actions. Although they admit it is not perfect, many grassroots organizations say this is preferable to a general trust-fund system. National environmental justice activists advocated the trust-fund approach. National environmental justice activists are not the only ones behind this type of reform; it is also supported by the Business Roundtable. Such public fragmentation may have unintentional consequences for the movement's place on the agenda. When policy communities become fragmented, issues tend to fade from the policy stream and return to the problem stream for redefinition, or they disappear completely. Government decisionmakers are less likely to address an issue if there are too many alternative solutions proposed, because the chances for receptivity are greatly diminished (Kingdon, 1984).

Environmental Groups Attack the EPA's Efforts

Despite the fact that national and grassroots activists began to split in their approaches to solving environmental inequities, they have remained cohesive in their criticism of the federal government's efforts to address the issue.

The early environmental justice efforts of the Bush administration were characterized as a public relations attempt to mollify the growing insistence on government action to address inequities. This characterization appeared to have some validity once an internal memo on the EPA's environmental equity communication plan was leaked to the public.[15] This memo was the focus of much debate during a House subcommittee hearing on the impacts of lead poisoning on low-income and minority communities. The memo acknowledged that the policy community forming between mainstream civil rights and environmental organizations needed to be dealt with before the issue exploded. In this light, the EPA proposed a two-prong plan that would primarily concentrate on addressing the concerns of mainstream groups, followed by working with the activists from affected communities as part of a secondary effort. The memo states:

> The goal of this strategy is to win the recognition the agency deserves for its environmental equity and cultural diversity programs before the minority fairness issue reaches the "flashpoint"—that stage in an emotionally charged public controversy when activist groups finally succeed in persuading the more influential mainstream groups (civil rights organizations, unions, churches) to take ill-advised actions. From what we've begun seeing in the news, this issue is reaching that point.

The memo sets forth several paths for bringing the EPA's environmental justice message to the public. Part of this process was to hold a roundtable media event consisting of a panel of experts on the issue. One of the recommended participants was Chavis. However, a handwritten note in the side margins of the memo discourages the inclusion of Chavis on the panel because EPA officials did not want to give him an open "platform." EPA could not be responsible for what he said and therefore wanted to go with a less controversial panel member. For obvious reasons, these statements, although only a small part of a proactive plan, tainted the activists' perceptions of the EPA's environmental justice efforts. This had been a longtime point of contention between government officials and activists.

Dissension also arose within the Environmental Equity Workgroup over the report, *Environmental Equity: Reducing Risk for All Communities.* Some members of the workgroup voiced concerns that the EPA was perpetuating the exclusionary practices of the past by not allowing members of the Michigan Coalition to review and give input on the report before it was released to the public. Robert Wolcott, chair of the workgroup, defended the release of the report, saying it was only a draft of the report that was released without the input of the coalition members. He said several members of the coalition stated that they would not be able to submit comments in time to meet the deadline for the draft copy. The draft copy was to be ready for the 1992 congressional hearing on the impacts of lead poisoning on low-income and minority communities.

Although environmental justice activists have tended to work well with the Clinton administration, the EPA's efforts have not been without controversy. For example, NEJAC comprises environmentalists, industry representatives, tribal members, state and local government interests, and academicians. NEJAC provides pertinent advice to the EPA on environmental justice–related issues. However, the stakeholders present within NEJAC have not always seen eye to eye. In May 1994, several activists wrote to Administrator Browner, who established NEJAC, to express their concern over the appointment of John Hall, head of the Texas Natural Resource Conservation Commission, as chair.[16] The activists' concerns stemmed from the fact that several environmental discrimination lawsuits were pending against the Texas commission. Hall stepped down as chair during NEJAC's first meeting in August 1994 (he remained as a member). Much of the insistence on Hall's resignation came from the grassroots wing of the movement, which shows that they are gaining legitimacy in the political stream in their own right. This may lead to greater conflict between the movement's factions in the future (Hall and Kerr, 1991:89).

Yet EPA has attempted to maintain its environmental justice initiatives by making an effort to involve affected communities in EPA planning strategies. On January 20, 1995, the EPA held the First Interagency Public Meeting on Environmental Justice. The purpose of the meeting was to provide citizens an opportunity to voice concerns about environmental issues affecting communities; it also served as a forum for public comment on federal agencies' environmental justice initiatives. In order to assure a wide spectrum of participation from across the country, the meeting was broadcast by satellite to various locations. These locations included historically black colleges and universities. It is estimated that more than 1,000 community residents, environmental justice leaders, and stakeholders participated in the meeting (U.S. Environmental Protection Agency, Office of Environmental Justice, 1995).

For the time being, EPA's commitment to environmental justice seems to be vigorous. Browner seems to be moving toward insulating the Office of Environmental Justice from future political attacks. In August 1995, she relocated it within the Office of Enforcement and Compliance Assurance (U.S. Environmental Protection Agency, Office of Environmental Justice, 1995). The reasoning was that the move would bring a multimedia approach to environmental justice and enhance environmental justice enforcement. Its previous home, the Office of Administration and Resource Management, did not have the high-profile status that was desired for the office.

Coalition-Building in Congress

Once civil rights organizations began to take an interest in the environmental justice movement, they brought the issue to their congressional allies—the Congressional Black Caucus. Delegate Fauntroy, a member of the CBC, was the first federal official to place the issue on Congress's policy agenda. The CBC's forum on environmental justice, held at its annual Legislative Weekend in 1990, strengthened the existing environmental justice policy coalition and gave it political clout (Dellums, 1992).

Members of Congress introduce legislation for a variety of reasons, from personal interest to political pressure. Environmental justice legislation is no exception to this rule, and a few examples will serve to illustrate the motivation behind the action. For example, the 1991 People of Color Environmental Leadership Summit reaffirmed the need for environmental justice legislation to Representative John Lewis. Lewis introduced the Environmental Equity Act of 1992 (H.R. 5326). Lewis wanted to see it addressed on its own, rather than tucked away in another piece of legislation such as the reauthorization of the Resource Conservation and Recovery Act, so that the relevance of the issue was not overridden by other concerns. The implications of the issue both as one of civil rights and environmental protection have kept environmental justice a priority in his office.[17]

In contrast, Representative Cardiss Collins's (D.–Ill.) interest in environmental justice was spurred by the experience of her constituents. Not only is Collins's district on the west side of Chicago, an area laden with environmental problems; it is bordered on the south by one of the most polluted areas in the country, known as the "toxic doughnut." Her personal interest in the issue led her to sponsor legislation to combat the problems of multiple exposure to pollutants (H.R. 1924). Collins would also like to see environmental justice legislation passed on its own; however, any type of legislation would be preferable to none. Legislation is preferable to the current executive order because it would be a permanent tool to assist communities. Although the political climate in Congress in 1996 did not favor the passage of such legislation, Collins nevertheless reintroduced the Environmental Equal Rights Act during the 104th Congress.[18]

Defining Alternate Solutions

As an issue matures, policy communities develop around it and begin to offer alternative solutions for problem-solving. Environmental justice is no exception. Initially, the policy communities consisted of inner-city environmental/civil rights activists who were attempting to improve their immediate living conditions. These individuals had little political clout, and as a result they did not have the connections needed to get the issue placed high upon the policy agenda. Environmental justice later attracted the attention of the civil rights movement. Civil rights entrepreneurs had the political connections needed to get decisionmakers interested in the issue. As the issue blossomed, it began to attract not only civil rights and grassroots social/environmental justice organizations but also mainstream environmental groups. By the late 1980s, this coalition seemed to be growing into a more vocal policy community. Its success in getting the issue onto the agenda seemed evident in the wide array of legislation dealing with environmental justice concerns that was introduced in the early 1990s. However, once legislation was introduced, the issue was recognized by other policy communities and viewed as possibly having an impact on their policy positions. Therefore, these groups are now beginning to vie for a place on the environmental justice policy agenda in order to assure that their interests are not ignored.

Competing policy communities do not vehemently deny that an environmental justice problem exists. The political backlash of such accusations would alienate too many government officials and, in the long run, detract from favorable action in other agenda areas. However, this growing coalition, made up of business and industry representatives and selected academicians, is posing questions about the proof given as evidence that environmental inequities exist. In cases where inequities are shown, they are offering alternative remedies.

The first question being raised is one of market dynamics. Most of the studies supporting claims of environmental racism have been cross-sectional rather than longitudinal. A study conducted by Vicki Been (1994) that longitudinally reanalyzed the community dynamics of two earlier environmental justice studies found support for the environmental racism thesis in one study but not the other, illustrating the discrepancies that could be hidden by an analysis with a limited scope. Another issue that has been raised concerning the early studies is the narrow range of variables employed in the analysis.

Although not totally disregarding environmental justice studies of the past, the Center for the Study of American Business outlines several options for mitigating exposure to environmental risks. A recognizably unrealistic goal of completely eliminating waste is the first option they discuss. This does not seem like a real choice given the constructs of our modern industrial society. However, it is the best option for resolving inequities. The political remedies they suggest include: developing regulations that would directly limit or prohibit future industrial siting in minority and disadvantaged communities, and invoking penalties against currently active polluting and waste facilities that disproportionately impact minorities (Boerner and Lambert, 1995). The third option is to compensate individuals who bear external costs.

Thus, business and industry are no longer standing by and allowing themselves to be painted as the perpetrators of environmental injustices. Their representatives are making their interests known both at congressional hearings and within agency environmental justice working groups such as NEJAC. In addition, several business associations, such as the National Association of Manufacturers (NAM), have established internal environmental justice working groups. NAM, for example, has adopted an environmental justice policy that includes support for open and informed dialogue with citizens about environmental decisions by industry that affect local communities, as well as continued research into factors affecting human health and the environment.[19] Industry has learned that it will be affected by the environmental justice movement's agenda-setting goals. Therefore, taking a proactive approach toward becoming involved in all three streams of the agenda-building process is in their best interest.

Summary of the Political Stream

In the late 1990s, the environmental justice movement reached a point where the political stream provided the necessary conditions to assist in opening windows of opportunities. There were several inhibitors of this in the past. For example, since the issue was initially defined in 1971 and through 1992, presidential administrations did not provide a stable, friendly forum for environmental justice concerns. It could be speculated that the issue would have been addressed in more depth during Nixon's second term; however, conditions following his departure from office left little room for the emergence of any new social concerns. Furthermore, the national mood was one of overall distrust toward government, and there were no environmental justice crises to keep the issue alive. The political stream seemed to open near the end of the Bush administration when the Michigan Coalition served to influence the establishment of the Environmental Equity Workgroup. At the same time, grassroots organizations were joining together at the First National People of Color Leadership Summit.

By 1992, the various factors of the environmental justice movement's political stream had coalesced. The 1992 Environmental Equity Act was introduced, clearing the way for the issue's movement from the government agenda onto the decisionmaking agenda. This act also signaled more diverse political support for environmental justice among policymakers as well. Following the 1992 presidential elections, a window of opportunity opened for the environmental justice movement. Bullard and Chavis, leading environmental justice entrepreneurs, were members of the transition team that offered advice to the incoming administration. Their efforts came to fruition with the signing of Executive Order No. 12898.

The future environmental justice political stream will most likely be characterized by efforts to maintain its current policy positions, and because environmental justice is not covered by legislative enactment, future activity may be lodged with Congress.

Summary and Conclusions

The environmental justice movement has competed for a place on the public agenda for about three decades. During this time the movement has undergone three periods of redefinition. In the 1970s, it was seen as an inner-city environmental movement whose primary aim was to get human health concerns addressed as part of the larger environmental movement. The civil rights aspect of the issue was present at this time; however, it was not the main focal point. This changed in the 1980s, when the issue fell under the rubric of environmental racism. The 1982 Warren County protest brought the issue to the attention of lawmakers, civil rights activists, and, at a less active level, environmental organizations. Although the issue did not receive the national legislative attention desired by many of the environmental justice activists, the issue was brought to the attention of established national policy communities such as the civil rights community and the Congressional Black Caucus. Academia began to take notice of the issue during this time, which led to the redefinition of the issue that emerged in the late 1980s—that of environmental justice. The redefinition of the issue as environmental justice has moved it to a more stable place on the public policy agenda.

In regard to the future of the environmental justice movement, much will hinge upon the political climate following the 2000 presidential elections. During the late 1990s, the only institutionalized federal environmental justice policy initiative has been within the executive office. However, a new presidential administration in 2000 might rescind the executive order of 1994. In such an event, there would be no binding federal commitment to environmental justice other than a general protection offered under the Equal Protection clause and the Civil Rights Act of 1964.

The political climate in Congress also presents a barrier to the advancement of environmental justice concerns. The conservative tone of Congress harkens back to the decentralizing agenda of the Reagan era. State power is increasing while federal budgets are decreasing. As seen during the Reagan era, this led to a polarization by the civil rights and environmental movements in order to protect their policy bargaining positions and retain past policy gains. During the 1980s, this led to a disappearance of environmental justice from the policy stream; it may do the same thing, at the federal level, after 2000. However, states have recently begun to take an interest in environmental justice. Events and policy communities within states have prompted legislative action. Therefore, the issue may be gaining the momentum needed to keep it on state-level agendas, thereby leading to continued recognition at the federal level, at least in terms of maintaining the executive order and the EPA Office of Environmental Justice.

Another setback for the movement at the national level was the dismissal of one of its most well-known entrepreneurs, Benjamin Chavis, from his position as executive director of the NAACP. He appeared at multiple congressional hearings on environmental justice issues and attended national events that effected the movement. It remains to be seen if he will continue to be involved in the promotion of environmental justice as a public figure or on behalf of another civil rights organization. Perhaps another nationally recognized environmental justice activist will take over where Chavis left off.

Overall, it appears that environmental justice has been legitimized as an issue on the policy agenda. Mechanisms have been put into place that will allow the issue to be studied in more depth and perhaps result in greater evidence supporting environmental justice claims. For example, national health studies will now be demographically characterized in order to examine adverse health conditions based on socioeconomic breakdowns. However, as illustrated by the Kingdon model, it is not enough to develop the problem stream. If the policy stream of environmental justice cannot be coupled with the problem stream, there will be no chance of the issue moving through the decisionmaking agenda. Moreover, if empirical research on this topic continues to call into question the basic validity of the thesis, then support within Congress for legislation may wane as well. In addition, if the traditional environmental and civil rights organizations abandon the issue of environmental justice, it remains to be seen if grassroots activists can form a policy community that will keep the issue on the national policy agenda.

We have discussed in this chapter how the issue of environmental injustice has emerged onto the public agenda. In Chapter 4, we discuss exactly how we propose to analyze the validity of the claims of environmental injustice discussed above. In the subsequent chapters, we present the results of our analyses at the state, county, and city levels before we finally suggest in Chapter 10 what might be done to alleviate this potential problem for public policy in the United States.

Notes

1. The fact that the environmental justice movement has been in progress since at least the early 1970s (and arguably since the 1960s) makes it well suited to an analysis

using the Kingdon model, in that the model is more suited to a chronological examination of an issue rather than one conducted in a limited time frame. A limited time frame does not allow one to fully comprehend the movements of the various streams and their effects on the overall agenda-setting process. This is because a stream, especially the problem stream, may be very active in times of issue redefinition while the other streams—policy and political—are dormant. Thus, if the scope of the analysis is limited in time, it will not capture the essence of the coupling of streams and the windows of opportunity needed to move the issue onto the decisionmaking agenda. Since the environmental justice movement has gone through three distinct periods of redefinition, the Kingdon model has allowed for a more comprehensive understanding of the agenda-setting process. Indeed, we conceptualize this process as stemming from the 1970s through the mid-1990s. We concentrate on this period in this chapter because we feel that the major events that placed environmental justice on the public agenda took place during this quarter century or so of political history.

2. The *Bean* case focused on opposition to a plan to site a municipal landfill near a suburban, middle-income neighborhood and a predominantly African American high school (National Conference of State Legislatures, 1995). In their move for a preliminary injunction against the Texas Department of Health's disposal facility permit, the plaintiffs' argued that their community, which was 82 percent African American, did not have characteristics preferable to siting such a facility—such as proximity to waste generators and access to good roads. The plaintiffs claimed the Texas Department of Health was also engaged in a broader pattern of historical discrimination by allowing the siting of disposal facilities in minority communities. In support of their claim, the plaintiffs' advanced statistical evidence compiled by Professor Robert Bullard that indicated that in Houston 82.4 percent of the seventeen disposal facilities in operation since 1978 were located in areas where the minority population was 50 percent or less. Of the total number of sites, 59 percent were in areas where the minority population was 25 percent or less. The court's opinion in *Bean* stated that the siting of a solid waste facility so close to a high school—while illogical—did not substantiate the claim of discrimination in that more that half of the sites were located in census tracts with minority populations of less than 25 percent. While setting aside the claim of racial discrimination, the court—as often occurs in cases of first impression—set forth the grounds necessary to support future claims of state agency discriminatory intent: the proximity of solid waste sites to minority communities within each census tract, the site-selection process and how many alternative sites are selected and examined by the state, and whether the racial composition of the potential site is taken into account and compared with the overall racial composition of all of the host communities so as not to discriminate (Mitchell, 1993).

3. This study examined the characteristics of Americans living in ZIP code areas surrounding commercial hazardous waste facilities and uncontrolled toxic waste sites throughout the United States. The United Church of Christ prefaced its study by saying that it was not designed to show cause and effect; rather, its purpose was purely exploratory. Nevertheless, the study argued strongly in favor of the environmental racism hypothesis.

4. Property owners were eligible to obtain the appraised market value of their home, $11,000 per acre of land, $4,000 per household for a moving allowance, and a premium on the value of their property. Renters were given a similarly lucrative of-

fer. No residents were forced to relocate to New Morrisonville. In fact, Dow provided assistance for relocation anywhere in the United States (Dow Chemical, 1989).

5. By choosing to rely upon networks rather than a single national environmental justice organization, leaders in the movement were aiming to prevent the centralization of the movement and assure the equal participation of all affected communities (Hill, 1996: 55).

6. EPA Region 4 includes Alabama, Florida, Georgia, Kentucky, Mississippi, North Carolina, South Carolina, and Tennessee.

7. U.S. House of Representatives, Subcommittee on Health and the Environment, Committee on Energy and Commerce, 1992, Impacts of Lead Poisoning on Low-Income and Minority Communities, 102nd Cong., 2nd Sess., February 25, 1992.

8. U.S. House of Representatives, Subcommittee on Transportation and Hazardous Materials, Committee on Energy and Commerce, 1993. H.R. 1924, 1925, and 2105: Bills to Amend Solid Waste Disposal Act, the Comprehensive Environmental Response, Compensation, and Liability Act, and to establish a program to assure compliance with all environmental health and safety laws, and for other purposes, 103rd, Cong., 1st Sess., November 18, 1993.

9. In retrospect, we can see that each prong has been addressed to some degree.

10. U.S. Senate, Committee on Environment and Public Works, 1994, A Bill to Amend the Comprehensive Environmental Response, Compensation, and Liability Act of 1980, and for other purposes (as reported by the Subcommittee on Superfund, Recycling, and Solid Waste Management), 103rd Cong., 2nd Sess., June 28, 1994.

11. The environmental justice strategy of the EPA appears to focus on the following key points: public participation, accountability, partnerships, outreach and communication with stakeholders, health and environmental research, data collection, analysis and stakeholder access to public participation, American Indian and indigenous environmental protection, and enforcement, compliance, assurance, and regulatory reviews.

12. The Big 10 organizations were the Sierra Club, Sierra Club Legal Defense Fund, National Parks and Conservation Association, Izzak Walton League, Friends of the Earth, Wilderness Society, National Audubon Society, National Resource Defense Council, Environmental Defense Fund, and National Wildlife Federation.

13. Much of the frustration for grassroots organizations stemmed from the feelings that mainstream groups used minority and low-income communities for personal gain in that working with grassroots organizations and their struggles brings national attention to mainstream groups (Hill, 1996: 84).

14. Prepared Statement of Florence T. Robinson, Superfund Reform Act of 1994 (S. 1834), Hearings Before the Subcommittee on Superfund, Recycling, and Solid Waste Management of the Committee on Environment and Public Works of the United States Senate, April 12, 1994, pp. 466–469.

15. November 15, 1991, U.S. Environmental Protection Agency Internal Memorandum from Associate Administrator Lewis S.W. Crampton to Chief of Staff Gordon Birder, submitted during testimony at a February 25, 1992, Hearing Before the Subcommittee on Health and the Environment of the Housing Committee on Energy and Commerce, p. 56.

16. U.S. Environmental Protection Agency, Office of Water, "Environmental Justice Council Develops Advice, Despite Chaotic State," *Water Policy Report*, August 17, 1994, p. 24.

17. Interview with Deborah Spielberg, legislative director for Representative John Lewis, conducted by Kelly M. Hill, November 20, 1995.

18. Interview with Sarah Wheat, legislative assistant to Representative Cardiss Collins, conducted by Kelly M. Hill, November 30, 1995.

19. National Association of Manufacturers Policy on Environment Justice, approved by NAM Board of Directors, September 24, 1994.

4

Modeling Environmental Injustice: Concepts, Measures, Hypotheses, and Method of Analysis

In developing a model to guide our analysis, we followed the steps suggested by W.T. Morris (1970). Specifically, we surveyed existing literature to piece together multiple explanations about the distribution of toxic hazards. The first wave of the existing literature indicated that race/ethnicity, social class, and political mobilization were integral to the study of environmental justice. The second wave of the literature review revealed an extensive set of additional concepts that are necessary to fully specify any inquiry regarding the frequency, distribution, or severity of any environmental harm. Many of the second-wave concepts had not been included in environmental justice studies.

The First-Wave Review of the Literature

In beginning with the first wave of the extant literature, we find several alternative explanations for environmental injustice—race/ethnicity, social class, and political mobilization. We review those preliminary explanations below and combine then into a simple tripartite model of environmental injustice.

Race/Ethnicity

There is a longitudinal body of literature that demonstrates a relationship between various minority groups and increased levels of a variety of environmental harms (Adeola, 1994; Allen, Lester, and Hill, 1995; Anderton, et al.,

1994a, 1994b; Arora and Carson, 1999; Asch and Seneca, 1978; Attah, 1992; Been, 1994, 1995; Berry, 1977; Boer, et al., 1997; Boerner and Lambert, 1995; Bowman and Crews-Meyer, 1995; Bullard, 1983, 1990a, 1990b; Burch, 1976; Burke, 1993; Clean Sites, Inc., 1990; Colquette and Robertson, 1991; Costner and Thornton, 1990; Crews-Meyer, 1994; Cutter, 1994; Dorfman, 1979; Downey, 1998; Fitton, 1992; Freeman, 1972; Gelobter, 1987; Gianessi, Peskin, and Wolfe, 1979; Gianessi and Peskin, 1980; Glickman and Hersh, 1995; Gould, 1986; Greenberg, 1993, 1994; Hamilton, 1993, 1995; Hird, 1993, 1994; Hird and Reese, 1998; Holm, 1994; Kohlhase, 1991; Krieg, 1995, 1998; Kruvant, 1975; Lavelle and Coyle, 1992; Lester, Allen, and Lauer, 1994; Lester and Allen, 1996; Mohai and Bryant, 1992; Moses, et al., 1993; Najem, et al., 1985; Perlin, et al., 1995; Polloch and Vittas, 1995; Ringquist, 1995, 1996, 1997; Rios, Poje, and Detels, 1993; Sexton and Anderson, 1993; Szasz, et al., 1992; United Church of Christ, 1987; West, 1992; White, 1992; Zimmerman, 1993, 1994). Within this body of literature we find statements that maintain that black communities, because of their economic and political vulnerability, have been routinely targeted for the siting of noxious facilities, locally unwanted land uses, and environmental hazards (Bullard, 1990a: xiv). Indeed, one author argues that "it is clear that environmental inequities, social injustice, and racism (individual and institutional) are not limited to the southern United States" (Bullard, 1990a: xv). Case studies of Michigan (Downey, 1998; West, 1992), Detroit (Downey, 1998; Mohai and Bryant, 1992), Ohio (Bowen, et al., 1995), Los Angeles (Boer, et al., 1997; Burke, 1993), and New Jersey (Greenberg, 1993, 1994), as well as more expanded research of U.S. counties (Allen, 2001; Allen, Lester, and Hill, 1995; Hird, 1993, 1994; Hird and Reese, 1998), cities (Lester and Allen, 1996), and ZIP codes (Ringquist, 1995, 1996, 1997; United Church of Christ, 1987) would tend to support this nonregional proposition. Although some research has demonstrated that race/ethnicity may not be the largest or most important measure when explaining environmental inequities, the predominant trend in the research on the subject indicates that as the percent of the minority population increases, so do the levels of environmental harms.

The race/ethnicity variable we employ consists of the percent of the population that is either black or Hispanic. For our state-level analysis, these demographic variables were taken from the 1980 U.S. Census Bureau figures. For our county- and city-level analyses, data for the two minority populations were taken from the 1990 *County and City Data Book*. In all instances, population data were subjected to log linear transformation to correct for skewed distributions.

We rejected the idea of creating a percent minority measure for several reasons. First, we are interested in the relationship between different minority populations and various environmental harms. Combining the race/ethnicity measure into a percent minority population would prohibit us from making the detailed statements we are interested in. Second, the U.S. Census classified Hispanics as being of any race—including black. As a consequence, combining these categories creates an inadvertent overcount and, in some cases, leads to population estimates in excess of 100 percent. Third, a previous large-scale study (United Church of Christ, 1987) focuses on these two groups at the ZIP code level. We can therefore engage in a partial replication of this previous research at the state, county, and city levels.

Thus, we have made a conscious research-design decision to limit our inquiry to the black and Hispanic populations at the state, county, and city levels for several reasons. We selected these two groups, in part, because of a simple question of allocating limited research resources—a broader inquiry that included Native Americans and Asian Pacific Islanders was simply beyond the scope of our financial wherewithal. Further, given the distribution of the Native American population in the United States and *within* the various states, counties, and cities, it seems that a different research strategy is needed to adequately assess the existence of environmental injustice for that section of the population. Additionally, the history of Asian Pacific Islanders in the United States also contains several idiosyncratic circumstances that we feel require a different research strategy than the one employed in this book. Thus, while we confine our investigation to the black and Hispanic populations at the state, county, and city levels, we encourage other scholars to investigate the relationship between environmental risk and race/ethnicity for groups that we have not included in our study.

The two groups we study are not bereft of a visible and well-documented history of discrimination, and, as such, we feel the study of these two groups in relationship to environmental injustice is quite relevant. In keeping with the predominant trend in this body of research, we should find a positive relationship between the percent of the population that is black or Hispanic and the environmental hazards that have been isolated for study.

Social Class

There is a class dimension to the environmental injustice thesis that maintains that poor communities are targeted for environmental hazards. Land is cheap in poor areas, possibly because of existing industry. New industries select these areas as potential locations because of depressed land prices and existing infrastructure. Additionally, wealthier locales, with well-educated, affluent individuals, want to protect against decreasing property values; thus, polluting industries meet opposition when trying to locate in upscale areas (O'Hare, Bascow, and Sanderson, 1983; Portney, 1991). As a consequence, studies have demonstrated a class dimension with regard to the location, frequency, and severity of a variety of environmental harms (Anderton, et al., 1994a, 1994b; Asch and Seneca, 1978; Berry, 1977; Boer, et al.,

1997; Boerner and Lambert, 1995; Bullard, 1983, 1990a; Burch, 1976; Clean Sites, Inc, 1990; Cutter, 1994; Freeman, 1972; Gelobter, 1987; Gould, 1986; Greenberg, 1993, 1994; Hamilton, 1995; Handy, 1977; Harrison, 1975; Hird, 1993, 1994; Hird and Reese, 1998; Krieg, 1995, 1998; Lavelle and Coyle, 1992; Lester, Allen, and Lauer, 1994; Ringquist, 1995, 1996, 1997; Shaikh, 1995; Shaikh and Loomis, 1998; Stretesky and Hogan, 1998; Stretesky and Lynch, 1999; Szasz, et al., 1992; United Church of Christ, 1987; U.S. Council on Environmental Quality, 1971; U.S. General Accounting Office, 1983; Zimmerman, 1993; Zupan, 1973).[1]

Measurement of social class was achieved by creating factor scales of traditional measures of income and education. Separate scales were created for the state-, county-, and city-level inquiries. In keeping with existing literature, we hypothesize a negative relationship between social class and the various environmental harms isolated for study, except for any measure of hazardous waste. In this instance, the hypotheses follow current research (Bowman and Crews-Meyer, 1995; Hird, 1993, 1994) and anticipate a positive relationship between social class and hazardous waste.[2]

Political Mobilization

It is also argued that politically mobilized communities capture the attention of decisionmakers. Thus, increased political mobilization should have the effect of minimizing environmental harms, because policymakers are likely to pay attention to problems articulated by this type of community. Some studies have examined the linkage between political mobilization and environmental hazards (Allen, Lester, and Hill, 1995; Crews-Meyer, 1994; Hird, 1993, 1994; Hird and Reese, 1998; Hamilton, 1995; Lester and Allen, 1996; Lester, Allen, and Lauer, 1994; Ringquist, 1995, 1996, 1997). Four studies indicate that political mobilization does play a role in diminishing levels of environmental hazards (Hamilton, 1995; Hird and Reese, 1998; Lester, Allen, and Lauer, 1994; Ringquist, 1997). At the state and county levels, political mobilization was measured by an indicator of voter turnout in each geographic area. For the state-level analysis, the votes cast in the 1984 presidential elections were divided by the 1980 total population. The county-level measure was created by dividing total votes cast in the 1992 presidential elections by 1990 total population.

The state- and county-level measures of political mobilization constitute a departure from the usual construction of this measure, which divides total votes cast in the election by the eligible electorate. Total population was selected as the denominator of the measure based on the logic that political influence of a population declines if either the eligible voters in that population tend to vote less often or more members of that population are ineligible to vote. The measure used in this research combines those two components of political activity. A similar argument was advanced in favor of constructing the measure in this fashion by S. Arora and T.N. Carson (1999:696–697), and similar measures had been used in other research (Allen, 2001; Allen, Lester, and Hill, 1995; Lester and Allen, 1996).

Unlike the previous measures of political mobilization, city mobilization is not measured in terms of voter turnout. In the United States, local elections are held at different times, and there is no agency that systematically collects election results. Further, some city-level presidential election results are reported for different geographic entities, making comparable measures difficult. Thus, the measure of political mobilization at the city level is the 1990 median value of owner-occupied housing measured in $1,000. On a conceptual level, we use the median value of owner-occupied housing because we feel that the higher the value of owner-occupied housing, the greater the stake in the community—and therefore the more likely a high level of mobilization will occur. Along other lines, we selected this measure because it has been used in similar fashion in other research (Hird, 1993, 1994; Hird and Reese, 1998; Lester and Allen, 1996).[3] In all instances, high scores on these measures equal a high level of political mobilization. The hypothesis states that higher levels of political mobilization will result in lower levels of environmental harms.

Simple Tripartite Model

The race/ethnicity, social class, and political mobilization components, when combined, create a simple formulation of the overall model and reflect the multivariate statistical hypothesis in Equation 4.1:

$$y_{env.\ harm} = a + b_1 Race - b_2 Class - b_3 Moblization$$

If race, class, and mobilization do matter, then the requisite signs and statistical significance should attach to each estimator in this simple equation.

The Second-Wave Review of the Literature

A second survey of the extant literature, usually associated with environmental politics and policy research, revealed an extensive list of additional measures that should be included when studying the nexus between the distribution of environmental harms and race, class, and political mobilization.

The additional sets of measures need to be included for a variety of reasons. First, correlating race and class, individually or in combination, with some level of an environmental harm does not, in any way, challenge or replace existing explanations for the distribution of environmental harms. Even adding political mobilization to an equation—though a step in the right direction—does not completely solve this problem. Thus, the tripartite model would merely assert, and to some degree justify, the existence of a potential rival explanation for the distribution of environmental harms.

Second, science is an activity that is based on comparisons—and science as comparison has a discrete set of outcomes. A new explanation can be shown to have no merit when compared to existing explanations. In the alternative, a new explanation can be shown to explain a phenomena better than existing theories. Under such conditions, the new explanation replaces the existing theory. However, there is a third possibility—the new explanation does not, by itself, explain the phenomena in question; instead, its adds to the existing explanation and therefore expands our understanding. The focus of this book is whether the environmental injustice thesis does tell us something more about the distribution of environmental harms. We doubt that the various dimensions of the simple tripartite model we test will replace competing theories, however, they might add to our existing understandings of the problem.

In order to achieve the goal of science as comparison, the race/class/mobilization model needs to be tested in comparison to rival explanations across the three different levels of analysis that we have chosen for this study: state, county, and city. Testing rival explanations across the three levels leads to a set of technical problems. First, whenever possible, similar measures should be constructed for the three levels of analysis. Second, two of our analyses—the county and the city—are subregions of states. As such, activities at subregional levels are to some degree affected by the actions at the state level. For example, highly organized environmental interests in states may affect the level of environmental harms in counties and cities by creating a statewide ethos that seeks to promote a higher degree of environmental protection. The fiscal capacity of a state may result in revenue-sharing, which enhances the ability of counties and cities to deal with environmental problems. A professional state legislature, having the institutional capability to deal with the complex interrelationships that mark environmental problems, may create policies that require counties and cities to deal with environmental problems. The overall business climate of the state—especially in states where business is favored by the actions of government—may dictate how counties and cities have to deal with them, which might be a major cause of pollution. State-level public opinion can create a climate that affects all aspects of state life, including actions within counties and cities that are part of the state. Finally, the overall political culture of a state may structure the responses counties and cities are capable of crafting. Thus, when assessing our primary topic of inquiry at the county and city levels, state-level effects need to be considered as well.

However, in addition to state effects, we also have county- and city-specific considerations. For example, at the county level, we need to consider county-specific pollution potential and fiscal capacity. Additionally, given the variation in size of counties, we need a control for county geographic size. Finally, because counties are spread across different broad sections of the nation, and because missing data on our county-level dependent variables vary by region, we need to include a regionalism surrogate to account for the varying distribution of this statistical problem. The city-level analysis presents similar problems. Our city-specific measures are pollution potential, city fiscal capacity, population density, and structural form of government—that is, either mayor-council or council-manager governments.

Pollution Potential

Pollution potential is a precondition of the levels of environmental harm selected for study at the state, county, and city levels. These harms exist within a context of large populations that are relatively densely situated in areas of high manufacturing capacity.

Many studies point to this concept as an explanation for the levels of environmental problems in any geographic locale, although these explanations have not necessarily been subsumed under the rubric of pollution potential (Lester, 1994). Four interrelated indicators capture the general cause of pollution: total population, population density, manufacturing establishments, and manufacturing employment.

Total population is not a commonly used variable in policy analysis, however, research has demonstrated a relationship between this measure and environmental harms (Allen, 2001; Allen, Lester, and Hill, 1995; Been, 1994; Bowman and Crews-Meyer, 1995, 1997; Lester and Allen, 1996). The nexus is rather straightforward: People produce waste material; as a consequence, the more people, the more waste. However, this premise regarding total population requires more specification; more people concentrated in close proximity, or population density, is also associated with the level of environmental problems. For example, population density explains the level of Toxic Release Inventory (TRI) facilities (Burke, 1993; Holm, 1994; Zimmerman, 1994); researchers (Allen, Lester, and Hill, 1995) have demonstrated a positive bivariate correlation between population density and eight different measures of environment harms in different samples of the sixty worst counties in the United States; James Lester and David Allen (1996)—using a weighted scale that included population density—report similar findings for two different samples of the largest cities in the United States. Further, high population density areas receive higher priorities for cleanup (Zimmerman, 1993), and airborne toxins are heavily concentrated in urban (high-density) areas (Cutter, 1995).

Population density needs to be considered for another reason. Most environmental contaminants are concentrated in urban areas (Ringquist, 1995, 1996, 1997). Indeed, E.J. Ringquist (1995) demonstrates a positive bivariate correlation between urbanism and hazardous waste facilities location (i.e., facilities covered under Title C of the Resource Conservation and Recovery Act). Population density is an acceptable surrogate for urbanism; in other words, states, counties, and cities with dense populations are likely to be highly urbanized.

A large population that is highly concentrated and coupled with industrialization that utilizes a high number of individuals employed in the manufacturing sector creates, as a byproduct of its endeavors, land, air, and water pollution. Several pieces of literature have demonstrated the relationship between existing and operating industrial concentrations and the presence of environmental problems. D.L. Anderton, et al. (1994a) demonstrated that the presence of industry had the most significant impact on TSD facility siting, and J.A. Hird (1993, 1994) confirms this finding with regard to the distribution of NPL sites. Hird and M. Reese (1998) have also shown the necessity of including this variable in their study of twenty-nine different environmental harms in U.S. counties, and E.J. Krieg (1998) demonstrates similar results regarding hazardous waste sites and TRI releases in the Boston area. Further, two studies focusing on the existence of a wide variety of environmental harms at county and city levels have demonstrated a strong relationship between existing manufacturing capacity and a wide range of environmental harms (Allen, Lester, and Hill, 1995; Lester and Allen, 1996).

Given the interrelationship among population and industry, and given the need to create separate state-, county-, and city-level measures for this concept, factor analysis of the relevant pool of variables was used to create sets of scales for the various levels of analysis. For the state-level measure, total population, population density, number of manufacturing establishments, and number of manufacturing employees were subjected to principal components factor analysis to create the state-level pollution potential scale. The resultant unidimensional factor explained 71 percent of variance among the four indicators.[4]

The county-specific measure of pollution potential, based on data abstracted from the 1994 *County and City Data Book*, was constructed using the same set of measures as was evident for the state-level measure of pollution potential. The unidimensional factor explained 80 percent of the variance with the pool of variables.[5]

In the state- and county-level analyses, four interrelated indicators could be subsumed into a single unidimensional factor scale. However, at the city level, we found that although the two manufacturing variables and total population did combine into a single factor, population density remained separate from the aforementioned measures. Because population density is a surrogate for urbanism (Ringquist, 1995, 1996), and because other research has demonstrated this measure's utility as a predictor of environmental harms (Allen, Lester, and Hill, 1995; Cutter, 1994; Lester and Allen, 1996; Ringquist, 1995, 1996, 1997; Zimmerman, 1993), we retained this variable in the city-level analysis as a separate indicator of pollution potential. Thus, our major measure of pollution potential at the city level is a factor scale of three indicators[6] augmented by population density as a separate indicator. High positive scores on all three scales indicate high levels of pollution potential; high negative scores indicate the opposite. A positive relationship is expected between pollution potential and the level of environmental harm.

Government Capacity

"Government capacity" refers to resources that are devoted to dealing with any societal problem. One means of assessing capacity is the financial resources of a government unit. Indeed, high government spending has been shown to reduce levels of water pollution (Ringquist, 1993) and other environmental problems at the state level (Lester and Lombard, 1990). At the state level, we were able to create a factor scale, using principal components factor analysis, that combines the percent of each state's budget obligated to natural resources in 1980, 1982, and 1985. The single factor explained 95 percent of the variance in the pool of variables. Besides being used in our state-level analysis, this scale was also used in the county- and city-level analyses to represent the state-level effect of government capacity on the two substate levels of government.[7]

At the county and city levels, we were unable to find reliable measures of fiscal resources devoted directly to the environment. Thus, for our county-level measure of fiscal capacity, we used overall county revenues and expenditures; again, a unidimensional scale generated by principal components factor analysis was used to measure the concept. The factor explained 40 percent of the variance in the pool of variables.[8]

At the city level, we found three measures (expenditures for sewers and sanitation, 1990–1991, per capita revenue, 1990–1991, and per capita expenditures, 1990–1991), which we use as surrogates for city capacity.[9] These measures are used individually at the city level because they could not be combined into a factor scale.

High scores on all measures indicate high fiscal capacity. We anticipate a negative relationship between these measures and the level of environmental harms.

Business Climate

States adopt a variety of policies designed to benefit various segments of society. Although these policies are caused by concerted lobbying in order to achieve a share of the pie, these policies also have a life of their own once adopted and can affect other segments of society. All states, to one degree or another, have adopted policies that are designed to encourage private enterprise to aid in economic development. These policies range from loan programs for construction of physical plants, to bond financing, to a variety of tax incentives. A state that favors business with a plethora of policy advantages might view the creation of a viable private economic sector as having a higher priority than environmental protection or, at least, may create a situation where the needs of business are given paramount consideration when balanced against environmental protection.

To measure business climate, three Guttman scales were subjected to principal components factor analysis, and a single factor, which explained 56 percent of the variance in the three Guttman scales, was produced. The Guttman scales were constructed from dichotomous data taken from the 1984–1985 *Book of the States*. Since high scores on each Guttman scale reflect a high level of support for business, the factor scale of the three Guttman components takes high positive values for a favorable business climate and high negative scores for the opposite. The hypothesis in this case is: As state policy favoring business increases, so does the level of environmental harm.

In the alternate, states that grant favorable conditions to business might attach a variety of riders to their largesse—forcing business to be a good environmental neighbor. Thus, we can also hypothesis that the level of environmental harm might decrease as a result of these business-oriented policies.[10]

The state-level measure was also used within the county- and city-level analyses for two reasons. First, one of the Guttman scales included in the factor speaks to the depth of support for business and contains policies that were supportive of business at the substate level. Second, state-level policies in support of business structure how counties and cities within the state must respond to business.

Legislative Professionalism

For decades, state legislatures were categorized as inefficient and corrupt (Sanford, 1967). However, during the 1960s and 1970s state legislatures reformed dramatically and added resources necessary for efficient government (Bowman and Kearney, 1986; National Conference of State Legislatures, 1986; Rosenthal, 1981). In many ways, state legislatures have come to resemble the U.S. Congress with regard to the role of committees, increased staff, longer tenure, and increased attention paid to constituency relations (Saffell, 1990:137). This has better prepared state legislatures to make policy and have a direct effect on the status of life within their respective states (Rosenthal, 1981). From a theoretical perspective, a more professional legislature should have more time to examine issues and develop more comprehensive and innovative solutions to societal problems (Ringquist, 1993:108). Under these conditions, professional legislatures should be more able to deal with the complex and technical area of environmental protection. In the main, research in this area has sought to couple legislative professionalism and more responsive policy outputs (Bulanowski, 1981; Lester, et al., 1983; Ringquist, 1993). Taking the next step and linking legislative professionalism directly to ameliorating environmental harms within the state is certainly plausible as well.

Several measures of legislative professionalism have been developed. These measures usually combine some set of weighted scores for length of tenure, staff size, length of session, and budget. However, more recent research has developed another method of measuring state legislative professionalism. Percival Squires (1992) created an index that compares each state legislature to the U.S. Congress and assigns a score to each state based on how closely the state legislature approximates the U.S. Congress.[11] High scores on Squires's index equal highly professionalized state legislatures.

State legislatures deal with problems on a statewide basis. As a consequence, they effect activities at the substate level. Thus, this measure was included in the county- and city-level analyses as a measure of state-level impact. The hypothesis, in keeping with the general tenor of existing research, predicts a negative relationship between legislative professionalism and level of environmental harm.

Public Opinion and Political Culture

In a democratic society, public opinion is supposed to shape governmental response. This linkage is too common and well known to require much in the way of explanation. Indeed, there is a long tradition that assesses the effect of opinion, measured in a variety of ways, on a variety of topics. However, this body of research has suffered from omission—that is, relevant survey data at the state and substate levels have not been available to directly measure public opinion.

More recently, however, researchers (Wright, Erickson, and McIver, 1985) have established a direct set of measures for the public opinion concepts of partisanship and ideology. These measures are based on CBS News–*New York Times* polling data that included questions regarding party affiliation and liberalism-conservatism. By aggregating respondents by state and over time, these measures of public opinion provide estimates of both the degree of partisanship (Republican-moderate-Democrat) and direction of ideological predisposition (in terms of a liberal-to-conservative continuum) for each state. Because both Democrats and liberals are viewed as holding more pro-environment views than Republicans and conservatives, the hypothesis is this: As the level of Democratic partisanship and liberalism in a state increases, lower levels of environmental harms should be evident. Because of the score patterns of each variable, the statistical hypothesis will consist of coefficients with negative signs. Further, since the state-level public opinion has an overarching effect across the state—determining what is expected from government by constituencies—we used these state-level measures of partisanship and ideology at the substate level. The hypothesis remains constant for the substate (county- and city-level) analyses.

"American political culture" has been defined as a subset of beliefs, values, and style of action derived from the general culture that constrain state political structure, political behavior, and modes of political action (Elazar, 1966:79–80). The patterns of the political culture are accepted at an unconscious level by those who participate in the polity, and its limits are "more effective because of their antiquity and subtly whereby those limited are unaware of the limitations placed on them" (Elazar, 1970:256–7). The cultural norms associated with political culture define what demands, decisionmakers and decisionmaking processes, policy outputs, and conditions are acceptable. The individuals living within the culture accept, at a subconscious level, the limitations of what is possible to ask for or expect from particular institutions.

Three dimensions of a general political culture have been identified in the United States: individualistic, moralistic, and traditionalistic. Of these three dimensions, the individualistic and moralistic cultures capture our attention because of their emphasis on the marketplace and because substantial segments of the American people operate within the confines of both of these cultures (Elazar, 1972:96). The individualistic culture "emphasizes the centrality of private concerns, it places a premium on limiting community intervention—whether governmental or non-governmental—into private activities to the minimum necessary to keep the marketplace in proper working order" (Elazar, 1972:94). The moralistic culture "emphasizes politics as activity centered on some notion of the public good and properly devoted to the advancement of the public interest" (Elazar, 1972:96). Within the moralistic culture, individualism is tempered by a general commitment to use institutions—preferably nongovernmental, but governmental if necessary—to "intervene into the sphere of 'private' activities when it is considered necessary to do so for the public good or the well-being of the community" (Elazar, 1972:97).

Both of these cultural dimensions generate expectations with regard to environmental harms. The individualistic culture would favor business-community needs over those of a more general community. As a consequence, we would anticipate that environmental harms—a byproduct of industry—would be more tolerated in an individualistic culture. A moralistic culture would have less tolerance for environmental pollution generated by industry. As such, we should expect a positive relationship between the individualistic culture and environmental harms and a slight negative relationship between the moralistic culture and environmental harms.

Johnson (1976) created indicators for the political cultures outlined by Daniel Elazar (1972) by averaging population percentages of major religious denominations in each state in four census years (1906, 1916, 1926, and 1936). Two of Johnson's indices, the moralistic and the individualistic, are used to measure political culture.[12]

Because state-level public opinion and political culture affect activities at the substate level—by structuring what responses can be expected from public officials—the measures were included as state-level effects in the county and city analyses. The hypothesized relationships for the state-level analysis are anticipated for the two substate analyses.

Environmental Interest Groups

In general, literature on political science (Banks and Weingast, 1992; Bentley, 1908; Bernstein, 1955; Downs, 1957; Edelman, 1964; Lowi, 1979; Meier, 1995; Posner, 1974; Stigler, 1971; Wilson, 1980), and specifically literature on environmental issues (Andrews, 1998; Kemp, 1981; Ringquist, 1993; Sabatier, 1975), have demonstrated the role that interest groups play with regard to public policy. A well-constructed equation regarding environmental harms needs to take into account the organized interests in the community that were concerned with the issue. One measure of environmental interests is membership in the Sierra Club, National Wildlife Federation, and Friends of the Earth per 1,000 persons in each state in 1987.[13] The hypothesis in this instance is this: The greater the size of environmental interests, the lower the level of environmental hazards. The state environmental interest measure was used to assess the state-level impact of environmental mobilization at the two substate levels.

Finally, there is a small subset of idiosyncratic variables that must be taken into account at the substate levels.

County Land Area

This variable is included in our county-level analysis as a control measure. Counties vary dramatically in size, and we felt this idiosyncratic feature of the analysis needed to be included. The land area, in square miles, of each county was used to measure this concept.

Region

At the county level, we are plagued by a paucity of missing data on our TRI indicators. These missing data appear to have a slight regional skew associated with it. As such, we have included EPA regions as follows: Northeast, North Central, and Sunbelt. These dummy variables were coded "1" for the region and "0" if otherwise. The Western region, with the most missing data, was used as the default category.

Form of Government

The structure of city government has been a mainstay of urban politics for an extended period, and the relationship between structure and policy outcomes at the city level has been well documented. Based on existing literature, a mayor-council form of government is more responsive to constituency needs, whereas a council-manager form has a higher level of technical competence. This technical competence serves as a precondition to deal with a broad range of problems found in urban areas. Each measure was scored in dichotomous form: 1 if mayor-council, 0 if otherwise; 1 if council-manager, 0 if otherwise—with the commission form of government constituting the default category. In both instances, we hypothesize negative relationships between the form of city government and the level of environmental harm.

Method of Analysis

Ordinary least squares regression is used to test the various models advanced in this book. This method of analysis is compatible with previous environmental injustice research at the state (e.g., Lester, Allen, and Lauer, 1994), county (e.g., Allen, 2001; Allen, Lester, and Hill, 1995; Bowman and Crews-Meyer, 1995, 1997), city (e.g., Holm, 1994; Lester and Allen, 1996), and other levels—such as SMSAs and ZIP codes (e.g., Anderton, et al., 1994a; Hamilton, 1995; Shaikh and Loomis, 1998).

The analyses in Chapters 5, 6, and 7 begin with a test of the simple tripartite model that, given the direction of the literature, should reflect the following: Increasing percentages of the black and Hispanic populations should be related to higher levels of any environmental harm, whereas increasing levels of social class and political mobilization should be related to lower levels of environmental harm.

However, as noted earlier, some previous studies were overly parsimonious in their construction of a test for incidence of environmental injustice. Thus, after arraying the results of the simple tripartite parsimonious test, the core concepts of environmental justice—race, class, and political mobilization—are placed in competition with our second-level set of variables. If the environmental justice thesis has merit, then when other explanations of environmental harms are held constant, race, class, and political mobilization should still matter and should still evidence the requisite relationships for environmental harms.

Our equations address only the direct effects of our independent variables on the various measures of environmental harms. Some may argue that glossing over indirect effects allows an error to creep into the research and that instead of a single equation a set of path analytic equations should be employed to understand the skein of interrelationships between our multiple explanations and environmental harms.

Path analysis, or causal modeling, does allow for identification and estimation of both direct and indirect effects and does allow a comparison of the relative impacts of each explanatory concept on the dependent variables. This is a task that multiple regression—in the manner specified in our equations—is incapable of performing; and if the estimation of direct and indirect paths is attempted using a single equation, one can obtain results that are simply wrong (Lewis-Beck, 1997:565).

Given that path analytic techniques can assess direct and indirect effects, why is this technique not used? First, we use linear equations because this has been the predominant trend in this literature, and we sought some degree of commonality with the more sophisticated work in the environmental injustice field. Second, and quite simply, when we passed beyond the simple tripartite model of environmental injustice we were not able to design a causal model that would allow—with scholarly confidence—the placement of variables in some order to allow for calculation of path coefficients. The key to this dilemma is the following question: How does race or ethnicity cause other independent variables in the model and, conversely, how do the other independent variables in the model cause race? Furthermore, the environmental injustice thesis does not assert that race/ethnicity causes environmental harms. Nowhere in the existing literature is a claim advanced that minorities create pollution problems. They do not own the factories that create the hazards. They do not create the landfills and Superfund sites. Instead, the existing literature advances the implied argument that minorities live in communities that have, for a variety of reasons and for a variety of causes, higher levels of environmental pollutants. Given the foregoing, the ability to assess a priori causal relationships—not merely associational linkages masquerading as causal chains—does not appear to exist in this research setting. Lacking this set of conditions, a set of path analytic equations—in our view—would not be appropriate.

Assessing the race/class/mobilization thesis in competition with other explanations of environmental harms produces a set of additional problems. First, in the state-level analysis we encounter the "Small N—Many Variables" problem. The complex test at the state level includes twelve variables for forty-eight cases. Multiple regression only allows an absolute minimum variable-to-cases ratio of 1:5 (Tabachnick and Fiddell, 1989: 128–129). Our state-level model violates this requirement. There are a number of solutions to this problem: enter into the equation only those variables that reveal a statistically significant bivariate correlation with the dependent variable—a technique that we eschew; use a backward or forward elimination technique based on an F-ratio—another technique that has fallen into disfavor; or use Christopher Achen's (1982:65) technique—which is not foolproof but does give the researcher some control over what is eliminated from an equation. We briefly discuss each technique to justify why we settled on Achen's.

Because of problems associated with classical suppression and homeostatic mechanisms in which force and counterforce tend to occur together and have counteractive effects, we eschew the technique that automatically eliminates any independent variables that do not evidence a significant simple bivariate relationship with any of our dependent variables. Further, a priori elimination of independent variables that evidence insignificant bivariate associations with dependent variables precludes tests to determine if the eliminated variable is exerting a conditional effect on relationships of interest.

Mechanical techniques based on backward and forward elimination based on some a priori significance level also exist. These techniques, included as subroutines in most standard data analysis packages, have proved—over time—to be both troublesome and misleading.

Instead of either a priori deletion based on simple bivariate correlations or mechanical backward and forward deletion of variables based on a priori significance levels, we have adopted a technique recommended by Achen (1982:65). Although this technique was required because of the "Small N— Many Variables" problem encountered in our state-level analysis, we also employed it in our county- and city-level analyses in order to ensure commonality of presentation across all our levels of analysis.

We first generate and report the results of an equation that contains the complete pool of variables. Next, variables with t-scores less than 1.40 (the square root of 2.00) are deleted one at a time—the first variable deleted is the variable with the smallest t-score below the 1.40 cutting point. A new equation is then generated with the remaining pool of variables, and again the variable with the smallest t-score below the 1.40 cutting point is eliminated. This process is repeated until all remaining variables have t-scores greater than or equal to 1.40. At that point, deleted variables are reentered one at a time in reverse order—that is, on a first-out, first-in basis—to determine if they achieve a t-score equal to or greater than 1.40. If a previously deleted variable achieves the minimum t-score, it is retained in the final reduced equation. However, if the previously deleted variables do not achieve the desired t-score, they are permanently left out of the equation. We report the original equation and the final reduced equation on our tables—not the entire set of intermediate reduced equations—and, for the sake of simplicity, discuss only the final reduced equations.[14]

We have three final comments to make. First, we noted a problem with skewed distributions on both independent and dependent variables that had the potential to adversely affect all statistical tests. To eliminate this problem, we normalized our data to the extent possible. We did this through a combination of recoding extreme values and, in some instances, using either a log linear or square root transformation (in accordance with procedures recommended by Tabachnick and Fiddell, 1989:68–89).

Second, we were interested in determining if conditional effects were present. To assess interactive effects, we created exhaustive sets of terms from our pool of independent variables and entered these terms one at a time. The term was retained if it achieved significance at the $p < .05$ level. Since this aspect of the analysis was exploratory—since interactive terms are usually not considered unless there is some prior theoretical justifications for their existence—we treat these results as advisory and recommend other researchers try to replicate our findings.

In order to test for conditional effects, we adopted the technique recommended primarily by R.J. Friedrich (1982) but repeated and explained elsewhere (Aiken and West, 1991; Cohen and Cohen, 1983:301–350). This technique requires that all variables are standardized before construction of interactive terms and that the equations be generated on the basis of standardized data. Under these conditions, reported results are regression coefficients (b) based on the standardized data.

Finally, multicollinearity is a problem with the type of data and measures we are using. We minimize this problem, in part, through the use of factor scales to subsume highly correlated measures of the same concept (for example, our social class scale). However, the problem could not be completely eliminated, and the data being the data, we simply had to accept that uncorrelated measures of the concepts of interest were simply not available. In order to produce a complete picture, we reproduce the tolerance statistics for each of our equations. Tolerance scores, which range from 0.00 to 1.00, indicate the degree of multicollinearity for respective independent variables and are interpreted as the smaller the tolerance score, the higher the level of multicollinearity. We note that the vast majority of the literature on the subject of environmental injustice does not report this statistic.

Summary

In this chapter, we have articulated the model that guides the analysis, its concepts and measures, the hypotheses that we will examine at the state, county, and city levels, and the method of analysis employed. In Chapters

5–7, we employ these variables to assess the validity of the environmental injustice argument. Specifically, Chapter 5 examines the argument within the context of U.S. states; Chapter 6 is concerned with the extent of environmental injustice at the county level; and Chapter 7 deals with this issue within the context of cities of more than 50,000 inhabitants. In each of these chapters, we discuss the nature of the environmental harms that are examined at each level, the sample of jurisdictional units that we utilized in each analysis, a justification for the use of each jurisdictional unit analyzed, and any idiosyncratic research problems that we encountered at each level of analysis. We begin with the state-level analysis before proceeding to the county and city level analyses.

Notes

1. Some research does report null class-risk relationships (Adeola, 1994; Allen, Lester, and Hill, 1995; Gianessi, Peskin, and Wolfe, 1979; Lester and Allen, 1996; West, 1992). Other research reports counterintuitive findings. Bowman and Crews-Meyer (1995, 1997) report that as per capita income increases, so does the presence of hazardous waste sites or generators in South Carolina counties. Hird (1993, 1994) also reports similar findings for the distribution of NPL sites in 3,000 U.S. counties.

2. Measurement of social class at the state level was achieved by a four-item factor scale that combined traditional measures of education and income. The variables included in the factor scale and their factor loadings were: median family income, 1980, in $1,000, .89; per capita income, 1985, in $1,000, .89; percent college graduates, 1980, .81; percent population 18–24 years of age in college, 1980, .65. The eigenvalue for the factor was 2.68, and the unidimensional factor generated by principal components analysis explained 67.1 percent of the variance in the pool of four variables. The county social-class scale resulted from a principal components factor analysis of six traditional indicators of social class. Two measures in the scale, median household income and percent of the population with a B.A. degree, were subjected to square root transformations in order to normalize univariate distributions, while median value of owner occupied housing was subjected to a log transformation for the same reason. Factor loadings for the single unrotated factor were: median family income, .85; median household income, .94; median value of owner occupied housing, .87; percent population B.A. degree, .84; percent population with high school degree, .77; and per capita income, .55. The factor has an eigenvalue of 4.17 and explains 69.6 percent of the variance in the pool of measures. The city-level social-class measure was constructed via a principal components factor analysis of 1990 per capita income, 1989 median family income, and 1990 percent of the population with B.A. degree or higher. The factor analysis was performed on data that had high values recoded to eliminate outliers. Once recoded, the measures were subjected to square root transformations (per capita income and median household income) or a log transformation (percent population with a bachelor's degree). Factor loadings on the city social-class scale are: per capita income, 1989, in $1,000, .95; median household income, 1989, in $1,000, .85; percent population, bachelor's degree or higher, 1990,

.79. The factor scale has an eigenvalue of 2.28 and explains 76.1 percent of the variance in the pool of variables.

3. We are not completely satisfied with the city-level measure of political mobilization; however, no other measure was readily available, and we did not want to run the risk of misspecifying the model. As a consequence, we were left with this indirect surrogate for the concept at the city level.

4. Prior to factor analysis, individual scale components were recoded to eliminate statistical outliers. After recoding, the number of manufacturing establishments, total population, and population density were subjected to square root transformations in order to normalize univariate distributions. The transformed values were multiplied by ten to restore variance. The source of data for these measures was the 1980 U.S. Census. The factor loadings for the scale are: number of manufacturing establishments, 1980, .92; total population, 1980, .90; number of manufacturing employees, .77; and population density, 1980, .75. The eigenvalue for the factor is 2.84. A careful inspection of factor scores revealed five states with exceptionally high scores. These scores were recoded in order to eliminate problems associated with extreme outliers. The recoded scores were: New York, 6.47 to 4.70; California, 5.76 to 4.60; Pennsylvania, 5.36 to 4.50; Ohio, 4.97 to 4.40; and, Illinois, 4.90 to 4.30. Although this recoding does alter the *magnitude* differences at the upper end of the scale, it does not affect the rank order of cases.

5. All variables in the scale were subjected to a log transformation prior to factor analysis in order to normalize, insofar as possible, the univariate distributions of the individual measures. The two manufacturing measures had a constant of .001 added to each value in order to eliminate zeros so that a log transformation could be used. The factor loadings for the scale are: number of manufacturing establishments, 1987, .95; total population, 1990, .95; population density, 1990, .90; number of manufacturing employees, 1987, .76. The eigenvalue for the factor is 3.20.

6. Prior to factor analysis, extreme scores were recoded for all measures. For the number of manufacturing establishments, a total of twenty cities was recoded. Nineteen cities were recoded on the total population and number of manufacturing employees measures. In order to normalize the univariate distributions of each measure, prior to factor analysis, a square root transformation was applied to the manufacturing employees measure while log transformation was used on the population and manufacturing establishment measures. The factor loadings for the scale are: number of manufacturing establishments, 1987, .94; number of manufacturing employees, 1987, .93; and total population, 1990, .89. The eigenvalue for the scale is 2.56.

7. The percentage of each year's budget devoted to natural resources was computed by dividing a state's natural resource expenditures by total expenditures for each year in question. The dividend was multiplied by 100 to establish a percentage. Source of data for these measures was the *1990 Statistical Abstract*. The percentages of 1982 and 1985 natural resource expenditures were slightly skewed. To eliminate this problem a square root transformation was applied to these two measures prior to factor analysis. The factor loadings are: percent of state budget expended for natural resources, 1982, .98; percent of state budget expended for natural resources, 1985, .97; percent of state budget expended for natural resources, 1980, .96. Eigen-

value for this factor scale is 2.85. Inspection of factor scores indicates that five states had extreme scores. The scores were recoded as follows: Alaska, 5.50 to 5.00; Idaho, 5.42 to 4.50; New York, −5.61 to −5.00; Montana, −5.50 to −4.50; South Dakota, −5.10 to −4.00. Although the recoding affected the magnitude of difference between the cases, it did not affect the rank ordering of cases.

8. All measures in the county-level factor scale were subjected to square root transformations prior to factor analysis in order to normalize univariate distributions. The factor loadings for the scale are: local government finances, per capita taxes, 1986–1987, .74; federal funds and grants, total expenditures, 1992, .66; general revenues per $1,000 personal income, 1986–1987, .55; and per capita expenditures, federal funds, 1992, .53. The eigenvalue for the factor is 1.62.

9. For the city-level capacity measure, two variables were corrected for nonnormal distributions: per capita expenditures and per capita revenues. For the former measure, fourteen cities were recoded; for the latter measure, sixteen cities were recoded. The recoded variables were subjected to a square root transformation to complete the normalization process. This procedure does affect the magnitude of difference between cases at the high end of the scale but does not affect the rank ordering of these cases.

10. This was a specially constructed measure that resulted from a principal components factor analysis of three separate Guttman scales. The first scale, a unidimensional Guttman scale of ten items (Cr=.87; Cs=.65), indicated state financial assistance for industry in 1984. Source of data: *Book of the States, 1984–1985*. The ten items, coded "+" for the presence of the item and "-" for the absence of the item were: privately sponsored development credit corporation, state-sponsored industrial development authority, state financial aid for existing plant expansion, state revenue bond financing, state loan for building construction, state loan for equipment and machinery, state loan guarantees for building construction, and state general obligation bond financing for industry. The second scale, depth of industry support in a state, consisted of a six-item unidimensional Guttman scale (Cr=.93, Cs=.78) and subsumes items indicating whether *some* cities and/or counties in the state provide special incentives to industry. Source of data: *Book of the States, 1984–1985*. The six items included in the scale, which scores "+" for the presence of the item and "-" for absence, are: city and/or county general obligation bond financing; city and/or county incentives for establishing industrial plants in areas of high unemployment; city and/or county loans for building construction; city and/or county loans for equipment and machinery; city and/or county guarantees for building construction; and city and/or county guarantees for equipment and machinery. The final item in this factor analysis is an eight-item unidimensional Guttman scale (Cr=.91, Cs=.65) indicating tax incentives to industry. Source of data: *Book of the States*, 1984–1985. The six items included in the scale, scored "+" for the presence of the item and "-" for absence, are: tax exemption on raw materials used in manufacturing; sales/use tax exemption on new equipment; tax exemption or moratorium on land capital improvement; tax exemption or moratorium on equipment and machinery; corporate income tax exemption; and excise tax exemption. The principal components factor analysis of the three Guttman scales produced a unidimensional factor with the following loadings for the three components: statewide financial assistance programs for industry, .88; depth of industry support in the state, .83; and statewide tax incen-

tive programs for industry, .45. The eigenvalue for the factor was 1.69 and the factor explained 56.3 percent of the variance among the three Guttman scales. Inspection of factor scores resulting from the analysis indicated that three states had extreme scores. These scores were recoded as follows: Arizona, –3.44 to –3.10; Connecticut, 3.36 to 2.55; and Michigan, 3.34 to 2.50. The descriptive statistics for the factor scores, before and after recoding, are shown below.

Business Climate	Mean	Std. D.	Skewness	Kurtosis	Variance	CV
Original	.00	1.69	–.03	–.09	2.86	–.131874E+17
Recoded	–.02	2.50	.03	–1.07	6.28	–42.70

11. The Squires index contains a series of outliers that was recoded as follows: New York, .659 to .309; Michigan, .635 to .308; California, .625 to .307; Massachusetts, .614 to .306; Pennsylvania, .336 to .305; Ohio, .329 to .304; Alaska, .311 to .302. Recoding did not affect the ranking of states on the index.

12. Johnson's traditionalistic index is correlated with both the moralistic index (r = -.59) and the individualistic index (r = -.81). If all three indices were entered into an equation, the problems associated with multicollinearity would adversely affect the statistical significance of estimators (Cohen and Cohen, 1983:100; Kmenta, 1971:380–391). Excluding the traditionalistic index is not fatal to the research. First, a preponderance of the population lives within the confines of the moralistic and individualistic cultures. Second, the negative correlations between the traditionalistic index and the other two measures indicate that low scores on the moralistic and individualistic measures are reflecting some level of traditionalism. Both the moralistic and individualistic indices contain outliers. Following our previous strategy, these outliers were recoded. Moralistic culture: Utah, .93 to .38; Idaho, .68 to .37; Kansas, .44 to .36; Wyoming, .42 to .35; and South Dakota, .37 to .34. Individualistic culture: New Mexico, .92 to .84; and Rhode Island, .87 to .83.

13. The data for the measure were taken from the *Green Index, 1991–1992*, p. 111. Extreme values were recoded as follows: Vermont, 20.2 to 13.3; New York, 15.3 to 13.2; and Connecticut, 14.2 to 13.1.

14. The aware reader will note that t-scores equal to 1.40 are not statistically significant at the p < .05 level. As such, this technique includes *some* insignificant variables in the equation. The insignificant variables are not discussed in our analysis. Overall, the reduction technique is not foolproof. However, this technique does allow the researcher more control over the reduction process—something the automatic statistical package–driven reduction techniques do not allow.

5

Environmental Injustice in America's States

In Chapter 4 we outlined our explanatory concepts, their measures, the hypotheses we would test, and our method of analysis. The purpose of this chapter is to examine the environmental injustice thesis as it applies to U.S. states. We begin by articulating the environmental hazards we plan to study.

Environmental Harms: The Dependent Variables at the State Level

The dependent variable is varying degrees of environmental hazards. Insofar as possible, we sought to replicate the environmental harms used in other environmental equity and racism research. For example, air quality has been a closely studied subject in this literature. Indeed, this harm was almost the exclusive focus of study prior to 1980 (e.g., Asch and Seneca, 1978; Berry, 1977; Burch, 1976; Freeman, 1972; Gianessi, Peskin, and Wolfe, 1979; Handy, 1977; Harrison, 1975; Kruvant, 1975; McCaull, 1976). This tradition has continued, as some (Allen, Lester, and Hill, 1995) studied hazardous chemicals and carcinogens discharged to the atmosphere; others (Cutter, 1994; Lester, Allen, and Lauer, 1994) studied airborne toxins; and some (Lester and Allen, 1996) have investigated so-called bad air days in forty-eight of the largest cities in the United States (see also Shaikh and Loomis, 1998, investigating stationary air sources). Thus, there is a long tradition of determining the environmental injustice dimension of air pollution.

Other literature has focused on aspects of hazardous waste. Indeed, one of the major events that put environmental justice on the national agenda was the U.S. General Accounting Office (1983) study and the subsequent United Church of Christ (1987) report on hazardous waste. Subsequent to these two studies, other scholars studied various aspects of hazardous waste in a wide variety of locales (Mohai and Bryant, 1992, investigating the location of hazardous waste sites in Detroit; see also Allen, Lester, and Hill, 1995, including hazardous waste generation and generators in their study of the sixty worst counties). TSD facilities have been studied at the county and ZIP code level (Anderton, et al., 1994a; Bowman and Crews-Meyer, 1997; Hamilton, 1995; Holm, 1994; Ringquist, 1995, 1996); and many scholars have assessed the location and scope of Superfund sites (Allen, Lester, and Hill, 1995; Greenberg, 1993, 1994; Hird, 1993; Lavelle and Coyle, 1992; Lester, Allen, and Lauer, 1994; Zimmerman, 1993). Indeed, a cottage industry seems to have sprung up with regard to this subject (Anderton, et al., 1994a; Bulanowski, 1981; Clean Sites, Inc., 1990; Costner and Thornton, 1990; Crews-Meyer, 1994; Fitton, 1992; Lester and Bowman, 1983; Lester, Bowman, and Kramer, 1983; Peck, 1989; Portney, 1991; White, 1992).

Solid waste has also been the subject of environmental injustice studies. Indeed, Bullard's (1983) first study focused on this environmental harm in urban areas. Since that date, other scholars have looking into a variety of aspects of solid waste (Adeola, 1994; Bullard, 1983; Lester, Allen, and Lauer, 1994). Toxic waste has also been a focus of inquiry. The first studies looked at the effect of pesticides on human epidemiology (Davies, 1972) or viewed this environmental problem as a drag factor on economic development (Colquette and Robertson, 1991; Goldman, 1991; Kazis and Grossman, 1983; Kohlhase, 1991; Peck, 1989; Szasz, 1994). Two more recent studies have also analyzed the distribution of carcinogens (Allen, Lester, and Hill, 1995) and cancer-causing toxins (Lester, Allen, and Lauer, 1994). There have also been many studies that have looked at overall toxic releases within a variety of geographic settings (e.g., Allen, 2001; Burke, 1993; Kohlhase, 1991; Krieg, 1998; Perlin, et al., 1995; Ringquist, 1997). Finally, our review of the literature reveals only one instance of the environmental equity and racism thesis being tested against incidents of water pollution (Gianessi and Peskin, 1980). We have, therefore, added a water pollution variable to our list of environmental hazards. By using multiple dependent variables, we expect to obtain a clearer picture of the relationships of various populations and exposure to various environmental hazards.

The dependent variables consist of factor scales for the following types of environmental harms: air pollution, hazardous waste, solid waste, toxic waste, and water pollution. We selected factor analysis to construct scales of environmental harms for several reasons. First, we isolated a total of thirty-one environmental harms in the areas of air, land, and water pollution at the state level. Factor analysis is an ideal means to reduce this unmanageable pool of indicators to a relatively understandable set of dimensions (Kim and Mueller, 1978a, 1978b). Equally important, all of the measures of environmental harm were correlated to some degree. Under such conditions, explanations of these different harms would share similar characteristics—and the reader would be inundated with an overwhelming degree of repetitive information. Thus, we create discrete scales so that—at the state level—the reader will have to process information only on several general categories of environmental harm and can process the information with a higher degree of conceptual understanding. Each of the scales is discussed in the following paragraphs.

Air Pollution

Air pollution has historically been a mainstay for the study of environmental equity. To create our measures of air pollution, nine indicators of air quality were selected from the *Green Index, 1991–1992*. The indicators, listed in Table 5.1, include ozone-depleting releases to the atmosphere, toxic chemical releases, high risk cancer facilities, and nitrogen oxide, carbon dioxide, and sulfur dioxide releases to the atmosphere.[1] The nine air pollution indicators were subject to principal components factor analysis with a varimax rotation that yielded an optimum two factor solution. The first factor is readily definable as the level of ozone depletion and toxic chemical releases to the atmosphere for each state. The second factor collects items that define the factor as indicating the level of nitrogen oxide, carbon dioxide, and sulfur dioxide releases to the atmosphere. High positive scores on each factor indicate high levels of the relevant air pollutants; high negative scores indicate low levels of relevant air pollutants. The eigenvalues for each factor are substantial, and the two factors combine to explain approximately 71 percent of the variance in the pool of nine variables.

Hazardous Waste

Hazardous waste is also studied in this chapter. Our measure of hazardous waste subsumes nine indicators—either in terms of sites, accidents, generators, or waste generated, into a single unidimensional scale. As shown in Table 5.2, the nine indicators of hazardous waste—when subjected to principal factor analysis[2]—produced a single factor solution that explained 60 percent of the variance in the pool of nine variables. High positive scores indicate high levels of hazardous waste; low negative scores reflect the opposite.

Solid Waste

We have also included a state-level measure of solid waste. As shown in Table 5.3, three solid waste indicators—number of tons per day of solid waste from municipal generators, tons per day of municipal solid waste generated, and number of open municipal landfills—were subjected to principal

TABLE 5.1 Principal Components Factor Analysis of Nine Air Pollution Indicta-tors in the Fifty U.S. States[1]

Variables	Factor 1 Loadings: Ozone Depletion and Toxic Chemical Releases to Atmosphere	Factor 2 Loadings: Nitrogen Oxide, Carbon Dioxide, and Sulfur Dioxide Releases to Atmosphere[2]
Ozone-Depleting Emissions (# of big facilities)	.91	−.09
Ozone-Depleting Emissions (output in 100 tons)	.89	−.01
Percent Population with Air Standards Violating Ozone Depletion	.80	−.06
Toxic Chemical Releases by Industry to Air (lbs/sq. mile)	.76	.03
Number of High-Risk Cancer Facilities	.52	−.07
U.S. Electric Utility Air Emissions, Nitrogen Oxide (lbs/capita)	−.02	.97
U.S. Electric Utility Air Emissions, Carbon Dioxide (tons/capita)	−.10	.96
U.S. Electric Utility Air Emissions, Sulfur Dioxide (lbs/capita)	.18	.85
Carbon Dioxide Emissions from All Fuel Sources (tons/capita)	−.27	.73
Eigenvalues	3.55	2.89
Percent of Explained Variance	39.54	31.18

NOTES:

[1]Data recoded to eliminate outliers and normalized with a square root transformation prior to factor analysis. Factor solution generated by principal components factor analysis with varimax rotation utilizing a two factor solution. Source of data: *Green Index, 1991–1992,* pp. 22–24.

[2]Inspection of factor scores for factor 2 indicated that eleven states had extreme scores. These scores were recoded as follows: Oregon, −6.64 to −4.30; Idaho, −6.37 to −4.20; Vermont, −6.32 to −4.10; California, −5.48 to −4.00; Rhode Island, −4.98 to −3.90; Montana, 4.15 to 2.70; Kentucky, 5.33 to 3.90; Indiana, 5.44 to 4.00; Wyoming, 6.29 to 4.10; West Virginia, 6.38 to 4.20; North Dakota, 6.52 to 4.30. The descriptive statistics for the factor scores, before and after recoding, are shown below:

Air Factor 2	Mean	Std. D.	Skewness	Kutosis	Variance	CV
Original	.00	3.28	.001	−.29	10.78	−246499E+17
Recoded	−.01	2.60	−.01	−1.01	6.78	−214.8

TABLE 5.2   Principal Components Factor Analysis of Nine Hazardous Waste Indicators in U.S. States[1]

Variables	Factor 1 Loadings: Degree of Hazardous Waste
*Number of Non-Superfund Waste Sites	.93
*Number of Hazardous Waste Management Sites	.91
Number of Hazardous Waste Transport Accidents	.91
*Number of Hazardous Waste RCRA Generators	.85
*Cost of Hazardous Waste Transport Accidents (millions of dollars)	.74
*Number of Military Hazardous Waste Sites	.72
*Number of Superfund (NPL) Sites	.70
*Hazardous Waste Generated (lbs/capita)	.55
*Hazardous Waste Stays in State (lbs/capita)	.50
Eigenvalue	5.40
Percent of Explained Variance	60.07

NOTE:

[1]Data recoded to eliminate outliers and variables marked with asterik (*) normalized with a square root transformation prior to factor analysis. Factor solution generated with principal components
factor analysis with no rotation for a single factor solution. Source of data: *Green Index, 1991–1992*, pp. 75–76. Inspection of factor scores indicated that four states had extreme scores. These scores were recoded as follows: California, 10.40 to 8.50; New Jersey, 8.88 to 8.40; Pennsylvania, 12.23 to 8.70; Texas, 12.13 to 8.60. The descriptive statistics for the factor scores, before and after recoding, are shown below:

Hazardous Waste	Mean	Std. D.	Skewness	Kutosis	Variance	CV
Original	.00	5.65	.39	−.61	30.9	.998471+16
Recoded	−.18	5.19	.16	−1.01	27.0	−27.49

components analysis.[3] A single factor emerged that reflects the degree of solid waste in the state. The factor explains 51 percent of the variance in the three scale components. High positive scores reflect a high degree of solid waste in the state; high negative scores reflect the opposite.

Toxic Waste

Toxic waste is also of concern to environmental scholars because of its far-reaching potential as a cause of health problems. As shown in Table 5.4, five indicators of toxic waste were subjected to principal components analysis.[4] The indicators include birth defects, cancer-causing and nerve-damaging toxins released to the atmosphere, toxic chemical transfers, and total chemi-

TABLE 5.3   Principal Components Factor Analysis of Three Solid Waste Indicators in U.S. States[1]

Variables	Factor 1: Degree of Solid Waste
*Number of Tons Per Day of Solid Waste from Municipal Incinerators	.81
Municipal Solild Waste Generated (tons/day)	.73
Number of Open Municipal Landfills	.58
Eigenvalue	1.53
Percent of Explained Variance	51.12

NOTE:
   [1]Data recoded to eliminate outliers and variable marked with an asterik (*) normalized with a square root transformation prior to factor analysis. Factor solution generated with principal components analysis with no rotation for a single factor solution. Source of data: *Green Index, 1991–1992*, p. 77. Inspection of factor scores indicated that two states had extreme scores. These scores were recoded as follows: California, 3.86 to 2.51; Virginia, 3.75 to 2.50. The descriptive statistics for the factor scores, before and after recoding, are shown below:

Solid Waste	Mean	Std. D.	Skewness	Kutosis	Variance	CV
Original	.00	1.53	.56	−.20	2.35	.391029+16
Recoded	−.05	1.42	.25	−.92	2.01	−27.17

cal releases to the environment. A single factor emerged that reflects the degree of toxic waste and explains 67.8 percent of the variance in the pool of five variables. High positive factor scores reflect high levels of toxic waste; negative scores indicate the opposite.

Water Pollution

Water pollution has been given some attention in the environmental justice literature. As shown in Table 5.5, five measures of water pollution were subjected to principal components factor analysis using a varimax solution.[5] Two factors were revealed that explained approximately 65 percent of the variance in the pool of five variables. The first factor is clearly identifiable as the degree of water-system violations. The second factor reflects the degree of toxic chemical pollution of the water supply. High positive scores reflect high levels of the two types of water pollution; negative scores reflect the opposite.

The Model Rearticulated

The exact concepts, the corresponding measures, and the detailed hypotheses submitted for testing at the state level are outlined in Chapter 4. To aid in

TABLE 5.4   Principal Components Factor Analysis of Five Toxic Waste Indicators in U.S. States[1]

Variables	Factor 1: Degree of Toxic, Birth Defect and Cancer-Causing Chemicals in Environment
Birth Defect Toxins Released to Environment (lbs/capita)	.90
Cancer-Causing Chemical Released to Environment (lbs/capita)	.90
Nerve Damaging Toxins Released to Environment (lbs/capita)	.84
Toxic Chemical Transfers Off-Site (lbs/capita)	.81
Total Chemical Releases to Environment (lbs/capita)	.62
Eigenvalue	3.39
Percent of Explained Variance	67.8

NOTE:

[1]Data recoded to eliminate outliers and normalized with square root transformation prior to factor analysis. Factor solution generated with principal components analysis with no rotation utilizing a single factor solution. Inspection of factor scores indicates six states had extreme scores. These scores were recoded as follows: Hawaii, –6.53 to –5.20; North Dakota, –5.55 to –5.10; New Mexico, –5.39 to –5.00; Tennessee, 6.42 to 5.00; Louisiana, 6.82 to 5.10; Indiana, 6.86 to 5.20. The descriptive statistics for the factor scores, before and after recoding, are shown below:

Toxic Waste	Mean	Std. D.	Skewness	Kutosis	Variance	CV
Original	.00	3.39	.04	–.76	11.51	.808604E+16
Recoded	–.05	3.13	–.09	–1.16	9.85	–59.75

refreshing the reader's memory, Figure 5.1 summarizes the concepts, measures, and hypotheses for the state-level analysis.

The Sample

The sample used for this first section of analysis is the states. Missing data on public opinion and political culture variables reduced the number of states analyzed to forty-eight in our complex equation, Alaska and Hawaii being the two missing data points.

Some may challenge us for using the states as a unit of analysis. However, we argue that using states as the first of several units of analysis is justified on several grounds. First, states are a valid arena for the study of any public policy problem. They are a primary actor in discourses about the formation

TABLE 5.5 Principal Components Factor Analysis of Five Water Pollution Indicators in U.S. States.[1]

Variables	Factor 1 Loadings: Degree of Water System Violations[2]	Factor 2 Loadings: Degree of Toxic Chemical Pollution of Surface and Groundwater Supply[3]
Percent Water System Violating SDWA	.86	.03
Percent Population with SDWA Violations	.80	.13
Percent of Water System with Significant Noncompliance with Standards	.75	−.30
Toxid Chemical Underground Injections (lbs/capita)	.10	.78
Toxic Chemicals Released to Surface Water (lbs/capita)	−.12	.74
Eigenvalue	2.00	1.26
Percent of Explained Variance	39.88	25.62

NOTES:

[1]Data recoded to eliminate outliers and normalized with a square root transformation prior to factor analysis. Factor solution generated by principal components analysis with varimax rotation utilizing a two factor solution. Source of data: *Green Index, 1991–1992*, pp. 35–39.

[2]Inspection of factor 1 factor scores indicated that eight states had extreme scores. These scores were recoded as follows: Maine, −4.20 to −2.54; Michigan, −3.20 to −2.53; Arkansas, −3.13 to −2.52; New Jersey, 2.73 to 2.51; Wyoming, 3.29 to 2.52; Washington, 3.70 to 2.53; Arizona, 4.38 to 2.54; Alaska, 4.73 to 2.55. The descriptive statistics for the factor scores, before and after recoding, are shown below:

Water Polution 1	Mean	Std. D.	Skewness	Kutosis	Variance	CV
Original	.00	1.99	.38	−.30	3.98	.686359E+16
Recoded	−.06	1.65	.22	−1.23	2.75	−25.69

[3]Inspection of factor 2 factor scores indicates four states with extreme scores. These scores were recoded as follows: Wyoming, 2.00 to 1.80; Arkansas, 2.25 to 1.90; Louisiana, 5.37 to 2.00; Nevada, −2.11 to −1.70. The descriptive statistics for the factor scores, before and after recoding, are shown below:

Water Polution 2	Mean	Std. D.	Skewness	Kutosis	Variance	CV
Original	.00	1.28	1.55	4.36	1.65	.167647E+16
Recoded	−.07	1.03	.04	−.73	1.06	−14.65

FIGURE 5.1 Summary of Concepts, Measures, and Hypotheses for the State-Level Analysis of Environmental Harms

Concept	Measure	Hypothesis
Race-Black	Percent Black Population, 1980.	Positive
Race-Hispanic	Percent Hispanic Population, 1980.	Positive
Social Class	Factor scale combining: median family income, 1980; per capita income, 1985; percent college graduates, 1980; percent population 18–24 years of age in college.	Negative
Political Mobilization	Votes cast in 1984 presidential election divided by 1980 total population.	Negative
Pollution Potential	Factor scale combining: number of manufacturing establishments, 1980; total population, 1980; number of manufacturing establishments, 1980; population density, 1980.	Positive
Environmental Interests	Membership in Sierra Club, National Wildlife Federation, and Friends of Earth.	Negative
Government Capacity	Factor scale combining percent of state budget expended for natural resources in each of three years: 1980, 1982, 1985.	Negative
Business Climate	Factor scale combining three Guttman scales of state policy support to business interests within the state, 1984–1985.	Positive
Legislative Professionalism	Squire's (1992) index of legislative professionalism.	Negative
Public Opinion-Partisanship	Wright, Erickson, and McIver (1985) index of partisanship.	Positive
Public Opinion-Ideology	Wright, Erickson, and McIver (1985) index of ideology.	Positive
Political Culture-Moralistic	Johnson's (1976) moralistic index.	Negative
Political Culture-Individualistic	Johnson's (1976) individualistic index.	Positive
Region	Dummy variable for Sunbelt and Western states—used as necessary to assess conditional relationships	

of public policy in the United States, both responding to federal requirements under the doctrine of partial preemption and generating their own policy solutions to immediate problems within their geographic boundaries. Furthermore, states, when creating policies, are governing substate entities, and they are the pass-through point for federal funds as well as the originator of funds used to solve problems within the state. Thus, state-level aware-

ness of a problem is an important step in allocating resources to a policy solution.

Additionally, states can become the focus of lawsuits regarding environmental injustice, as was the case in Mississippi. As such, the possibility of
environmental injustice arising from state action or inaction in this policy
arena makes them a fit subject for study. Finally, not all pollutants are localized; they can disperse across wide areas. Thus, relationships between race,
class, and environmental harms can take on a statewide coloring.

We acknowledge that there is a continuing controversy in the environmental justice literature regarding the proper level of analysis. Some argue
that small units are preferable (Anderton, 1996; Bowen, et al., 1995). Others
argue that it is preferable to create areal units that preserve intra-area homogeneity for the variables of interest (Haining, 1990). Although there is no
reason to expect that relationships on one geographic level will behave in the
same fashion at another level it will be valuable to determine if similar relationship patterns can be uncovered as between the state unit of analysis and
the results reported in other research that uses more finely graduated units
(e.g., SMSAs, census tracts, and ZIP codes). Indeed, as Glynis Daniels and
Samantha Friedman (1999:250) state: "Rather than argue for the inherent superiority of one unit over another, we believe that relationships at a variety
of analytical levels are inherently interesting and should be investigated."

We fully acknowledge the problems associated with testing the thesis at
the state level. State-level data do indeed mask the demographic and socioeconomic variations within a state. However, if we obtain similar findings
across three levels of analysis (state, county, and city), then we feel that a
higher degree of confidence may be placed in the validity of the environmental justice thesis.

Testing a Simple Model of
Environmental Injustice

A noted in Chapters 1 and 2, existing literature has established a positive relationship between race and increasing levels of a variety of environmental
harms. This may be the result of a conscious effort to place these hazards in
minority communities or may be simply the unintentional consequences of
industrial development and existing demographic patterns. Regardless of
the debated and debatable origins of the pattern, the outcome is the same for
purposes of our research: a positive relationship between race and a variety
of environmental harms will indicate the existence of race-based environmental injustice.

Additionally, the environmental classism hypothesis leads to a similar
conclusion, that is, for a variety of reasons lower-income areas—either
through accident or design, or a combination of both—are also alleged to be

recipients of increasing levels of environmental hazards. As a consequence, given the construction of our social-class measure, a negative relationship is expected between this concept and environmental hazards.

Finally, the simple tripartite model maintains that political mobilization has an effect on the distribution of environmental hazards: where communities are mobilized, political actors are responsive, and industry encounters some difficulty in releasing high levels of pollution into the community. Thus, a negative relationship is expected between political mobilization and environmental hazards.

Tables 5.6 and 5.7 array the results of the tests of the simple race/class/ mobilization model for our state-level measures of environmental hazards. Table 5.6 deals with the percent black population, Table 5.7 with the Hispanic population.

The state-level results in Table 5.6 provide interesting findings: For five out of seven measures of environmental hazards, given controls for social class and political mobilization, the relationship between the percent black measure and the various dependent variables is, as hypothesized, positive. In the alternate, Table 5.6 indicates no relationship between the percent black measure on one of our measures of air pollution: nitrogen oxide, carbon dioxide, and sulphur dioxide released to the atmosphere. Finally, the relationship between the percent black indicator and one of our measures of water pollution—the degree of water-system violations—is negative, the opposite of the hypothesized relationship. Thus, in five out of seven instances, the results from our simple test conform to existing research. In contrast, the class and mobilization results in Table 5.6 do not provide support for the remaining hypotheses. When controlling for race and mobilization, evidence of environmental classism is evident for only three out of seven incidences of environmental hazards: nitrogen oxide, carbon dioxide, and sulphur dioxide released to the atmosphere; toxic, birth defect–causing, and cancer-causing chemicals in the environment; and toxic and chemical pollution of surface and groundwater. In the other four instances the relationship between class and environmental harms is either in the wrong direction or nonexistent. Finally, we find support for the political mobilization hypothesis only with regard to the degree of water-system violations. In the remaining six instances the relationship between political mobilization and our measures of environmental harms is either opposite to the hypothesis or nonexistent.

Table 5.7 arrays the state-level results for the percent Hispanic population. In this instance, the results indicate no relationship between race and five out of seven measures of environmental hazards. In one remaining instance, the relationship between the Hispanic population and toxic, birth defect–causing, and cancer-causing chemicals is the opposite of the hypothesis. Indeed, we find evidence only to support the race-based hypothesis for

TABLE 5.6   Simple Model of Environmental Inequities in the Fifty U.S. States, Black Population[1]

Variables	Coeff.	Constant	Percent Black	Social Class	Political Mobilization	Adj. R. Sq.	F-Ratio
Eq. 1 Ozone Depletion/Toxic Chemicals Released to Atmosphere	b Seb	.004 .37	2.56*** .46	.15 .15	.86** .46	.39	11.85***
Eq. 2 Nitrogen Oxide, Carbon Dioxide, and Sulphur Dioxide Released to Atmosphere	b Seb	−.02 .34	.07 .41	−.42*** .14	−.25 .42	.14	3.65***
Eq. 3 Hazardous Waste	b Seb	−.18 .51	4.12*** .61	.20 .21	.69 .63	.51	18.29***
Eq. 4 Solid Waste	b Seb	−.04 .17	.61*** .21	.20*** .07	.02 .21	.26	6.91***
Eq. 5 Toxic, Birth Defect and Cancer-Causing Chemicals in Environment	b Seb	−.06 .32	2.40*** .39	−.45** .13	1.07* .39	.47	15.53***
Eq. 6 Degree of Water-System Violations	b Seb	−.06 .22	−.73*** .27	.05 .09	−.47* .27	.08	2.44*
Eq. 7 Toxic Chemical Pollution of Surface and Groundwater Supply	b Seb	−.07 .13	.54*** .16	−.19* .05	.21 .16	.19	8.46***

NOTES:

[1]Entries are regression coefficients based on standardized normal distribution of all variables. Tolerate statistics: percent black population, .68; social class, .96; political mobilization, .66.

   ***p < .01   **p < .05   *p < .10

the degree of water-system violations. Results in Table 5.7 also provide scant support for the class and mobilization hypotheses. We find no evidence to support a class-based relationship when we control for the size of the Hispanic population and political mobilization. And when controlling for race

TABLE 5.7 Simple Model of Environmental Inequities in the Fifty U.S. States, Hispanic Population[1]

Variables	Coeff.	Constant	Percent Hispanic	Social Class	Political Mobilization	Adj. R. Sq.	F-Ratio
Eq. 1: Ozone Depletion, Toxic Chemicals Released to Atmosphere	b Seb	.01 .48	−.64 .64	.40 .25	−.82 .54	.01	1.22
Eq. 2: Nitrogen Oxide, Carbon Dioxide, and Sulphur Dioxide Released to Atmosphere	b Seb	−.02 .34	.14 .45	−.45 .17	−.25 .33	.14	3.67***
Eq. 3: Hazardous Waste	b Seb	−.18 .71	.54 .94	.22 .37	−1.46* .79	.06	2.09
Eq. 4: Solid Waste	b Seb	−.04 .18	−.26 .24	.28*** .09	−.41** .20	.15	3.88***
Eq. 5: Toxic, Birth and Cancer-Causing Chemicals in Environment	b Seb	−.05 .41	−1.11** .55	−.09 .21	−.66 .46	.12	3.22**
Eq. 6: Degree of Water System Violations	b Seb	−.06 .22	.75*** .30	−.15 .11	.19 .25	.06	2.10
Eq. 7: Toxic Chemical Pollution of Surface and Groundwater Supply	b Seb	−.07 .14	−.19 .19	−.02 .07	−.16 .16	.01	1.15

NOTES:
[1]Entries are regression coefficients based on standardized normal distributions of all variables. Tolerance statistics are: Percent Hispanic population, .57; social class, .59; and political mobilization, .81.
  ***p < .01   **p < .05   *p < .10

and class, we find support for the political mobilization hypothesis in only two out of seven instances. In the remaining five instances, we find the absence of a relationship between political mobilization and the applicable environmental hazards.

A Complex Test

In Chapter 4, we explained the shortcomings of the tripartite model—namely, its restrictive nature, its inability to account for other known explanations of environmental harms, and its simple construction, which precluded testing for conditional relationships. Thus, we reanalyze our state data using a more complex model that includes a wide range of additional known explanations for levels of environmental harms.

Again, we continue with our separate analysis for the percent black and Hispanic populations. We organize our presentation of results according to our seven measures of environmental harm. For the sake of simplicity, we discuss only the results from reduced equations.

Air Pollution

Tables 5.8 and 5.9 array the results of our analysis for the two dimensions of air pollution. Table 5.8 contains the results for ozone depletion and toxic chemicals released to the atmosphere, whereas Table 5.9 arrays the results for nitrogen, carbon dioxide, and sulphur dioxide released to the atmosphere. Each table reports separate results for the percent black and percent Hispanic populations.

Ozone Depletion and Toxic Chemicals.   With regard to our first measure of air pollution—ozone depletion and toxic chemicals released to the atmosphere—the reduced equation in Table 5.8 confirms the existence of a race-based inequity associated with the percent black population. In contrast, the relationship between the Hispanic population and this measure of environmental harm is negative—the opposite of the hypothesized relationship. Although the magnitude of the race relationships in Table 5.8 are different from those reported in Tables 5.6 and 5.7, the direction of the relationships remains constant as between the two sets of analysis.

Table 5.8 also reveals a class-based relationship when analyzing results in conjunction with the percent black population. However, as was the case for our simple analysis in Table 5.7, we find no class-based relationship associated with the Hispanic population. Additionally, Table 5.8 reveals no support for the political mobilization hypothesis. For the reduced black population equation, the relationship is the opposite of the hypothesis, and when using the percent Hispanic measure, the political mobilization indicator does not even appear in the equation.

We turn now to our additional explanations of environmental hazards. In our reduced percent black equation, we find that the environmental interest measure evidences a positive relationship with our first measure of air pollution—the opposite of the hypothesis.[6] Conversely, the environmental inter-

TABLE 5.8 Complex Model of Environmental Inequities in U.S. States (Full and Reduced Equations) for the Percent Black Population and the Percent Hispanic Population for First Air Pollution Indicator—Ozone Depletion and Toxic Chemicals Releases to Atmosphere[1]

Variables	Full Equation Ozone Depletion and Toxic Chemicals to Air		Reduced Equation Ozone Depletion and Toxic Chemicals to Air		Full Equation Ozone Depletion and Toxic Chemicals to Air		Reduced Equation Ozone Depletion and Toxic Chemicals to Air	
	b	Tol.	b	Tol.	b	Tol.	b	Tol.
Percent Black	.80***	.14	.46**	.31				
Percent Hispanic					−.40	.49	−.42**	.92
Social Class	−.33**	.18	−.22*	.33	−.02	.16		
Political Mobilization	.47*	.39	.39*	.52	.12	.38		
Environmental Interests	1.09***	.16	.81**	.21	.38	.20		
Pollution Potential	.99***	.26	.90***	.40	1.00***	.26	.98***	.53
Government Capacity	−.33***	.33	−.33***	.36	−.32	.31	−.29***	.51
Business Climate	−.17	.51			−.07	.56		
Legislative Professionalism	−.28	.29			.16	.37		
Public Opinion–Partisanship	.02	.41			−.09	.42		
Public Opinion–Ideology	.57**	.40	.41*	.50	.29	.46		
Moralistic Culture	.37	.24			−.04	.31		
Individualistic Culture	−.38	.36	−.55***	.43	−.58***	.40	−.58***	.94
Constant	−1.01		−.57		.41		.42	
Adj. R sqr.	.87		.87		.85		.87	
F-Ratio	28.37***		43.58***		24.84***		84.22***	
N	48		48		48		48	

NOTES:

[1]Cell entries are regression coefficients computed on standardized normalized data. Alaska and Hawaii deleted because of missing data on the public opinion and culture variables.

***$p < .01$ **$p < .05$ *$p < .10$

est measure does not enter into the equation when analyzing our results in conjunction with the percent Hispanic indicator.

Interestingly, across both reduced equations in Table 5.8, we find that pollution potential is a major explanation of the level of ozone depletion and toxic chemicals released to the atmosphere. This is not surprising. We would expect highly and densely populated industrial states to have high levels of pollution. Further, government capacity also reduces the level of this environmental harm in both reduced equations. We also find one instance of public opinion having an effect on this measure of air pollution. States with high scores on the ideology measure have high levels of ozone-depleting and

TABLE 5.9   Complex Model of Environmental Inequities in U.S. States (Full and Reduced Equations) for the Percent Black Population and the Percent Hispanic Population for Second Air Pollution Indicator—Nitrogen Oxide, Carbon Dioxide, and Sulphur Dioxide Released to the Atmosphere[1]

Variables	Full Equation Nitrogen Oxide, Carbon and Sulphur Dioxide to Air		Reduced Equation Nitrogen Oxide, Carbon and Sulphur Dioxide to Air		Full Equation Nitrogen Oxide, Carbon and Sulphur Dioxide to Air		Reduced Equation Nitrogen Oxide, Carbon and Sulphur Dioxide to Air	
	b	Tol.	b	Tol.	b	Tol.	b	Tol.
Percent Black	.39	.12	.48	.28				
Percent Hispanic					.03	.48		
Social Class	−.15	.14	−.17	.23	.14	.16	.11	.42
Political Mobilization	−.09	.37			−.02	.38		
Environmental Interests	−1.81**	.14	−1.78***	.24	−2.20***	.20	−2.12***	.33
Pollution Potential	−.10	.24	−.21	.46	−.21	.26	−.20*	.83
Government Capacity	.01	.31			−.09	.31		
Business Climate	−.003	.41			.13	.51		
Legislative Professionalism	−.45	.29			−.47	.36		
Public Opinion-Partisanship	−.45	.31			.04	.42		
Public Opinion-Ideology	.01	.35			−.22	.44		
Moralitic Culture	−.23	.20			−.09	.31		
Individualistic Culture	.55	.28	.60	.36	1.10**	.40	1.15***	.53
Sunbelt	−.99	.15	.15	.26				
Sunbelt x Percent Black	−3.24**	.17	−2.98**	.20				
Class x Pollution Potential	−.15**	.70	−.15***	.87	−.16***	.76	−.15***	.93
Constant	.72		.24		.36		.38	
Adj. R sqr.	.42		.48		.36		.45	
F-Ratio	3.30***		6.62***		3.05***		8.87***	
N	48		48		48		48	

NOTES:

[1]Cell entries are regression coefficients computed on standardized normalized data. Alaska and Hawaii deleted because of missing data on the public opinion and culture variables.

***$p < .01$ **$p < .05$ *$p < .10$

toxic chemicals released to the atmosphere. However, contrary to our hypothesis, states with an individualistic cultural ethos evidence lower levels of these types of airborne pollutants.

Nitrogen Oxide, Carbon Dioxide, and Sulphur Dioxide Released to the Atmosphere. Our analysis of the second indicator of air pollution—the levels of nitrogen oxide, carbon dioxide, and sulphur dioxide released to the atmosphere—is shown in Table 5.9. This table reveals an unforeseen set of conditional race- and class-based results for the reduced equation that focus on the black population. Further, although the reduced equation that focuses on the Hispanic population reveals no relationship between this population group and our measure of air pollution, this equation also reveals a class-based conditional relationship. We find that the relationship between the black population and level of this type of air pollution is negative in Sunbelt states and positive throughout the rest of the nation.[7] The algebraic factoring of this relationship (see Aiken and West, 1991:12–14), shown below, demonstrates this claim.

Region	b_0	$b_1 black$
Sunbelt States	.39	−2.50
Non-Sunbelt States	.24	.48

The same reduced equation indicates that class moderates the relationship between pollution potential and the level of nitrogen oxide, carbon dioxide, and sulphur dioxide releases. Below is the algebraic factoring of this relationship for three different levels of social class.

Social Class Level	b_0	$b_1 Pollution\ Potential$
High Social Class (+1.00)	.07	−.36
Middle Social Class (0.00)	.24	−.21
Low Social Class (−1.00)	.07	−.07

These factored coefficients indicate that states with a wealthier and more educated polity seem to be able to mitigate the relationship between pollution potential and air pollution, resulting in incidences of lower levels of this form of air pollution. We also note the poor showing for the political mobilization variable.

Additional results in Table 5.9 indicate that environmental interest decreases the level of this type of air pollutant, whereas an individualistic cultural ethos allows for increased levels of nitrogen oxide, carbon dioxide, and sulphur dioxide releases.[8]

TABLE 5.10   Complex Model of Environmental Inequities in U.S. States (Full and Reduced Equations) for the Percent Black Population and the Percent Hispanic Population for Hazardous Waste[1]

Variables	Full Equation Hazardous Waste		Reduced Equation Hazardous Waste		Full Equation Hazardous Waste		Reduced Equation Hazardous Waste	
	b	Tol.	b	Tol.	b	Tol.	b	Tol.
Percent Black	2.22***	.13	2.27***	.27				
Percent Hispanic					.31	.49	.69**	.86
Social Class	−.15	.15			.23	.16		
Political Mobilization	.08	.37			−.14	.38		
Environmental Interests	−.20	.15			−1.28*	.20	−1.23***	.50
Pollution Potential	1.83***	.25	1.84***	.34	1.67***	.26	1.56***	.47
Government Capacity	.30	.31	.36**	.36	.09	.31		
Business Climate	−.58***	.48	−.56***	.61	−.24	.56		
Legislative Professionalism	.17	.29			.69	.37	.77*	.41
Public Opinion-Partisanship	−.97*	.31	−.89**	.34	−.77	.42		
Public Opinion-Ideology	.64	.39	.74**	.54	.14	.46		
Moralistic Culture	1.07*	.20	1.05**	.28	.44	.31		
Individualistic Culture	.82*	.28	−.79*	.32	−.06	.40	−.82**	.51
Sunbelt	.66	.15	1.03	.17				
Sunbelt x Percent Black	−4.13***	.17	−3.81***	.20				
Constant	.76		.61		.08		.03	
Adj. R sqr.	.87		.88		.83		.84	
F-Ratio	25.03***		37.43***		21.06***		51.73***	
N	48		48		48		48	

NOTES:

[1]Cell entries are regression coefficients computed on standardized normalized data. Alaska and Hawaii deleted because of missing data on the public opinion and culture variables.

***$p < .01$ **$p < .05$ *$p < .10$

Hazardous Waste

Equations that explain the level of hazardous waste in a state are shown in Table 5.10. The first two columns on this table represent full and reduced equations for hazardous waste that include the black population measure; columns three and four represent similar equations for the Hispanic population measure.

The reduced equation that focuses on the black population reveals another region-based conditional finding. As was the case in the prior analysis of air pollution, the black population outside the Sunbelt is associated with higher levels of hazardous waste.[9] Based on the results of the equation, the relationship between the black population and our measure of hazardous waste is also strongest in states outside the Sunbelt region.

Region	b_0	$b_1 black$
Sunbelt States	1.64	−1.54
Non-Sunbelt States	.61	2.27

The reduced percent black equation evidences no support for either a class, political-mobilization, or interest-group explanation for the level of hazardous waste in a state. Also, in both reduced equations, we see the effect of the pollution potential measure—highly and densely populated industrial states have high levels of hazardous waste. The remaining measures in this equation produce contradictory results. The results for the government-capacity, business-climate, partisanship, and cultural measures are contrary to our hypotheses. However, the results for the ideology measure conform to our original hypothesis.

The reduced equation for the Hispanic population does reveal that as the Hispanic population increases, so does the level of hazardous waste. Environmental interests also reduce the level of hazardous waste while pollution potential, as previously noted, increases the level of this harm. The results from this reduced equation are opposite to our hypotheses for the legislative-professionalism and the individualistic-cultural measures.

Solid Waste

Table 5.11 shows our results for the degree of solid waste in a state. Columns 1 and 2 on this table are the full and reduced equations for the black population; columns 3 and 4 array the results for the Hispanic population.

The degree of solid waste in U.S. states, when the additional explanations are taken into account, reveals no race- or class-based inequities or any effect attributable to political mobilization. Of the explanations we have available, the reduced equations contain only environmental interests, pollution potential, and one measure of political culture as statistically significant predictors of solid waste. These results differ substantially from the findings based on the simple tests arrayed in Tables 5.6 and 5.7 and indicate that the simple equation was probably misspecified.

TABLE 5.11   Complex Model of Environmental Inequities in U.S. States (Full and Reduced Equations) for the Percent Black Population and the Percent Hispanic Population for Solid Waste[1]

Variables	Full Equation Solid Waste		Reduced Equation Solid Waste		Full Equation Solid Waste		Reduced Equation Solid Waste	
	b	Tol.	b	Tol.	b	Tol.	b	Tol.
Percent Black	−.24	.14						
Percent Hispanic					−.16	.49		
Social Class	.09	.18			.12	.16		
Political Mobilization	−.18	.39			−.20	.38		
Environmental Interests	.31	.16	.38*	.51	.36	.20	.38*	.51
Pollution Potential	.35***	.26	.39***	.95	.36***	.26	.39***	.95
Government Capacity	−.009	.33			.02	.31		
Business Climate	.07	.51			.03	.56		
Legislative Professionalism	.10	.29			.04	.37		
Public Opinion-Partisanship	−.31	.41			−.28	.42		
Public Opinion-Ideology	.07	.40			.11	.46		
Moralistic Culture	.10	.24			.18	.31		
Individualistic Culture	−.43*	.36	−.47***	.53	−.36	.40	−.47***	.53
Constant	−.02		−.05		−.02		−.05	
Adj. R sqr.	.50		.55		.51		.55	
F-Ratio	5.03***		20.82***		5.08***		20.82***	
N	48		48		48		48	

Notes:

[1]Cell entries are regression coefficients computed on standardized normalized data. Alaska and Hawaii deleted because of missing data on the public opinion and culture variables.

***$p < .01$ **$p < .05$ *$p < .10$

Toxic Waste

Table 5.12 shows the results of state-level data on toxic waste. Our measure of toxic waste is a rather deadly combination of environmental harms, including birth-defect toxins, cancer-causing and nerve-damaging chemicals released to the environment, along with toxic chemical transfers off-site and total chemical releases to the environment. Indeed, of all our dependent variables, this constitutes the ultimate witch's brew of environmental harms.

Employing the reduced percent black equation in Table 5.12, we find a race-based inequity for this segment of the population.[10] The class-based re-

TABLE 5.12 Complex Model of Environmental Inequities in U.S. States (Full and Reduced Equations) for the Percent Black Population and the Percent Hispanic Population for Toxic Waste[1]

Variables	Full Equation Toxic Waste		Reduced Equation Toxic Waste		Full Equation Toxic Waste		Reduced Equation Toxic Waste	
	b	Tol.	b	Tol.	b	Tol.	b	Tol.
Percent Black	2.21***	.13	1.93***	.30				
Percent Hispanic					−1.15***	.38	−1.31***	.40
Social Class	−.39	.17	−.23	.29	.38	.15	.56***	.24
Political Mobilization	1.68***	.39	1.55***	.56	1.25***	.35	.79**	.54
Environmental Interests	−.55	.14	−.67	.28	−2.41***	.17	−2.41***	.31
Pollution Potential	.49	.26	.41*	.28	.51**	.24	.39**	.40
Government Capacity	−.41*.	.32	−.33*	.38	−.19	.28		
Business Climate	−.09	.44			−.04	.53		
Legislative Professionalism	1.63***	.29	1.34***	.37	−1.15**	.32	−.63	.44
Public Opinion-Partisanship	.03	.41			−.21	.42		
Public Opinion-Ideology	−.07	.37			−.26	.45		
Moralistic Culture	.23	.24			−.09	.25		
Individualistic Culture	.007	.36			−.11	.38		
Social Class x Pollution Potential	−.12*	.70	−.16***	.75				
West					−3.46***	.33	−3.80***	.45
West x Percent Hispanic					2.53***	.40	2.21***	.43
Constant	.02		.21		1.31		1.73	
Adj. R sqr.	.57		.63		.61		.62	
F-Ratio	5.93***		11.72***		6.30***		10.97***	
N	48		48		48		48	

NOTES:
[1] Cell entries are regression coefficients computed on standardized normalized data. Alaska and Hawaii deleted because of missing data on the public opinion and culture variables.

***p < .01   **p < .05   *p < .10

sults from this analysis produce an unforeseen result in that class is part of a conditional relationship involving pollution potential. The results of the algebraic factoring of these results, shown below, indicate that high social class mitigates the impact of pollution potential. Conversely, in low-social-class states, the relationship between pollution potential and toxic waste is quite pronounced.

Social Class Level	b_0	b_1 Pollution Potential
High Social Class (+1.00)	−.02	.18
Middle Social Class (0.00)	.21	.41
Low Social Class (−1.00)	.44	.64

This equation also reveals that political mobilization and legislative professionalism are positively related to toxic waste—both contrary to our initial hypotheses. Government capacity, in keeping with our initial hypothesis, is related to toxic waste in the proper direction.

The reduced equation analyzing the relationship between the percent Hispanic population and toxic waste reveals a conditional relationship. The relationship between the Hispanic population and this environmental harm is stronger in Western states. Indeed, as shown below in the algebraic factored results, the relationship between Hispanics and toxic waste elsewhere in the nation is negative.

Region	b_0	b_1 Hispanic
Western States	−2.07	.90
Nonwestern States	1.73	−1.31

Results from the reduced Hispanic equation also reveal a set of findings that is both consistent and inconsistent with our initial hypotheses: Environmental interests reduce the level of toxic waste, whereas pollution potential increases the level of toxic waste. Contrary to initial hypotheses, both social class and political mobilization are positively related to the level of toxic waste.[11]

Water Pollution

Tables 5.13 and 5.14 array the results from our analysis of water pollution. Table 5.13 includes our first measure of water pollution: degree of water-system violations. Columns 1 and 2 array the full and reduced equations for our analysis of the percent black populations; the third and fourth columns are the corresponding results for the percent Hispanic population. Table 5.14, arranged in the same fashion, arrays our results for the second measure of water pollution: toxic chemical pollution of surface and groundwater.

Degree of Water System Violations. We begin with a discussion of the first isolated dimension of water quality: the degree of water-system violations. The first point that is obvious is the absence of race- and class-based

TABLE 5.13   Complex Model of Environmental Inequities in U.S. States (Full and Reduced Equations) for the Percent Black Population and the Percent Hispanic Population for First Water Quality Indicator—Degree of Water-System Violations[1]

Variables	Full Equation Water System Violations		Reduced Equation Water System Violations		Full Equation Water System Violations		Reduced Equation Water System Violations	
	b	Tol.	b	Tol.	b	Tol.	b	Tol.
Percent Black	−1.13**	.14	−.62**	.46				
Percent Hispanic					.79***	.38	.67***	.60
Social Class	.26	.18	.34***	.35	−.24	.15		
Political Mobilization	−.64*	.39	−.40	.63	−.48	.35		
Environmental Interests	−.81	.16	−.70*	.31	.40	.17		
Pollution Potential	.01	.26			−.05	.24		
Government Capacity	.18	.33	.22**	.58	.02	.28		
Business Climate	−.11	.51			−.22	.53	−.24**	.85
Legislative Professionalism	.52	.29			.42	.32		
Public Opinion-Partisanship	−.21	.41			−.12	.42		
Public Opinion-Ideology	−.09	.40			.08	.45		
Moralistic Culture	.16	.24			.36	.25		
Individualistic Culture	.009	.36			.02	.38		
West					1.91**	.33	1.91***	.74
West x Hispanic					2.55***	.40	−1.42***	.56
Constant	−.001		−.03		−.34		−.39	
Adj. R sqr.	.12		.19		.31		.41	
F-Ratio	1.54		3.41***		2.55**		9.81***	
N	48		48		48		48	

NOTES:
[1]Cell entries are regression coefficients computed on standardized normalized data. Alaska and Hawaii deleted because of missing data on the public opinion and culture variables.
  ***$p < .01$ **$p < .05$ *$p < .10$

inequities. For the reduced percent black equation in Table 5.13, we find that as the percent of the black population decreases, the level of water-system violations increases. The reduced Hispanic equation in Table 5.13 reveals a conditional relationship between the Hispanic population and this measure of water pollution. An algebraic factoring of this relationship, shown below, indicates that Hispanics living outside of Western states are subjected to far higher levels of water-system violations than is the case for Hispanics living in Western states.

TABLE 5.14   Complex Model of Environmental Inequities in U.S. States (Full and Reduced Equations) for the Percent Black Population and the Percent Hispanic Population for Second Water Pollution Indicator—Toxic Chemical Pollution of Surface and Groundwater Supply

Variables	Full Equation Toxic and Chemical Pollution— Surface and Groundwater b	Tol.	Reduced Equation Toxic and Chemical Pollution— Surface and Groundwater b	Tol.	Full Equation Toxic and Chemical Pollution— Surface and Groundwater b	Tol.	Reduced Equation Toxic and Chemical Pollution— Surface and Groundwater b	Tol.
Percent Black	.71**	.14	.73***	.28				
Percent Hispanic					−.21	.38	−.23	.41
Social Class	.07	.18			.29***	.15	.30***	.19
Political Mobilization	.55***	.39	.50***	.49	.47***	.35	.43***	.41
Environmental Interests	−.19	.16			−.78***	.17	−.76***	.29
Pollution Potential	.18**	.26	.10*	.42	.20**	.24	.22***	.29
Government Capacity	.07	.33			.14*	.28	.15*	.30
Business Climate	−.04	.51			.01	.53		
Legislative Professionalism	−.81**	.29	−.77***	.38	−.71***	.32	−.71***	.34
Public Opinion- Partisanship	−.34*	.41	−.27*	.51	−.42**	.42	−.42***	.57
Public Opinion- Ideology	−.10	.40			−.20	.45		
Moralistic Culture	.09	.24			.0006	.25		
Individualistic Culture	−.09	.36			−.16	.38		
West					−1.14***	.33	−1.15***	.39
West x Hispanic					.76**	.40	.83***	.43
Constant	−.11		−.13		.12		.11	
Adj. R sqr.	.38		.43		.43		.46	
F-Ratio	3.44***		8.15***		3.55***		5.04***	
N	48		48		48		48	

NOTES:

[1]Cell entries are regression coefficients computed on standardized normalized data. Alaska and Hawaii deleted because of missing data on the public opinion and culture variables.

***$p < .01$ **$p < .05$ *$p < .10$

Region	b_0	b_1 Hispanic
Western States	2.32	−.75
Nonwestern States	.41	.67

For both reduced equations in Table 5.13, we find no evidence of the hypothesized class-based inequity. For the reduced equation dealing with the black population, the class and water pollution relationship is inconsistent with our initial hypothesis; for the reduced Hispanic equation, social class is not present. Further, neither reduced equation provides any support for the political-mobilization hypothesis. In one instance, political mobilization is statistically insignificant, and in the remaining reduced equation it is absent.

Overall, the reduced equations provide the following portraits. When controlling for relevant extraneous variables, the degree of water-system violations is a function of decreasing levels of the black population located in relatively high social class states. And whereas high levels of organized interests depress the degree of water-system violations, government capacity to deal with the problem appears to be lacking in that the higher the level of natural resource expenditure, the higher the level of water-system violations. Quite possibly, the money expended for natural resources is not going to the maintenance of the water system in these states.

When dealing with the reduced equation for the Hispanic population, the Hispanic population located in states outside the West seems to be exposed to far greater levels of water system violations; the level of water system violation is further decreased by a favorable business climate—contrary to our initial hypothesis.

Toxic and Chemical Pollution of Surface and Ground Water. The results from Table 5.14 indicate the presence of a race-based inequity for both the percent black and percent Hispanic populations and the absence of any class-based inequity with regard to this measure of water pollution. For the reduced equation focusing on the black population, the results indicate that as the black population increases, so does the level of toxic and chemical pollution of the surface and groundwater supplies.[12] For the reduced equation focusing on the Hispanic population, a conditional relationship is present. The algebraic factor of this relationship, shown below, indicates that increasing levels of the Hispanic population located in Western states are associated with higher levels of toxic and chemical water pollution than is the case elsewhere in the nation.

Region	b_0	$b_1 Hispanic$
Western States	−1.04	.60
Nonwestern States	.11	−.23

The class variable does not survive the reduction technique in the reduced black equation, and the reduced Hispanic equation is opposite to the initial hypothesis—indicating that increasingly wealthier states are faced with higher levels of water pollution problems.[13]

Summary of Complex State-Level Analysis

This chapter assesses race, class, and political-mobilization explanations of seven environmental harms in the forty-eight contiguous U.S. states. We began the analysis with a simple, three-variable model and then tested the three concepts in competition with other known explanations for environmental hazards. Our simple tripartite model produced some interesting results. For the percent black equation (Table 5.6), we found evidence to confirm race-based environmental injustice in five out of seven instances. In contrast, the simple equations that focused on the Hispanic population (Table 5.7) only produced evidence to confirm race-based environmental injustice in one out of seven instances. Additionally, solid evidence of class-based environmental injustice was evidenced in only one instance, and we found only minor evidence indicating that political mobilization reduced levels of environmental hazards.

We developed a more complex test to assess the race, class, and mobilization effects (the core concepts in the environmental injustice literature) on environmental hazards by adding a pool of explanations from the existing literature. The findings from this analysis were mixed but interesting. We provide a summary of these results in Figure 5.2.

We begin this summary with our most consistently negative findings from the complex test. Results indicate that political mobilization did not perform as expected in our complex state-level analysis. In five out of seven instances, political mobilization bore no relationship to the level of environmental hazards. In the remaining two instances—toxic waste and toxic and chemical pollution of surface and groundwater—the direction of the relationship ran counter to the initial hypothesis, that is, our results indicate that instead of decreasing the level of environmental harms, the political mobilization increased the level of the two hazards.

The class measure also evidenced mixed results—although its performance was marginally better than the mobilization measure due to conditional relationships. At the outset, the class measure was either unrelated to environmental harms or evidenced a direct positive sign—the opposite of the initial hypothesis—in five out of seven instances. In the remaining two instances, class moderated the relationship between pollution potential and two environmental harms—nitrogen oxide, dioxide carbon, and sulphur dioxide released to the atmosphere, and toxic waste. In both instances, high social class weakened the relationship between pollution potential and environmental hazards such that higher levels of pollution potential produced less in the way of environmental pollutants. Possibly the wealth and education level of the polities in higher social class states means they seek to protect lives and therefore tolerate less environmental damage.

FIGURE 5.2   Summary of State-Level Findings (based on reduced equations)

Environmental Harm	Race Inequity	Class Inequity	Political Mobilization	Other Explanations***
Ozone Depletion and Toxic Chemicals Released to Air	Black (yes) Hispanic (no)	no	no	Environmental Interests, *Pollution Potential, Government Capacity, Ideology,* Individualistic Culture
Level of Nitrogen Oxide, Carbon Dioxide, and Sulphur Dioxide Released to Air	Black (yes)* Hispanic (no)	yes**	no	*Environmental Interest, Pollution Potential, Individualistic Culture*
Hazardous Waste	Black (yes)* Hispanic (yes)	no	no	*Environmental Interests, Pollution Potential,* Government Capacity, Business Climate, Legislative Professionalism, Partisanship, *Ideology, Moralistic Culture,* Individualistic Culture
Solid Waste	Black (no) Hispanic (no)	no	no	Environmental Interests, *Pollution Potential,* Individualistic Culture
Toxic Waste	Black (yes) Hispanic (yes)*	yes**	no	*Environmental Interest, Pollution Potential, Government Capacity,* Legislative Professionalism
Degree of Water-System Violations	Black (no) Hispanic (yes)*	no	no	*Environmental Interest,* Government Capacity, Business Climate
Toxic and Chemical Pollution of Surface and Groundwater	Black (yes) Hispanic (yes)*	no	no	*Environmental Interest, Pollution Potential,* Government Capacity, *Legislative Professionalism,* Partisanship

Notes:
    *Region-based conditional relationship
    **Class-based conditional relationship with pollution potential
    ***Other variables included in either or both reduced equations; entries that are italicized evidenced the hypothesized relationship.

The race-based findings produced the most interesting results, although some findings are perplexing. We begin with a summary of findings for the percent black population. For this group, we found three instances of the simple positive hypothesized relationship between race and pollution, that is, increasing proportions of the black population were associated with increasing levels of ozone depletion and toxic chemicals released to the atmosphere, toxic waste, and toxic and chemical pollution of surface and groundwater. In two other instances, we found either no relationship between the black population (solid waste) or a relationship contrary to the initial hypothesis (degree of water-system violations). However, by far the most interesting and perplexing finding focused on the black population–Sunbelt conditional relationship. In both instances, the results indicate that black populations residing outside Sunbelt states were associated with higher levels of nitrogen oxide, carbon dioxide, and sulphur dioxide air pollutants and hazardous waste than was the case for black Americans residing in the Sunbelt. This finding, exploratory as it is, is perplexing. We would expect to find that black Americans living in Sunbelt states were exposed to higher levels of pollution. First, the Sunbelt has undergone unrivaled development leading to higher levels of environmental pollution. Second, large proportions of the black population reside in the Sunbelt region. Nevertheless, this bears closer scrutiny.

We also have interesting race-based findings for the Hispanic population. First, in three out of seven instances, we found either no relationship between this group and environmental harms or a negative relationship that was contrary to the initial hypothesis. In one instance—hazardous waste—we did find the requisite positive relationship that conforms to the initial hypothesis. However, in three instances we found conditional relationships based on region. For our two measures of water pollution, we found that Hispanics living outside Western states were subjected to higher levels of harms. In contrast, we found that Hispanics residing within Western states were subjected to higher levels of toxic waste. Like our region-based black conditional findings, this set of results bears closer investigation.

One additional statistical finding is of interest: The pollution-potential measure was a consistent feature in establishing the level of environmental hazards in six out of seven instances—either in the form of a direct positive relationship or as part of a conditional relationship expressing social class. As a consequence, any environmental injustice research needs to account for this key concept.

Chapter 6 replicates our state-level results using the 2,000-plus counties in the United States for which toxic release inventory data were available. We want to see if the findings from the state-level investigation stand up at a different level of analysis.

Notes

1. Elimination of extreme outliers, to correct skewed distributions on each air pollution indicator, was partially achieved by recoding data. Recoded data was sub-

jected to a square root transformation (with the resultant value multiplied by ten to restore variance) in order to normalized univariate distributions. The recoded states are shown below:

Variables	States Recoded
A1, Ozone Depleting Emissions (# of big facilities)	California, 353 to 189
A2, Ozone Depleting Emissions (output in 100 tons)	California, 121 to 61
A3, Percent Population with Air Standards Violating Ozone Depletion	No recode
A4, Toxic Chemical Releases by Industry to Air (lbs/sq. mile)	Connecticut, 4,772 to 3,600; New Jersey, 4,690 to 3,400; Rhode Island, 4,764 to 3,500
A5, Number of High Risk Cancer Facilities	California, 11 to 9; Georgia, 11 to 9; Washington, 10 to 8
A6, U.S. Electric Utility Air Emissions, Nitrogen Oxide (lbs/capita)	Wyoming, 93.9 to 26; North Dakota, 45.5 to 25; West Virginia, 43.9 to 24
A7, U.S. Electric Utility Air Emissions, Carbon Dioxide (lbs/capita)	North Dakota, 45.5 to 25; Washington, 43.9 to 24; Wyoming, 93.9 to 26
A8, U.S. Electric Utility Air Amissions, Sulfur Dioxide (lbs/capita)	West Virginia, 1041.6 to 540
A9, Carbon Dioxide Emissions for all Fuel Sources (tons/capita)	Alaska, 58.6 to 40; Louisiana, 46.3 to 39; North Dakota, 72.9 to 42; West Virginia, 64 to 41; Wyoming, 126 to 43

The descriptive statistics for the original and the recoded/transformed value of each air pollution indicator are shown below:

Variables	Mean	Std. D.	Skewness	Kutosis	Variance	CV
A1, Original	59.6	64.7	2.19	6.68	4198.8	1.08
A1, Transformed	65.4	37.1	.12	−.76	1381.2	.56
A2, Original	20.4	22.8	2.14	6.09	520.0	1.11
A2, Transformed	37.8	22.2	.17	−.78	495.9	.58
A3, Original	38.8	35.2	.35	−1.20	1245.4	.90
A3, Transformed	50.3	37.1	−.25	−1.46	1383.3	.73
A4, Original	1311.7	1314.6	1.14	.51	1728323	1.00
A4, Transformed	803.9	187.8	.04	−1.12	31973.4	.58
A5, Original	3.5	5.5	3.44	14.56	30.6	1.54
A5, Transformed	13.4	10.3	.06	−1.10	459.9	.77
A6, Original	80.7	104.2	3.28	12.30	10804.2	1.29
A6, Transformed	72.1	35.1	−.36	−.32	1247.2	.48

A7, Original	11.2	15.07	3.80	16.90	227.9	1.34
A7, Transformed	27.9	14.0	.15	.31	197.9	.50
A8, Original	151.7	187.8	2.60	8.49	35279	1.23
A8, Transformed	102.8	60.4	.48	−.29	3659.1	.58
A9, Original	26.8	19.7	3.09	11.8	390.5	.74
A9, Transformed	47.0	9.9	.29	−.99	98.8	.21

2. Elimination of extreme outliers and normalization of univariate distributions was achieved by recoding outliers and then subjecting each indicator to a square root transformation (multiplied by ten to restore variance). Recoded states are shown below:

Variables	Recode
HW1, Number of Non-Superfund Sites	California, 2400 to 1520; Pennsylvania, 2363 to 1510; Texas, 2324 to 1500
HW2, Number of Hazardous Waste Management Facilities	Texas, 1153 to 500
HW3, Number of Hazardous Waste Transportation Accidents	California, 676 to 500; Illinois, 880 to 510; Ohio, 908 to 520; Pennsylvania, 989 to 580; Texas, 880 to 510
HW4, Number of Hazardous Waste RCRA Generators	California, 3972 to 820; Massachusetts, 1013 to 720; New Jersey, 1480 to 780; Pennsylvania, 2607 to 800; Texas, 2450 to 790
HW5, Cost of Hazardous Waste Transportation Accidents	Delaware, 2183 to 1400; California, 3665 to 140; North Carolina, 4495 to 1420; Texas, 8733 to 1430
HW6, Number of Military Hazardous Waste Sites	California, 1713 to 710; Virginia, 812 to 700
HW7, Number of Superfund (NPL) Sites	California, 88 to 54; Michigan, 78 to 52; New Jersey, 109 to 56; New York, 83 to 53; Pennsylvania, 95 to 55
HW8, Hazardous Waste Generated	Georgia, 12498 to 6300; Virginia, 8769 to 6100; Virginia, 12426 to 6200; Tennessee, 13932 to 6400
HW9, Hazardous Waste Stays in State	Georgia, 12496 to 6300; Louisiana, 6555 to 6000; Virginia, 8760 to 6100; West Virginia, 12443 to 6200

Descriptive statistics for original and recoded/transformed indicators are shown below:

Variables	Mean	Std. D.	Skewness	Kutosis	Variance	CV
HW1, Original	611	587	1.70	2.40	345840	.96
HW1, Transformed	560	452	.99	−.27	204663	.80
HW2, Original	97.6	179	4.42	22.3	32279	1.83
HW2, Recoded Only	77.0	49	1.27	1.23	2460	.63
HW3, Original	245	249	1.52	1.79	62433	1.01
HW3, Recoded Only	210	167	.48	−1.06	28096	.79

HW4, Original	431	735	3.26	11.06	541198	1.70
HW4, Transformed	147	79.3	.24	−1.02	6302	.53
HW5, Original	863	1412	4.03	18.35	1994551	1.63
HW5, Transformed	595	466	.51	−1.15	217479	.78
HW6, Original	283	271	3.15	13.64	73560	.95
HW6, Transformed	261	181	.84	−.05	32907	.69
HW7, Original	24.5	25.7	1.78	2.42	665.1	1.05
HW7, Transformed	20.8	16.6	.87	−.59	277.7	.80
HW8, Original	1830	3391	2.39	4.93	.115021+.08	1.85
HW8, Transformed	271	255	.95	−.45	65442	.94
HW9, Original	1665	2998	2.34	5.04	8988551	1.80
HW9, Transformed	266	255	.97	−.42	65442	.95

3. Elimination of extreme outliers was achieved by recoding data. Only two of the three indicators required recoding. No square root transformations were required to normalize the data. The recoded states are shown below:

Variables	Recode
SW1, Number of Tons Per Day of Solid Waste from Municipal Incinerators	California, 2500 to 1470; Connecticut, 5700 to 1520; Florida, 9200 to 1540; Indiana, 3000 to 1480; Maryland, 5000 to 1510; Massachusetts, 8600 to 1530; Minnesota, 2000 to 1460; New York, 9877 to 1550; Ohio, 3750 to 1490; Virginia, 4000 to 1500
SW2, Municipal Solid Waste Generated (tons/day)	No recode
SW3, Number of Open Municipal Landfills	Alaska, 740 to 270; California, 423 to 260; Texas, 934 to 290; Wisconsin, 775 to 280

The descriptive statistics for the original and recoded variables are shown below:

Variables	Mean	Std. D.	Skewness	Kutosis	Variance	CV
SW1, Original	1375.7	2401.8	2.34	4.74	5768701	1.74
SW1, Recode	191.9	155.0	.01	−1.56	24039.9	.80
SW2, Original	1898.5	501.5	.63	−.50	251513	.26
SW3, Original	147.0	185.1	3.05	8.83	34279.5	1.25
SW3, Recode	112.0	70.6	.96	.41	4986.3	.62

4. Elimination of extreme outliers, in order to normalize univariate distributions, was accomplished by recoding extreme scores on four out of the five indicators. Recoded states are shown below:

Variables	Recode
TW1, Birth Defect Toxins Released to Environment (lbs/capita)	No recode
TW2, Cancer-Causing Chemicals Released to Environment (lbs/capita)	Indiana, 5.7 to 4.4; Louisiana, 5.4 to 4.0; West Virginia, 5.8 to 4.5
TW3, Nerve Damaging Toxins Released to Environment (lbs/capita)	Louisiana, 8.6 to 7.0; Tennessee, 9.8 to 7.5; West Virginia, 12.3 to 8.0
TW4, Toxic Chemical Transfers Off-site (lbs/capita)	Kansas, 21.9 to 12
TW5, Total Chemical Releases to Environment (lbs/capita)	Kansas, 70 to 60; Louisiana, 167 to 90; Utah, 86 to 70; Wyoming, 96 to 80

The descriptive statistics for the five indicators are shown below:

Variables	Mean	Std. D.	Skewness	Kutosis	Variance	CV
TW1, Original	5.35	3.19	.37	−.41	10.2	.59
TW2, Original	3.72	3.95	2.30	7.25	15.6	1.06
TW2, Recode	16.6	8.75	.21	−.63	76.7	.52
TW3, Original	3.17	2.58	1.33	2.17	6.6	.81
TW3, Recode	3.00	2.14	.52	−.57	4.9	.71
TW4, Original	3.72	3.95	2.30	2.25	15.6	1.06
TW4, Recode	16.6	8.76	.21	−.65	76.7	.52
TW5, Original	27.9	28.3	2.89	10.5	800.9	1.01
TW5, Recode	47.2	18.6	.55	−.07	346.2	.39

5. Elimination of extreme outliers was achieved by recoding data. Data was then normalized, in most instances, using a square root transformation (with resultant values multiplied by ten to restore variance. The recoded states are shown below:

Variables	Recode
WP1, Percent Water System Violating SDWA	No recode
WP2, Percent Population with SDWA Violations	Alaska, 48 to 25; Arizona, 59.9 to 26; New Jersey, 100 to 27; Washington, 44.5 to 24
WP3, Percent Water System with Significant Noncompliance with Standards	Alaska, 72.2 to 8; Arizona, 24.1 to 6; Nevada, 28.3 to 7; Washington, 18.6 to 5
WP4, Toxic Chemicals Underground Injections (lbs/capita)	Kansas, 36.5 to 12; Louisiana, 95.77 to 14; Mississippi, 17.8 to 10; Tennessee, 10.1 to 9; Texas, 29.2 to 11; Wyoming, 57.5 to 13
WP5, Toxic Chemicals Released to Surface Water (lbs/capita)	Alaska, 8.3 to 3.4; Louisiana, 36.5 to 3.5

The descriptive statistics for the original and recoded/transformed indicators are shown below:

Variable	Mean	Std. D.	Skewness	Kutosis	Variance	CV
WP1, Original	23.6	21.0	1.00	.13	443.7	.89
WP2, Original	14.2	16.9	3.31	12.6	285.7	1.19
WP2, Transformed	31.4	11.0	.09	−.86	121.8	.35
WP3, Original	4.36	12.0	5.07	27.39	144.2	2.74
WP3, Transformed	12.2	6.3	.31	.05	40.2	.51
WP4, Original	5.5	16.7	4.0	16.9	279.8	3.02
WP4, Transformed	9.8	20.2	2.7	7.6	41102	2.06
WP5, Original	1.49	5.10	6.19	38.6	26.0	3.42
WP5, Transformed	6.69	5.20	.74	−.10	27.0	.74

6. The tolerance statistic associated with this measure has a value of .21.

7. The tolerance statistics associated with the percent black, Sunbelt, and black-Sunbelt measures are .28, .26, and .20, respectively.

8. The tolerance statistic associated with the individualistic political culture measure is .53.

9. The tolerance statistics associated with the percent black, Sunbelt, and black-Sunbelt measures are .27, .17, and .20, respectively.

10. The tolerance statistic associated with this measure is .30.

11. The tolerance statistic associated with social class is .24.

12. The tolerance statistic associated with the percent Hispanic measure is .28.

13. The tolerance statistic associated with the social-class measure in the reduced Hispanic equation is .19.

6

Environmental Injustice in America's Counties

This chapter examines the environmental injustice thesis within the context of U.S. counties. We begin this chapter by specifying our dependent variables for this level of analysis. Then, after a brief recapitulation of the model established in Chapter 4 and a discussion of the sample, we present our results, first in the form of a simple tripartite model that includes race, class, and political mobilization, and second in the form of a longer reduced equation using all of our additional measures in addition to the race/class/mobilization measures.

Toxic Releases as the Dependent Variable

Because of the toxic pollutant–related findings in Chapter 5 regarding the linkage between race/ethnicity and toxic environmental hazards, we decided to shift our inquiry to toxic hazards for subsequent sections of our analysis. Using data from the Toxic Release Inventory, we constructed three measures at the county level: global toxic releases to air, land, and water, stack air toxic releases, and fugitive air toxic releases. All data for the county level analysis were extracted from the 1995 Toxic Release Inventory and is coded in thousands of pounds of toxins released.

Before we proceed, some comments need to be made about the use of TRI data. Other research has worked with this particular hazard (Bowen, et al., 1995; Burke, 1993; Cutter, 1994; Downey, 1998; Gould, 1986; Krieg, 1998; Lester and Allen, 1996; Perlin, et al., 1995; Polloch and Vittas, 1995; Ringquist, 1997; Szasz, et al., 1992). However, some of these articles only looked at the number of toxic release facilities in relation to race and did not measure the actual level of toxic emissions (Burke, 1993; Cutter, 1994; Perlin, et al., 1995; Polloch and Vittas, 1995). Additionally, some findings on race and toxic release exhibit problems of external validity because of restricted samples, that is, while four studies did involve broad samples (Gould, 1986—urban neighborhoods; Lester, Allen, and Lauer, 1994—all U.S. states; Perlin, et al., 1995—U.S. counties; Ringquist, 1997—all urban ZIP codes), the remaining articles studied far more discrete areas (e.g., Krieg, 1998, only studied Route 128 towns in Boston; Burke, 1993, and Szasz, et al., 1992, focused only on Los Angeles County; Cutter, 1994, studied only South Carolina counties; Lester and Allen, 1996, restricted their inquiry to the seventy-five largest cities in the United States; Polloch and Vittas, 1995, only studied Florida; Downey, 1998, limited the sample to Michigan; and, Bowen, et al., 1995, dealt only with Cuyahoga County, Ohio).

Furthermore, some of these articles used very simple race/class models to analyze the data, therefore precluding any chance of assessing if spurious relationships were present (Bowen, et al., 1995; Burke, 1993; Downey, 1998; Krieg, 1998; Perlin, et al., 1995; Polloch and Vittas, 1995; Szasz, et al., 1992). Finally, contradictory findings are present (Krieg, 1998, and Cutter, 1994, did not report clear-cut relationships between race and toxic hazards; Bowen, et al., 1995, report income as a better predictor of TRI emissions than is the case for race in Cuyahoga County, Ohio). Other research, however, reports significant relationships between race and toxic hazards (Burke, 1993; Downey, 1998; Gould, 1986; Lester and Allen, 1996; Lester, Allen, and Lauer, 1994; Perlin, et al., 1995; Polloch and Vittas, 1995; Ringquist, 1997; Szasz, et al., 1992). By focusing on toxic releases, using a broad sample, and employing more complex equations, this research can both provide more generalizable findings about the race-risk nexus with regard to this environmental hazard and determine if the predominantly positive results about race and toxic hazards can be replicated at the county level.

Using TRI data is not, however, without its problems. First, the database includes only manufacturing facilities with primary Standard Industrial Codes 20–39. Thus, not all toxic release facilities file reports with the inventory. Second, only SIC 20–39 facilities with ten or more employees that either process more than 25,000 pounds of the 350 1995 TRI list chemicals and chemical compounds annually or who use more than 10,000 pounds of these chemicals and chemical compounds per year file reports. Therefore, toxic releases from small firms and firms that do not reach the processing or use thresholds are not included, indicating that reasonably significant amounts of toxic releases are not reflected in the inventory. Third, TRI data are the result of industry self-reporting, and their reports receive only spot-checks by the Environmental Protection Agency. This may mean that producers are underreporting emission levels (Krieg, 1998:192–193). Finally, TRI data are a product of currently industrialized areas with active processors and users of a restrictive list of toxins. It does not reflect other toxins at abandoned waste dumps, landfills, and other storage facilities. As a consequence, the TRI data should not be conceptualized as measuring the exact amounts of toxic waste in any community.

However, studying environmental injustice in terms of the Toxic Release Inventory is still valid. For example, toxic waste sites of defunct industry, albeit still dangerous, represent a fixed amount of environmental hazard. The industry has closed down, and the sources of environmental degradation cannot expand. Furthermore, although toxins moved to storage facilities and active dumps do constitute an expanding supply of environmental hazards, these locations are fixed and, to some degree, do contain the spread of the waste. In contrast, the TRI data represent a continually expanding supply of environmental hazards directly discharged to the land, air, and water by a known set of companies within the community. Thus, the data used in this study do represent the annual amount of new toxins released to air, land, and water within a specific community that is not necessarily accounted for in other databases. Finally, even though the industry reports do not cover all toxic chemicals and all firms, the amounts reported are substantial and a cause for concern. Thus, this source of pollution should not be ignored.

Another problem to consider when using TRI data is how to quantify a toxic release measure. The following hypothetical example clarifies part of the situation. Assume the existence of three counties: County A, with six facilities producing 50,000 pounds of toxic release per year; County B, with eight facilities producing 40,000 pounds annually; and County C, with five facilities with 100,000 pounds per year of releases. Using the number of facilities as the environmental hazard measure, the countries would be listed, on a more to less continuum, as B-A-C. However, if pounds of toxic release are measured, then the ranking is C-A-B, that is, the high and low cases reverse as between the two measures. Given this example, the number of facilities and the level of toxic releases could be inversely related, and since the level of toxic releases is what causes environmental degradation, it appears that the level of toxic releases, not the number of facilities, would be a more valid measure.

The decision to measure toxic releases presents another problem. Simply reporting total pounds released masks the method of release. Releases occur as stack air and fugitive air, land, and water releases, and the amounts of these individual release modes can vary dramatically even though total amounts released can be highly similar for different locales. An example based on North Carolina data clarifies this problem. As shown in Table 6.1, the two counties have almost identical total release volumes. However, Columbus County has a high level of stack air releases, relatively low levels of fugitive air releases, and noticeable amounts of land and water releases.

TABLE 6.1   Comparison of Components of Total Toxic Releases in Two North
Carolina Counties (thousands of pounds)

Type of Release	Columbus County	Catawba County
Stack Air	3856.6	3327.3
Fugitive Air	315.6	920.9
Land Releases	37.0	0.0
Water Releases	231.2	.001
Total Releases	4440.4	4248.2

SOURCE: *Toxic Release Inventory, 1995.*

By comparison, all of Catawba County's toxic releases occur in the form of
stack and fugitive air. One way to account for the variation in modes of release is to create a weighted factor scale, and an accepted method of creating
a weighted scale is factor analysis. Although not an ideal solution, a factor
scale of release modes is better than using total releases, because the
weighted scale at least gives some consideration to varying levels of dis-
charge in the four modes. A simple additive measure of total releases would
not be capable of achieving this outcome.[1] Principal components factor
analysis of thousands of pounds of stack air and fugitive air, land, and water
releases, abstracted from the 1995 Toxic Release Inventory and transformed
to eliminate extreme outliers, produced a single unrotated factor.[2] High positive scores reflect high levels of toxic releases; high negative scores reflect
the opposite.

To augment the global TRI release measure, we used two of the factor
components—stack air and fugitive air TRI releases—as separate measures
of toxic hazards in U.S. counties. We selected the two air-quality measures
for several reasons. Air pollution, although initially concentrated around the
source point of emissions, moves with wind direction. Thus, air pollution
represents a particularly invidious form of environmental hazard. Second,
air pollution has historically been a mainstay for the study of environmental
injustice. Thus, we focus on a harm that will be comparable to measures in
earlier research for purposes of replication.

Our auxiliary measures of air pollution consist of thousands of pounds of
toxic releases through stack air and fugitive air in 1995 in U.S. counties.[3]

The Sample of Counties

The sample used in this level of analysis includes approximately 2,100 counties in the United States. Alaskan and Hawaiian counties were excluded because of missing data on two explanatory concepts: public opinion and political culture. The loss of these counties was not detrimental to our analysis
for two reasons. First, both states have very low percentages of the racial

and ethnic groups of interest to our study. Second, the deletion of Alaska resulted in the loss of only eleven counties, and the deletion of Hawaii resulted only in the loss of a few counties. Indeed, some of the deleted Alaskan and Hawaiian counties had missing data on the dependent variables.

However, the largest reduction in number of cases resulted from missing data on the dependent variables. The lack of TRI reports for slightly more than 1,000 counties resulted in an N of cases equal to 2,095.[4] In some instances, the results reported herein are based on slightly less than 2,095 counties. The additional marginal reduction in cases was produced by the presence of statistically significant residual outliers that were deleted from the relevant analysis. In sum, the results reported here are based on between 2,082 and 2,092 U.S. counties in 1995, or roughly 69 percent of all U.S. counties.[5]

Some may argue with using counties as the unit of analysis. We argue that using counties as our second level of analysis is justified. Counties are governing units of states and, as such, do have substate responsibilities for many issues of societal concern. Thus, county-level awareness of a problem within their geographic area is an important first step toward allocating resources to policy solutions. Furthermore, counties can become the focus of lawsuits (i.e., from activists) regarding environmental injustice, a host of other pressures from the state government to which they are subordinate, or investigations by the federal government. As such, the possibility of environmental injustice arising from county-level action or inaction in this policy area makes them a fit subject for study. Furthermore, not all pollutants are localized—they can disperse across counties. Thus, relationships between race/class and environmental harms can take on a countywide coloring. Finally, several environmental injustice studies have made use of this level of analysis (e.g., Allen, 2001; Allen, Lester, and Hill, 1995; Bowman and Crews-Meyer, 1995, 1997; Hird, 1993, 1994; Hird and Reese, 1998). Thus, this study will have a means of comparison with existing literature.

As noted in Chapter 5, there is a continuing controversy in environmental justice literature regarding the level of analysis. Some argue that small units are preferable (Anderton, 1996; Bowen, et al., 1995). Others argue that it is preferable to create areal units that preserve intra-area homogeneity for the variables of interest (Haining, 1990). The county unit does obscure some intracounty heterogeneity in the distribution of residents. Furthermore, although there is no reason to expect that relationships at one geographic level will behave in the same fashion at another level it will be valuable to determine if similar relationship patterns can be uncovered as between the county unit of analysis and the results reported in other research that uses more finely graduated units (e.g., SMSAs, census tract, and ZIP codes). Additionally, as John Hird (1993:323, n. 1) points out—with any analysis, trade-offs exist between aggregation problems (variation within the region of analysis) and the availability of data (the finer the resolution, the lower the availability of region-specific data). The county is large enough to include the effects of the hazard and small enough to record significant variation on relevant measures. Finally, as Daniels and Friedman (1999:250) state: "Rather than argue for the inherent superiority of one unit over another, we believe that relationships at a variety of analytical levels are inherently interesting and should be investigated."

Rearticulating the Model

We combine both county-level measures of key concepts and state-level effects when analyzing the race-risk nexus at the county level. The exact concepts, the corresponding measures, and the detailed hypotheses submitted for testing are outlined in Chapter 4. In essence, we are interested in whether race, class, and political mobilization are related to our three environmental harms when all other explanations are held constant. To aid readers in refreshing their memory, Figure 6.1 summarizes the measures and hypotheses for the county-level analysis

Testing a Simple Model of Environmental Justice

A large amount of the existing research established positive relationships between race and increasing levels of a variety of environmental harms. This may be the result of a conscious effort to place these hazards in minority communities or may simply be the unintentional consequences of industrial development and existing demographic patterns. However, regardless of the debatable origins of this pattern, the outcome is the same for purposes of our research: a positive relationship is expected between race and toxic releases.

Additionally, the environmental classism hypothesis leads to a similar conclusion, that is, for a variety of reasons outlined in Chapter 4, lower-income areas—either through accident or design or a combination of both—are also the recipient of increasing levels of toxic releases. As a consequence, given the construction of our social-class measure, a negative relationship is expected between class and toxic releases.

Finally, the simple tripartite model maintains that political mobilization has an effect on the distribution of toxic waste. Where communities are mobilized, political actors are responsive, and so industry encounters some difficulty in releasing high levels of toxic chemicals into the community. Thus, a negative relationship is expected between political mobilization and toxic releases.

FIGURE 6.1   Summary of Concepts, Measures, and Hypotheses for the County-Level Analysis of Toxic Releases

Concept	Measure	Hypothesis
County-Level Measures		
Percent Black	Percent black population, 1990.	Positive
Percent Hispanic	Percent Hispanic population, 1990.	Positive
Social Class	Factor scale combining median family income, 1989; median household income, 1989; percent population B.A. degree, 1990; percent population H.S. degree, 1990; per capita income, 1989.	Negative
Political Mobilization	Votes cast in 1992 presidential election/total population, 1990.	Negative
Government Capacity	Factor scale combining local government finances, per capita taxes, 1986–1987; federal funds and grants, total expenditures, 1992; general revenues per $1,000 personal income, 1986–1987; per capita expenditures, federal funds, 1992.	Negative
Pollution Potential	Factor scale combining manufacturing establishments, 1987; total population, 1990; population density, 1990; number of manufacturing employees, 1987.	Positive
Land Area	Land area in square kilometers, 1990.	?
State-Level Measures		
Environmental Interests	Membership in Sierra Club, National Wildlife Federation, and Friends of the Earth, 1987.	Negative
Capacity	Factor scale combining percent of state budget expended for natural resources in each of three years: 1980, 1982, 1985.	Negative
Business Climate	Factor scale combining three Guttman scales of state policy support to business interests within the state, 1984–1985.	Positive
Legislative Professionalism	Squire's (1992) index of legislative professionalism.	Negative
Public Opinion-Partisanship	Wright, Erickson, and McIver (1985) index of partisanship.	Positive
Public Opinion-Ideology	Wright, Erickson, and McIver (1985) index of ideology.	Positive
Political Culture-Moralistic	Johnson (1976) Moralistic index.	Negative
Political Culture-Individualistic	Johnson (1976) Individualistic index.	Positive
Region	Dummy variables for EPA's Northeastern, North Central, and Sunbelt regions. Western region is the default category.	?

TABLE 6.2   Simple Model of Environmental Inequities in U.S. Counties, Black Population[1]

Variables	Coeff.	Constant	Percent Black	Social Class	Political Mobilization	Adj. R. Sq.	F-Ratio
Toxic Release	b	.0008	.19**	.27**	−.06**	.12	98.4**
Factor (N=2094)	Seb	.02	.02	.02	.02		
Stack Air Toxic	b	.001	.13**	.25**	−.05*	.09	69.6**
Releases (N=2094)	Seb	.02	.02	.02	.02		
Fugitive Air Toxic	b	.0005	.15**	.28**	−.11**		93.7**
Releases (N=2091)	Seb	.02	.02	.02	.02	.11	

NOTES:

[1]Entries are regression coefficients based on standardized normalized distribution of all variables. Tolerance statistics: percent black population, .74; social class, .87; political mobilization, .66.

**p < .01   *p < .05

Tables 6.2 and 6.3 array the results of the test of the simple race/class/mobilization model for our three measures of toxic releases. Table 6.2 deals with the percent black population, Table 6.3 with the Hispanic population.

The results in Table 6.2 provide interesting findings. For all three measures of toxic releases, given controls for social class and political mobilization, the relationship between the percent black measure and the dependent variables is, as hypothesized, a positive one. These results thus conform to existing research. Yet the relationship between class and toxic releases is not as hypothesized: Higher social-class counties have greater levels of toxic re-

TABLE 6.3   Simple Model of Environmental Inequities in U.S. Counties, Hispanic Population[1]

Variables	Coeff.	Constant	Percent Hispanic	Social Class	Political Mobilization	Adj. R. Sq.	F-Ratio
Toxic Release	b	−.0004	−.03	.31**	−.18**	.09	75.04**
Factor (N=2095)	Seb	.02	.02	.02	.02		
Stack Air Toxic	b	.001	−.07**	.30**	−.15**	.08	61.93**
Releases (N=2094)	Seb	.02	.02	.02	.05		
Fugitive Air Toxic	b	.005	−.04	.31**	−.20**	.10	80.39**
Releases (N=2091)	Seb	.02	.02	.02	.02		

NOTES:

[1]Entries are regression coefficients based on standardized normalized distribution of all variables. Tolerance statistics: percent Hispanic population, .74; social class, .79; political mobilization, .80.

**p < .01   *p < .05

leases. This finding could be spurious in that the equation does not include relevant controls for a wide variety of known explanations for this environmental harm. Finally, this simple three-variable model reveals the hypothesized relationship between political mobilization and toxic releases: As mobilization increases, the level of toxic releases decreases.

Table 6.3 arrays the results of the tripartite test for the percent Hispanic population. In this instance, the results indicate no relationship between race and two measures of toxic releases—and in one case the relationship is opposite of the hypothesized relationship. However, as was the case in Table 6.2, we find a positive relationship between social class and all measures of toxic releases—a finding opposite to the hypothesized relationship—and a negative relationship between political mobilization and toxic releases. The latter findings indicate that high social-class counties have increasing levels of toxic relations but that the level of political mobilization decreases the level of this environmental hazard.

A Complex Test of Environmental Justice

In Chapter 4, we explained the shortcomings of the tripartite model— namely its restrictive nature, its inability to account for other known explanations of environmental harms, and its simple construction. Thus, we reanalyze our county data using a more complex model that includes a wide range of well-known explanations for the level of environmental harms. Again, we continue with our separate analysis for the percent black and Hispanic populations.

Toxic Releases and the Percent Black Population

Tables 6.4 and 6.5 array our results for the three measures of toxic releases for the percent black population using our expanded pool of variables. For the sake of simplicity, we discuss only the results from the reduced equation for each measure of toxic releases.

The first noticeable difference between these results and the previous tripartite analysis deals with the relationship between social class and toxic releases. Social class, in the current analysis, is unrelated to any of our measures of toxic releases. Apparently neither the rich nor the nonrich are specifically targeted for toxic releases in U.S. counties. Furthermore, the complex analysis indicates that political mobilization is unrelated to toxic releases. The complex analysis also reveals that the race/toxic release nexus is more complex than initially hypothesized. For both our global TRI measure and stack air toxic releases, a conditional relationship is present. The relationship between increasing percentages of the black population and increasing levels of toxic releases is stronger in counties in Sunbelt states than

TABLE 6.4   Multiple Regression Results (Full and Reduced Equations) for Toxic Releases to Air, Land, and Water in U.S. Counties, 1995 (percent black population only)[1]

Variables	Full Equation		Reduced Equation	
	b	Tol.	b	Tol.
Percent Black	−.033	.24	−.032	.25
Social Class	−.050	.41	−.052	.42
County Mobilization	.010	.54		
County Capacity	.081**	.63	.076**	.68
Pollution Potential	.560**	.26	.546**	.30
State Impact				
Environmental Interests	−.186**	.25	−.170**	.28
State Capacity	−.024*	.59	−.024*	.60
Business Climate	.008	.63		
Legislative Professionalism	−.059	.45	−.052*	.48
Public Opinion-Partisanship	.085**	.29	.071*	.32
Public Opinion-Ideology	−.041	.42		
Moralistic Culture	−.073*	.23	−.061	.25
Individualistic Culture	.033	.30	.047	.33
Land Area 1990	.075**	.82	.069**	.85
Sunbelt States	−.162	.14	−.182*	.15
Percent Black* Sunbelt States	.235**	.34	.226**	.36
Constant	−.004		.006	
Adj. R Sqr.	.296		.297	
F-Ratio	55.96**		69.72**	
N of Cases	2089		2089	

NOTES:
   [1]Cell entries are regression coefficients based on standardized normalized data. Six cases with significant studentized residual outliers deleted from the analysis.
   **$p < .01$ *$p < .05$

is evident in other regions. The manipulation of the intercept and slope, possible when an interactive term is used in a multiple regression equation, demonstrates the difference between the relationship in the Sunbelt region and elsewhere in the United States.

Global TRI Releases	b_0	b_1 % black
Sunbelt Region	−.176	.194
Non-Sunbelt Regions	.006	−.032

Stack Air TRI	b_0	b_1 % black
Sunbelt Region	−.414	.16
Non-Sunbelt Regions	−.036	−.10

TABLE 6.5 Multiple Regression Results (Full and Reduced Equations) for Toxic Releases in Stack Air and Fugitive Air in U.S. Counties, 1995 (percent black population only)[1]

Variables	Toxic Stack Air Full Equation		Toxic Stack Air Reduced Equation		Toxic Fugitive Air Full Equation		Toxic Fugitive Air Reduced Equation	
	b	Tol.	b	Tol.	b	Tol.	b	Tol.
Percent Black	−.093**	.24	−.107**	.26	−.084*	.16	−.043	.24
Social Class	.0001	.41			.022	.42		
County Mobilization	.015	.54			−.055*	.53	−.044	.57
County Capacity	−.019	.63			.014	.61		
Pollution Potential	.495**	.26	.489**	.38	.516**	.26	.539**	.33
State Impact Environmental	−.138**	.25	−.142**	.32	−.151**	.24		
Interests								
State Capacity	−.049**	.59	−.048**	.60	−.022*	.59	−.171**	.73
Business Climate	−.015	.63	.021	.70	.016	.63	−.017	.79
Legislative Professionalism	−.063*	.45	−.058*	.51	−.037	.45		
Public Opinion-Partisanship	.050*	.29	.052	.31	.071*	.29		
Public Opinion-Ideology	.013	.42			.038	.41	.055	.53
Moralistic Culture	−.053	.23	−.058	.28	−.047	.21	.033	.28
Individualistic Culture	.036	.30			.020	.23		
Land Area 1990	.074**	.87	.071**	.87	.034	.81	.039*	.88
Sunbelt	−.188*	.14	−.218*	.16	−.203*	.13	−.194*	.24
Percent Black* Sunbelt	.267**	.34	.267**	.37	.220**	.14	.144*	.28
Percent Black* Ideology					.101**	.50	.085**	.52
Percent Black* Individualistic					.066*	.24		
Constant	−.015		−.036		.030		.029	
Adj R Sqr.	.219		.220		.268		.268	
F-Ratio	37.6**		54.68**		43.30**		69.9**	
N of Cases	2091		2091		2086		2086	

NOTES:

[1]Cell entries are regression coefficients based on standardized normalized data. The number of cases varies between the two dependent variables. For toxic stack air, four cases were deleted because of significant studentized residual outliers. Nine cases were deleted for toxic fugitive air for the same reason.

**p < .01 *p < .05

This set of results is understandable. Larger proportions of the black population reside in the Sunbelt region. Further, this region is home to a large number of polluting industries. Apparently, the highest levels of toxic releases are present in counties in the Sunbelt that have high proportions of the black population. Conversely, in other regions of the country, increased proportions of the black population are not disproportionately exposed to these two types of toxic releases.

The relationship between the black population and fugitive air toxic releases is slightly more complex than the previous results would indicate. In this instance, there are two conditional relationships that need to be explained: one centering on the Sunbelt region, the other centering on the state's ideological bias. As was evident for the other two measures of toxic releases, we also find that the relationship between the percent black population and fugitive air TRI is stronger in the Sunbelt states than is the case for regions elsewhere in the nation. The manipulation of the intercept and slope demonstrate this statement.

Fugitive Air TRI	b_0	b_1 % black
Sunbelt Region	−.11	.11
Non-Sunbelt Regions	.02	−.04

However, we also find another conditional effect. The relationship between the percent black population and fugitive air toxic releases is marginally stronger in counties within states with a strong conservative ideological bias. Conversely, there is a negative slope in counties within states with a strong liberal ideological bias. The manipulation of the intercepts and slopes for three values of ideology demonstrate this finding.

Fugitive Air TRI	b_0	b_1 black
+1.00 Conservative	.076	.042
0.00 Moderate	.005	−.043
−1.00 Liberal	.003	−.128

Under conditions of conservative politics, the black population is marginally more likely to be exposed to increased levels of fugitive air toxic releases. However, as this conservative bias is replaced by either a moderate ideological stance or a liberal ideological bias, the black population is less likely to be exposed to fugitive air toxic releases. The conditional effect of ideology on the race-risk nexus may be a function of a liberal ideological bias being more concerned with overall environmental protection—resulting in the black population in such areas benefiting from the overall concern with cleaner air (Lester and Lombard, 1990).

Additional findings, outside of the race/class/mobilization concerns, are also evident from the expanded equations in Tables 6.4 and 6.5. Again, using results from reduced equations, we find that explaining levels of toxic releases is more amenable to a complex equation. We discuss only the significant findings in this regard.

First, the relationship between pollution potential and all measures of toxic releases is large, significant, and in the expected direction. This finding is expected given the nature of our dependent variables. Constant production of toxic releases is a function of highly and densely populated areas with existing and operating manufacturing capacity.

Second, the relationship between county fiscal capacity and toxic releases is somewhat surprising. With regard to our measure of global toxic releases, counties with more revenues have higher levels of toxic releases. Possibly, the general revenue sources that combine to create the capacity measure are obligated to other community needs and not to environmental protection. Indeed, for stack and fugitive air toxic releases, the relationship to country fiscal capacity is null.

As hypothesized, environmental interests—with their known desire for better environmental quality—are related to toxic releases in a negative fashion in two instances: global toxic releases and stack air toxic releases. States' fiscal and institutional capacities also reduce the level of toxic releases in all three areas. Obviously, higher state spending for environmental quality translates to substate regions as well. A professional legislature also results in lower levels of toxic releases in two instances: global toxic releases and stack air toxic releases. Apparently, a professional legislature can more easily come to grips with these technical problems and thus exert pressure to diminish environmental harms within all regions of a state. Partisanship exerts an influence only with regard to global toxic releases. As anticipated, states that have a significant Republican slant evidence higher levels of toxic releases. Finally, we included county land area in 1990 as a control variable. The results for this measure are consistent across all three measures of toxic releases: larger counties produce more toxic releases.

Toxic Releases and the Percent Hispanic Population

We now turn to our separate complex analysis dealing with the Hispanic population and toxic releases. The results of this analysis are shown in Tables 6.6 and 6.7. Again, we discuss only the results from our reduced equations.

Once again, the complex reduced equations shown in Tables 6.6 and 6.7 reveal, unlike the results from the tripartite analysis, that social class has no direct relationship with the level of toxic releases in U.S. counties. Instead of

TABLE 6.6 Multiple Regression Results (Full and Reduced Equations) for Toxic Releases to Air, Land, and Water in U.S. Counties (percent Hispanic population only)[1]

Variables	Full Equation		Reduced Equation	
	b	Tol.	b	Tol.
Percent Hispanic	.066	.20	.071*	.20
Social Class	.012	.31	.004	.32
County Mobilization	−.022	.38		
County Capacity	.182**	.47	.180**	.47
Pollution Potential	.550*	.28	.556**	.33
State Impact				
Environmental Interests	−.186**	.24	−.188**	.24
State Capacity	−.028*	.54	−.030**	.54
Business Climate	.025	.60	.028*	.68
Legislative Professionalism	−.050	.43	−.053*	.44
Public Opinion-Partisanship	.059	.29	.059	.29
Public Opinion-Ideology	−.035	.37	−.046	.39
Moralistic Culture	−.116**	.22	−.118**	.22
Individualistic Culture	.026	.29		
Land Area 1990	.061**	.69	.064**	.69
Sunbelt States	−.141	.12	−.160	.14
Northeastern States	−.210**	.48	−.215**	.50
Hispanic* Sunbelt	−.211**	.43	−.201**	.44
Hispanic* Northeastern	−.279**	.50	−.277**	.50
Hispanic* Class	−.107**	.39	−.108**	.49
Hispanic* County Capacity	−.073**	.57	−.072**	.62
Constant	.140		.148	
Adj R Sqr.	.314		.314	
F-Ratio	48.75**		54.13**	
N of Cases	2092		2092	

NOTES:

[1]Cell entries are regression coefficients computed on the basis of standardized normalized data. Three cases were deleted because of significant studentized residual outliers.

**p < .01   *p < .05

a direct relationship, social class moderates the relationship between the Hispanic population and the level of toxic releases. We will discuss this set of results in detail when discussing the nature of the relationship between the Hispanic population and toxic releases.

Again, unlike the political mobilization results from the tripartite analysis, the complex reduced equation demonstrates that political mobilization is unrelated to two out of three measures of toxic releases: global toxic releases and stack air toxic releases. Only in the area of fugitive air does political mobilization minimize the level of this environmental harm.

TABLE 6.7 Multiple Regression Results (Full and Reduced Equations) for Toxic Releases in Stack Air and Fugutive Air in U.S. Counties, 1995 (percent Hispanic population only)[1]

Variables	Toxic Stack Air Full Equation		Toxic Stack Air Reduced Equation		Toxic Fugitive Air Full Equation		Toxic Fugitive Air Reduced Equation	
	b	Tol.	b	Tol.	b	Tol.	b	Tol.
Percent Hispanic	−.071**	.30	−.060**	.35	−.037	.29	−.031	.35
Social Class	.051	.32	.037	.35	.065*	.31	.066*	.33
County Mobilization	−.029	.42			−.063**	.41	−.072**	.42
County Capacity	.025	.64			.037	.64	.041	.71
Pollution Potential	.478**	.29	.507**	.35	.521**	.29	.514**	.31
State Impact Environmental Interests	−.093**	.28	−.118*	.46	−.145**	.28	−.135**	.43
State Capacity	.031**	.65	-.032**	.85	-.023*	.54	-.017	.72
Business Climate	.028	.64	.019	.83	.036**	.62	.033**	.83
Legislative Professionalism	−.065*	.45			−.020	.45		
Public Opinion-Partisanship	−.014	.36	−.065*	.52	−.065*	.38	.062**	.63
Public Opinion-Ideology	.007	.41			−.019	.39		
Moralistic Culture	−.023	.26			−.052	.26		
Individualistic Culture	−.022	.31			−.042	.34		
Land Area 1990	.105**	.71	.104**	.74	.036	.72		
North Central States	.288**	.54	.238**	.66				
Northeast States					−.232**	.54	−.222**	.59
Percent Hispanic* Northeast States					−.193**	.59	−.205**	.61
Percent Hispanic* Social Class	−.102**	.41	−.101**	.59	−.122**	.40	−.108**	.41
Constant	−.065		−.054		.073		.073	
Ajd R Sqr.	.234		.235		.276		.277	
F-Ratio	40.83**		65.01**		47.71**		67.32**	
N of Cases	2090		2090		2082		2082	

NOTES:

[1]Cell entries are regression coefficients based on standardized normalized data. The number of cases varies between the two dependent variables. For toxic stack air, five cases were deleted because of significant studentized residual outliers. Thirteen cases were deleted for toxic fugitive air for the same reason.

**$p < .01$ *$p < .05$

Our central interest in this analysis is the relationship between the Hispanic population and toxic releases in U.S. counties. This relationship was nonexistent in our tripartite analysis for our global and fugitive air measures of toxic releases. Additionally, the tripartite analysis demonstrated a negative relationship between the Hispanic population and stack air releases. However, in our more complex analysis a different picture is present. As previously reported, the relationship between the Hispanic population and toxic releases is conditional and depends on the level of social class within the county. The moderating effect of three levels of social class is demonstrated by manipulating the intercept and slope characteristics of the three equations.

Intercept & Slope	Global Releases b_0	b_1 % Hispanic	Stack Air Releases b_0	b_1 % Hispanic	Fugitive Air Releases b_0	b_1 % Hispanic
+1.00 High Social Class	.15	−.03	−.01	−.16	.13	−.13
0.00 Middle Class	.14	.07	−.05	−.06	.07	−.03
−1.00 Low Social Class	.14	.17	−.09	.04	−.01	.06

In all instances, the relationship between the Hispanic population and toxic releases is negative in counties with high social class. However, as is also evident from the preceding manipulated intercept and slope coefficients, Hispanics are marginally more likely to be exposed to increasing levels of toxic releases in counties with low social class. This finding is substantially different than results revealed by the tripartite model, which revealed either no relationship or a negative relationship between the Hispanic population and toxic releases. In sum, where lower income and lower education are the norm, Hispanics are more likely to be exposed to higher levels of toxic releases.

The same type of effect is also evident for the remaining set of interactive terms in the three equations. For example, the relationship between the Hispanic population and global toxic releases is conditional. In all instances, exposure rates of Hispanics to global toxic releases are lower within the Sunbelt, the Northeast, and in counties with high levels of fiscal capacity. Conversely, exposure of Hispanics to global toxic releases is higher in the West (the regional default category) and in counties with low fiscal capacity. Additionally, although exposure of Hispanics to fugitive air toxic releases is lower in the Northeast, in other regions the exposure to environmental harm increases.

As was the case with the analysis of the complex equations in Chapter 5, our pool of additional explanations for environmental pollution produces additional findings that are separate and apart from our race/class/political mobilization concerns tied to the environmental justice question. Again, using results from the reduced equations, we find the hypothesized relationship between pollution potential and all measures of toxic releases. This finding, again, is expected given the fact that we are examining toxic releases, and the construction of this measure equates with existing and operating manufacturing capacity. Environmental interests are also related to all three measures of toxic releases in the hypothesized direction. State-level environmental interests are concerned with maximizing environmental quality, and the size of these interests throughout the state appears to lower the level of toxic releases in the substate regions. The state business climate, in this phase of the analysis, increases the level of toxic releases. Most probably, state-level actions to encourage and support economic development are having an effect at the substate level, and this effect is to minimize concerns about environmental protection—leading to higher levels of toxic releases. Apparently, the substate regions have little control over either the benefits the state awards to business or to the consequences of those benefits—increased pollution.

Although legislative professionalism exerts the hypothesized effect on the level of global toxic releases—that is, a professional legislature decreases this level of environmental harm—its effect disappears when dealing with the specific air-pollution measures of toxic releases. Partisanship also evidences a marginal effect on two measures of toxic releases. Although Republican partisanship is marginally related to decreased levels of state air toxic releases, it is positively related to fugitive air toxic releases. Finally, large counties appear to have higher global TRI releases and stack air toxic releases.

Conclusion

This chapter has assessed the environmental racism hypothesis with regard to three measures of toxic pollutants within roughly 70 percent of U.S. counties as of 1995. In both instances, our simple tripartite model produced misleading results when compared to our more complex analysis. Indeed, in all instances, the results from our more complex model provided evidence of complicated relationships between our measures of race and toxic releases. To aid the reader, our findings from the reduced complex test are summarized in Figure 6.2.

Overall, our findings do tend to confirm that our two minority classifications were exposed to higher levels of toxic releases; and insofar as other research has reported similar, but less complicated, results, our findings are compatible (Burke, 1993; Downey, 1998; Gould, 1986; Lester and Allen, 1996; Lester, Allen, and Lauer, 1994; Polloch and Vittas, 1995; Ringquist, 1997; Szasz, 1994). However, our results also go beyond simple formulations of the race-risk nexus. Instead of simple linear relationships between the percent black population and toxic releases, we found that this relationship was considerably stronger within the Sunbelt. Furthermore, the rela-

FIGURE 6.2   Summary of County-Level Findings (based on reduced equations)

Environmental Harm	Race Inequity	Class Inequity	Political Mobilization	Other Explanations*
Total Toxic Releases	Black (yes)** Hispanic (yes)**	No No	No No	County Capacity, Business Climate, *Pollution Potential, Environmental Interests, State Capacity, Legislative Professionalism, Partisanship, Moralistic Culture, Land Area*
Stack Air Releases	Black (yes)** Hispanic (yes)**	No Yes**	No No	*Pollution Potential, Environmental Interests, State Capacity, Legislative Professionalism,* Partisanship, *Land Area*
Fugitive Air Releases	Black (yes)** Hispanic (yes)**	No Yes**	No Yes	*Pollution Potential, State Capacity,* **Ideology, **County Capacity, Business Climate, Partisanship, **Sunbelt

NOTES:
*Other variables included in either or both reduced equations. Entries that are italicized evidenced the hypothesized relationship.
**Conditional relationship.

tionship between the black population and fugitive air releases was not only conditioned by the Sunbelt but by ideology as well.

Although the tripartite model revealed either no relationship between the Hispanic population and toxic release—or a negative relationship between these two measures—we found that a set of conditional relationships was evident that did indicate that under certain conditions the Hispanic population is exposed to higher levels of toxic releases in U.S. counties. Specifically, we found that under conditions of low social class, western regionalism, and low county fiscal capacity, the Hispanic population was exposed to marginally higher levels of toxic releases within 70 percent of U.S. counties.

Notes

1. It should be noted that in Chapter 7, our city level analysis, we do employ an additive measure of total TRI releases. We made this conscious decision in order to determine if different measures of the dependent variable lead to different results.

2. Each release component had extremely high values that were sequentially recoded at one integer higher than the highest break in the distribution. This technique reduces value magnitude yet preserves the difference ordering of cases; see Tabachnick and Fiddell (1998) for a justification of this procedure. Recoded measures were subjected to log transformations to normalize univariate distributions. A constant of 1 was added to all variables on each release component in order to eliminate zeros so that a log transformation could be employed. The recoded log transformed measures were subjected to principal components factor analysis. The factor loadings for the single unrotated factor were: stack air releases, .812; fugitive air releases, .812; water releases, .764; and land releases, .654. Eigenvalue: 2.33. The factor explained 58.3 percent of the variance in the pool of four variables.

3. These two measures, which had the highest factor loadings on the global TRI release measure, both had significant outliers. The outliers were sequentially recoded at one integer higher than the highest break in their individual distributions. This technique reduced value magnitude yet preserved case-difference ordering. See Tabachnick and Fiddell (1998) for a justification of this technique. Recoded measures were subjected to log transformations to normalize univariate distributions. A constant of 1 was added to all values in order to eliminate zeros so that a log transformation could be employed.

4. Missing data could not be coded as zero because of the nature of the reporting requirements for the Toxic Release Inventory. For example, no reports for a county does not mean no toxic releases in the county. It could mean that there were several firms with ten or fewer employees. These firms, regardless of toxic releases, are not required to file reports. Furthermore, larger firms that do not process or use the threshold amounts do not need to file reports. As such, absence of reports could reflect any level of toxic releases. Therefore, given the nature of the data source, the only viable option was to treat the cases as "missing data."

5. There is some regional variation in missing data. The western region of the United States has the largest incidence of deleted counties because of no TRI reports. This is predominantly a function of counties within nine states in this region: Colorado, Idaho, Montana, Nevada, North Dakota, South Dakota, Utah, Washington, and Wyoming. The north-central and Sunbelt regions are approximately tied in the incidence of missing TRI data. The north-central region's missing counties are predominantly a function of two states: Kansas and Nebraska. The Sunbelt region has five states with high percentages of counties with no TRI reports: Georgia, Kentucky, New Mexico, Oklahoma, and Texas. The Northeast evidences the smallest number of deleted counties. However, this figure is slightly misleading because of complete reports on all counties in two small states: Connecticut and Delaware. Within this region, three states do evidence high percentages of deleted counties: Maryland, Virginia, and West Virginia. To account for this problem, the western region was used as the default category when the regional dummy variables were included in equations. The states with each region are:

Region	States
Northeast	Connecticut, Delaware, Maine, Maryland, Massachusetts, New Hampshire, New Jersey, New York, Ohio, Pennsylvania, Rhode Island, Vermont, Virginia, West Virginia
North-central	Illinois, Indiana, Iowa, Kansas, Michigan, Minnesota, Missouri, Nebraska, Wisconsin
Sunbelt	Alabama, Arkansas, Florida, Georgia, Kentucky, Louisiana, Mississippi, North Carolina, Oklahoma, South Carolina, Tennessee, Texas
Western	Arizona, California, Colorado, Idaho, Montana, Nevada, New Mexico, North Dakota, Oregon, South Dakota, Utah, Washington, Wyoming

7

Environmental Injustice in America's Cities

=====

In Chapter 4, we outlined out explanatory concepts, their measures, the hypotheses we would test, and our method of analysis. The purpose of this chapter is to examine the environmental injustice thesis at the level of U.S. cities. We begin by articulating the environmental hazards we plan to study.

Environmental Harms: The Dependent Variables at the City Level

As noted in our county-level analysis, we have made a conscious decision to study toxic hazards at the substate level. The data from the TRI also allows us to focus on a specific finding from our state-level analysis as well. In the state-level analysis, we found a strong positive relationship between the percent black population in a state and the level of toxic waste present in a state. Similar findings were replicated in our county-level analysis. Furthermore, toxic waste has also been subjected to study in the literature (Allen, 2001; Allen, Lester, and Hill, 1995; Bowen, et al., 1995; Burke, 1993; Cutter, 1994; Davies, 1972; Gould, 1986; Krieg, 1998; Lester, Allen, and Lauer, 1994; Lester and Allen, 1996; Polloch and Vittas, 1995; Ringquist, 1997). We abstracted four measures from the 1993 Toxic Release Inventory: total TRI released to the environment, TRI released through fugitive and stack air, and lead TRI released to air, land, and water.

The reader will notice different measures for total TRI releases between our county-level analysis in Chapter 6 and the measures employed in this chapter. We are using the additive total TRI Releases in U.S. cities in order to determine if different results occur if different measures of a dependent variable are employed. It should be noted that the additive version of total TRI releases is the most frequently employed measure in existing literature. Furthermore, in Chapter 6 we used data from the 1995 Toxic Release Inventory. Using 1993

TRI data for the city-level analysis provides us with a rudimentary cross-time picture. In sum, if we can obtain similar findings across different time periods with moderately different measures of a dependent variable, then we can place a bit more confidence in our combined multilevel results.[1]

In addition to our Total Toxic Release measure, we also employed two measures of air pollution. As previously noted, air pollution has been one of the most closely studied subjects in this literature (Council of Environmental Quality, 1971; Freeman, 1972; Harrison, 1975; Kruvant, 1975; Burch, 1976; Berry, 1977; Handy, 1977; Asch and Seneca, 1978; Gianessi et. al., 1979; Gelobter, 1987, 1992; McCaull, 1976). We were able to create two discrete measures for this environmental harm based on the TRI data: 1993 stack air TRI releases in 1,000 pounds and fugitive air TRI releases in 1,000 pounds.[2] These measures are similar to the measures we employed in Chapter Six—although in the case of Chapter Six these measures were abstracted from the 1995 Toxic Release Inventory.

In addition to the three previous measures we also extracted an additional measure of a specific type of toxic release: lead released to the environment. This type of environmental harm can have far reaching adverse implications, and it is therefore important to study this specific environmental harm. The measure reflects the lead TRI releases to air, land, and water and is measured in pounds released.[3]

As noted in Chapter 6, using data from the Toxic Release Inventory is not without problems. The inventory does not include all manufacturing facilities—nor does it contain reports on all possible toxic chemicals/chemical compounds. Further, only release/use levels which exceed certain parameters are reported. Additionally, the reports are self-generated by industry and only subjected to spot checks by the Environmental Protection Agency. This may mean that producers are under reporting emissions (Krieg, 1998: 192–193). Finally, TRI data is a product of currently industrialized areas with active processors/users of restrictive lists of toxins. It does not reflect other toxins at abandoned waste dumps, landfills, or other storage facilities. As a consequence, the TRI data should not be conceptualized as measuring the total level of toxic waste in any community.

Nonetheless, as we explained in Chapter Six, use of the Toxic Release Inventory is still valid—mainly because TRI data represents a continually expanding supply of known pollutants directly discharged into the environment by a known set of companies within the community. Thus, the data does represent the annual amount of new toxins released into the community that is not necessarily accounted for in other data bases—and these amounts are substantial and a cause for concern. Further, as we explained in Chapter Six, we continue the inquiry using the *level* of toxic releases—not the number of facilities. This step is taken because the level of toxic releases is what causes environmental degradation, rather than the total number of toxic facilities in an area.

The Sample

The sample used for this section of analysis is cities in the United States with populations in excess of 50,000 people according to the 1990 U.S. Census. Missing data on the state level public opinion and political culture variables eliminated cities in Alaska and Hawaii—but this condition only resulted in dropping two cities from the analysis. The chief cause of sample reduction from the originally isolated 514 cities was the lack of Toxic Release Inventory reports for many smaller cities. This reduced the sample size from the original 514 cities to between 401 and 429 cities. In addition to missing reports, the sample was also reduced by deleting cases that preliminary analysis revealed as having significant residual outliers. Even with the variety of circumstances that reduced the number of cases, the analysis is still based on roughly 79 to 84 percent of all cities with populations in excess of 50,000 people.

Some may argue with using cities as the unit of analysis. We argue that using cities as our third level of analysis is clearly justified. Cities are governing units and, as such, do have substate responsibilities for many issues of societal concern. Thus, city-level awareness of a problem is an important first step toward allocating resources to policy problems. Furthermore, cities can become the focus of lawsuits regarding environmental injustice from activists, as well as a host of other pressures from the state government and federal agencies. As such, the possibility of environmental injustice arising from city action (or inaction) in this policy area makes them an appropriate subject for study. Furthermore, not all pollutants are localized—they can disperse across areas of a city. Thus, relationships between race, class, and environmental harms can take on a citywide coloring.

Finally, as we have noted about both the state and county sample, we recognize that there is a continuing controversy in environmental justice literature regarding the level of analysis. Some argue that small units are preferable (Anderton, 1996; Bowen, et al., 1995). Others argue that it is preferable to create areal units that preserve intra-area homogeneity for the variables of interest (Haining, 1990). The city unit does obscure some intracity heterogeneity in the distribution of residents. Furthermore, although there is no reason to expect that relationships at one geographic level will behave in the same fashion at another level—given the structure of the ecological fallacy—it will be valuable to determine if similar relationship patterns can be uncovered between the county unit of analysis and the results reported in other research that uses more finely graduated units (e.g., SMSAs, census tracts, and ZIP codes). Finally, as Daniels and Friedman (1999:250) state: "Rather than argue for the inherent superiority of one unit over another, we believe that relationships at a variety of analytical levels are inherently interesting and should be investigated."

Recapitulating the Model

We combine both city-level measures of key concepts and state-level effects when analyzing our city data. The exact concepts, their measures, and the detailed hypotheses submitted for testing are outlined in Chapter 4. To aid in refreshing the reader's memory, Figure 7.1 summarizes the concepts, measures and hypotheses for the city-level analysis.

Testing a Simple Model of Environmental Justice

As noted in Chapters 1 and 2, existing literature has established a positive relationship between race and increasing levels of environmental harms. This may be the result of a conscious effort to place hazards in minority communities or may simply be the unintentional consequences of industrial development and existing demographic patterns. Regardless of the debatable origins of the pattern, the outcome is the same: a positive relationship between race and environmental harms constitutes evidence of environmental injustice.

Additionally, the environmental classism hypothesis leads to similar conclusions: Lower-income areas, either through accident or design or a combination of both, are also allegedly recipients of increasing levels of environmental harms.

Finally, the simple tripartite model maintains that political mobilization has an effect on the level of environmental hazards. Where communities are mobilized, political actors are responsive to community demands, and industry encounters some difficulty in releasing high levels of pollutants into the community. Thus, a negative relationship is expected between political mobilization and environmental hazards.

Tables 7.1 and 7.2 array the results of the tests of the simple race/class/mobilization model for our city-level measures of environmental hazards. Table 7.1 deals with the percent black population, Table 7.2 with the Hispanic population.

The city-level results in Table 7.1 are interesting. For all the environmental hazards studied at the city level, the relationship between the percent black measure and the various dependent variables is, as hypothesized, positive. Thus, in all instances, the results of our simple test—for this population group—conform to existing literature.

However, the class-based findings in Table 7.1 do not conform to the initial hypothesis. Given controls for race and political mobilization—when analyzing results for the black city population—no evidence of class-based environmental injustice is evident for any of the environmental hazards. Yet the political mobilization results shown in Table 7.1 do conform to the initial hypothesis. In all four instances, increasing levels of political mobilization are related to reduced levels of these environmental hazards.

Although these findings are consistent with existing literature, the results for our analysis based on the Hispanic population, arrayed in Table 7.2, do

FIGURE 7.1 Summary of Concepts, Measures, and Hypotheses for the
City-Level Analysis of Environmental Harms

Concept	Measure	Hypothesis
City-Level Measures		
Percent Black	Percent black population, 1990.	Positive
Percent Hispanic	Percent Hispanic population, 1990.	Positive
Social Class	Factor scale combining: per capita income, 1990; median family income, 1989; percent population with bachelors degree, 1990.	Negative
Political Mobilization	Median value of owner occupied housing, 1990.	Negative
Capacity	Three separate measures: expenditures for sewers and sanitation, 1990–1991; per capita revenues, 1990–1991; per capita expenditures, 1990–1991.	Negative
Pollution Potential	Factor scale combining: number of manufacturing establishments, 1987; number of manufacturing employees, 1987; total population, 1990.	Positive
Population Density	Population density per square mile, 1990.	Positive
Mayor-Council	Dummy variable: 1=mayor-council; 0, if otherwise. (Commission form of government is the default category.)	Negative
Council-Manager	Dummy variable: 1=council-manager; 0, if otherwise. (Commission form of government is the default category.)	Negative
State-Level Measures		
Environmental Interests	Membership in Sierra Club. National Wildlife Federation, and Friends of the Earth.	Negative
Capacity	Factor scale combining percent of state budget expended for natural resources in each of three years: 1980, 1982, 1985.	Negative
Business Climate	Factor scale combining three Guttman scales of state policy support to business interests in the state, 1984–1985.	Positive
Legislative Professionalism	Squire's (1992) index of legislative professionalism.	Negative
Public Opinion-Partisanship	Wright, Erickson, and McIver (1985) index of partisanship.	Positive
Public Opinion-Ideology	Wright, Erickson, and McIver (1985) index of ideology.	Positive
Political Culture-Moralistic	Johnson's (1976) moralistic index.	Negative
Political Culture-Individualistic	Johnson's (1976) individualistic index.	Positive

TABLE 7.1   Simple Model of Environmental Inequities in U.S. Cities, 1993—
Black Population[1]

Dependent Variables		Constant	Percent Black	Social Class	Political Mobilization	Adj. R sq.	F ratio
Total TRI Releases in 1,000 lbs. (N = 464)	b	−.02	.27**	−.01	−.30**	.20	41.43**
	Seb		.04	.02	.05		
Fugitive Air TRI Releases in 1,000 lbs. (N = 464)	b	−.03	.30**	−.04	−.23**	.22	45.87**
	Seb		.04	.02	.05		
Stack Air TRI Releases in 1,000 lbs. (N = 464)	b	−.03	.30**	−.002	−.33**	.21	50.81**
	Seb		.04	.02	.05		
Total Lead TRI Releases (N = 461)	b	−.02	.20**	−.02	−.24**	.13	25.70**
	Seb		.04	.02	.05		

NOTE: Entries are regression coefficients based on standardized normal distributions. The tolerance statistics for the independent variables are: percent black, .92; social class, .57; and political mobilization, .59.
    **$p < .01$ *$p < .05$

not support the initial hypothesis. In three out of four instances, given controls for social class and political mobilization, no relationship is evident for the percent Hispanic population. Furthermore, the relationship for the Hispanic measure and stack air TRI releases is opposite to our initial hypothesis, indicating that cities with larger Hispanic populations have lower levels of this specific environmental harm.

Although the race-based findings in Table 7.2 do not support the initial hypothesis, the class and mobilization findings in this table do support existing literature. Given controls for race and political mobilization, social class is related to environmental hazards in three out of four instances. Only in the case of lead TRI releases is there an absence of any demonstrable linkage between class and environmental hazards. Furthermore, the political mobilization results in Table 7.2 are all in line with our initial hypothesis. In all four instances, cities with higher levels of political mobilization have lower levels of the four environmental hazards.

A Complex Test of Environmental Justice

In Chapter 4, we explained the shortcomings of the tripartite model, namely, its restrictive nature, its inability to account for other known explanations of environmental harms, and its overly simplistic construction. Thus, we reanalyze our city data using a more complex model that includes a range of additional known explanations for environmental harms. Again,

TABLE 7.2   Simple Model of Environmental Inequities in U.S. Cities, 1993—Hispanic Population[1]

Dependent Variables		Constant	Percent Hispanic	Social Class	Political Mobilization	Adj. R sq.	F ratio
Total TRI Releases in 1,000 lbs. (N = 464)	b	−.02	−.03	−.04*	−.28**	.14	26.37**
	Seb		.05	.02	.07		
Fugitive Air TRI Releases in 1,000 lbs. (N = 464)	b	−.02	−.01	−.07**	−.24**	.14	26.15**
	Seb		.05	.02	.07		
Stack Air TRI Releases in 1,000 lbs. (N = 464)	b	−.02	−.09**	−.05**	−.27**	.16	31.51**
	Seb		.04	.02	.06		
Total Lead TRI Releases (N = 461)	b	−.02	.02	−.03	−.27**	.10	13.81**
	Seb		.05	.02	.07		

NOTE: [1]Entries are regression coefficients based on standardized normal distributions. The tolerance statistics for the independent variables are: percent Hispanic, .64; social class, .47; and political mobilization, .38.
    **p < .01   *p < .05

we continue with a separate analysis for the percent black and Hispanic populations. We organize our presentation of results according to our measures of environmental harms. For the sake of simplicity, we discuss only the results from the reduced equations.

Total TRI Releases

Table 7.3 arrays the results of our analysis for 1993 total toxic releases. The first two columns array the analysis results for the full and reduced equations using the black population; columns 3 and 4 provide the same results for the Hispanic population.

This table confirms the existence of a race-based inequity associated with the percent black population. Contrarily, the relationship between the Hispanic population and this measure of environmental harm is negative—the opposite of the hypothesized relationship.

Table 7.3 also reveals class-based inequities for the two separate sets of analyses. In both instances, as hypothesized, increased levels of social class are associated with decreasing levels of environmental harms. Finally, as shown in Table 7.3—and contrary to the results from the simple analysis—no evidence is present to support the political-mobilization hypothesis.

We turn now to our additional explanations of environmental hazards. In both reduced equations, we find that city-level pollution potential is related in positive fashion to this measure of environmental harm. This is not a surprising finding—toxic releases are a function of currently industrialized ar-

TABLE 7.3 Multiple Regression Results (Full and Reduced Equations) for Total TRI in 1,000 pounds in U.S. Cities, 1993[1]

Variables	Full Equation b	Tol.	Reduced Equation b	Tol.	Full Equation b	Tol.	Reduced Equation b	Tol.
Percent Black	.15**	.56	.14**	.64				
Percent Hispanic					−.12**	.49	−.11**	.66
Social Class	−.05*	.36	−.06**	.79	−.10**	.32	−.08**	.81
City Mobilization	−.01	.20			.08	.17		
City Capacity Sewer and Sanitation	.02	.20			.03	.79		
Per Capita Revenue	−.05	.43			−.03	.43		
Per Capita Expenditure	−.01	.78			.01	.43		
City Pollution Potential	.20**	.78	.19**	.86	.21**	.77	.21**	.94
Population Density	−.06	.56	−.07	.66	−.03	.52		
Mayor-Council	−.19*	.54			−.20	.17		
Council-Manager	−.29*	.17	−.15*	.83	−.27	.17	−.09	.80
State Impact Environmental Interests	−.24**	.13	−.27**	.22	−.24**	.13	−.24**	.19
Capacity	−.01	.55			−.004	.55		
Business Climate	−.03	.46	−.05*	.51	−.03	.48		
Legislative Professionalism	−.06	.36			−.01	.35		
Public Opinion-Partisanship	.16**	.42	.13**	.73	.13**	.42	.07**	.77
Public Opinion-Ideology	−.16*	.16	−.14*	.19	−.14*	.15	−.10	.28
Moralistic Culture	−.05	.36			−.07	.35		
Individualistic Culture	.06	.35	.04	.40	.02	.36		
Constant	.15		.02		.14		−.04	
Adj R Sqr.	.51		.51		.51		.51	
F-Ratio	26.17**		46.11**		25.80**		64.85**	
Standard Error of Estimate	.64		.63		.63		.63	
N of Cases	428		429		425		429	

NOTES:

[1]Cell entries are regression coefficients based on standardized normal distributions. Missing data and deletion of cases with significant outliers resulted in the number of cases used in the analysis.

**p < .01   *p < .05

eas, and the pollution potential measure takes this range of events into account. Furthermore, in one instance—the analysis associated with the percent black population—the council-manager form of government, as hypothesized, is associated with lower levels of total TRI releases.

Some of the state-level measures also explain the level of this environmental hazard. We begin with the findings that mirror the initial hypotheses. State-level environmental interests and partisanship are related to environmental harms in negative and positive fashion, respectively. Cities in states with well-organized interests have lower levels of total TRI releases, whereas cities in Republican-dominated states are associated with higher levels of this specific environmental harm. Still, the business-climate measure and ideology are related to total TRI releases in negative fashion—the opposite of the initial hypotheses.

Air Pollution: Stack and Fugitive Air TRI Releases

Tables 7.4 and 7.5 array the results of our analysis of 1993 stack and fugitive air TRI releases, respectively.[4] Once again, columns 1 and 2 in each table array the results of the full and reduced equations for the black population measure; columns 3 and 4 array full and reduced equations based on the Hispanic population.

For both air-quality measures, we find both race- and class-based inequities for the percent black population. In both instances, as the percent black population increases and social class decreases, the levels of stack and fugitive air TRI releases are high. Contrarily, the analysis that involves the Hispanic population indicates—contrary to the initial hypothesis—that higher levels of stack and fugitive air TRI releases are associated with decreasing percentages of the Hispanic population. Conversely, the same analysis also reveals class-based inequities—as hypothesized—in the Hispanic equations. Finally, for all equations in Tables 7.4 and 7.5, we find no support for the political-mobilization hypothesis.

We turn now to our additional explanations for environmental hazards. First, we discuss city-specific variables, then we discuss the findings resulting from our state-level measures. For both the percent black and Hispanic equations in Table 7.3, we find a contradictory pattern with regard to the fiscal capacity of cities and stack air TRI releases. The funds expended for sewers and sanitation, a surrogate for environmental spending, is related to stack air TRI releases in hypothesized fashion; however, the second measure of fiscal capacity—per capita revenue—is negatively related to stack air TRI releases. Yet when considering fugitive TRI releases, none of the measures of city fiscal capacity is related to this measure of air pollution.

Our global measure of city pollution potential performs as expected; higher levels of pollution potential lead to higher levels of both stack and fugitive air TRI releases. Again, this is expected, as TRI releases are a function of currently industrialized areas. Yet population density—in nearly uniform fash-

TABLE 7.4   Multiple Regression Results (Full and Reduced Equations) for Stack Air TRI Releases in 1,000 pounds in U.S. Cities, 1993[1]

Variables	Full Equation b	Tol.	Reduced Equation b	Tol.	Full Equation b	Tol.	Reduced Equation b	Tol.
Percent Black	.11**	.58	.13**	.72				
Percent Hispanic					−.17**	.48	−.23**	.55
Social Class	−.05**	.37	−.06**	.73	−.10**	.33	−.18**	.36
City Mobilization	−.05	.20			.08	.17	.09	.18
City Capacity Sewer and Sanitation	.10**	.79	.10**	.86	.08**	.79	.08**	.83
Per Capita Revenue	−.10**	.42	−.08**	.70	−.09*	.42	−.09**	.45
Per Capita Expenditure	.03	.39			.05	.40	.06	.47
City Pollution Potential	.14**	.77	.14**	.84	.17**	.75	.16**	.81
Population Density	−.11**	.53	−.12**	.74	−.09**	.52	−.09	.60
Mayor-Council	−.07	.16			−.18	.17		
Council-Manager	−.18	.16	−.15**	.82	−.17	.16		
State Impact Environmental Interests	−.04	.13			−.05	.13	−.07	.34
Capacity	−.006	.51			−.003	.13		
Business Climate	−.02	.48			.0007	.50		
Legislative Professionalism	−.10*	.36	−.10**	.73	−.03	.36		
Public Opinion-Partisanship	.07	.42	.08**	.84	.10**	.42	.09**	.72
Public Opinion-Ideology	−.11	.15			−.04	.14		
Moralistic Culture	.02	.35			−.02	.36		
Individualistic Culture	−.04	.36			−.02	.38		
Constant	−.03		−.09		−.06		−.23	
Adj R Sqr.	.44		.45		.47		.48	
F-Ratio	19.69**		38.90**		21.58**		39.93**	
Standard Error of Estimate	.57		.57		.53		.52	
N of Cases	414		414		404		404	

NOTES:
[1]Cell entries are regression coefficients based on standardized normal distributions. Missing data and deletion of cases with significant outliers resulted in the number of cases used in the analysis.
**p < .01   *p < .05

TABLE 7.5   Multiple Regression Results (Full and Reduced Equations) for Fugitive Air TRI Releases in 1,000 pounds in U.S. Cities, 1993[1]

Variables	Full Equation b	Tol.	Reduced Equation b	Tol.	Full Equation b	Tol.	Reduced Equation b	Tol.
Percent Black	.17**	.56	.17**	.64				
Percent Hispanic					−.08	.50	−.09*	.67
Social Class	−.09**	.53	−.10**	.76	−.12**	.32	−.13**	.81
City Mobilization	−.06	.19			−.009	.17		
City Capacity								
Sewer and Sanitation	−.01	.29			−.01	.79		
Per Capita Revenue	.02	.43			.03	.43		
Per Capita Expenditure	−.09	.41	−.08	.67	−.06	.42		
City Pollution Potential	.18**	.76	.19**	.53	.20**	.76	.20**	.93
Population Density	−.09	.52	−.10**	.55	−.08	.51	−.08*	.68
Mayor-Council	−.25	.17	−.11	.86	−.26	.17	−.18*	.83
Council-Manager	−.16	.16			−.13	.16		
State Impact								
Environmental Interests	−.07	.13	−.10	.40	−.10	.13	−.12**	.58
Capacity	.01	.54			.01	.54		
Business Climate	−.02	.47			−.009	.48		
Legislative Professionalism	−.06	.36	−.07	.55	−.04	.35		
Public Opinion-Partisanship	.10	.42	.07	.77	.08	.42		
Public Opinion-Ideology	−.04	.15			−.06	.15		
Moralistic Culture	−.07	.34			−.09	.34		
Individualistic Culture	.009	.35			−.02	.37		
Constant	.17		−.005		.14		.01	
Adj R Sqr.	.42		.42		.40		.41	
F-Ratio	18.8**		37.6**		17.9**		53.1**	
Standard Error of Estimate	.75		.75		.76		.76	
N of Cases	442		428		442		446	

NOTES:
[1]Cell entries are regression coefficients based on standardized normal distributions. Missing data and deletion of cases with significant outliers resulted in the number of cases used in the analysis.
   **p < .01   *p < .05

ion—shows a negative relationship with both measures of air pollution, a finding that is contrary to our initial hypothesis. Furthermore, Tables 7.4 and 7.5 provide scant support for our form-of-government hypotheses: Only in the percent black analysis is one form of city government—the council-manager arrangement—related in hypothesized fashion to air pollution.

The effects of state-level measures produce scattered and inconsistent results. State-level environmental interests are related, in hypothesized fashion, only to fugitive air TRI releases in the percent Hispanic analysis. Legislative professionalism, in the percent black analysis of stack air TRI releases, does diminish this form of air pollution; partisanship, in the same equation, is related to stack air TRI releases in the hypothesized fashion.

Lead TRI Releases

Table 7.6 arrays the results of our analysis of lead TRI releases to the environment in U.S. cities. Once again, columns 1 and 2 contain the full and reduced equations for the percent black population; columns 3 and 4 array similar equations for the percent Hispanic population.

Table 7.6 confirms the existence of a race-based inequity for the percent black population: Cities with large black populations have higher levels of lead TRI releases. Yet the relationship between the Hispanic population and lead TRI releases is opposite to the initial hypothesis. Once again, however, Table 7.6 does reveal class-based inequities with regard to TRI releases, and both the percent black and percent Hispanic analyses reveal no support for the political-mobilization hypothesis. Furthermore, the pollution potential measure performs as anticipated; however, the mayor-council form of government in the percent black equation is related to lead TRI releases in a fashion contrary to the initial hypothesis.

Our state-level measures provide sparse and, in one instance, contradictory results. Both the state-level environmental interests and partisanship measures are related, in hypothesized fashion, to lead TRI releases. However, in the percent Hispanic equation, the moralistic culture measure is related to lead TRI releases in a fashion that is contrary to the initial hypothesis.

Conclusion

This chapter has assessed race, class, and political mobilization explanations for 1993 toxic-release measures in 79–84 percent of U.S. cities with populations in excess of 50,000 people. We began the analysis with a simple three-concept model and then tested the three concepts in competition with other well-known explanations for environmental hazards. Our simple tripartite model produced some interesting results. For the percent black equation (Table 7.1), we found evidence to confirm race-based environmental injustice in all four instances. Yet the simple equations that focused on the Hispanic population (Table 7.2) did not produce any evidence to confirm race-

TABLE 7.6   Multiple Regression Results (Full and Reduced Equations) for Lead TRI Releases in U.S. Cities, 1993[1]

Variables	Full Equation b	Tol.	Reduced Equation b	Tol.	Full Equation b	Tol.	Reduced Equation b	Tol.
Percent Black	.08*	.55	.08*	.72				
Percent Hispanic					−.06	.49	−.08*	.71
Social Class	−.02	.36	−.04**	.81	−.05*	.32	−.06**	.89
City Mobilization	−.08	.20			−.04	.17		
City Capacity Sewer and Sanitation	−.03	.80			−.03	.80		
Per Capita Revenue	−.01	.44			−.01	.44		
Per Capita Expenditure	.007	.42			.02	.44		
City Pollution Potential	.12**	.78	.12**	.89	.13**	.77	.13**	.96
Population Density	.02	.52			.03	.51		
Mayor-Council	.13	.15	.15*	.92	.13	.16		
Council-Manager	.07	.15			.10	.16		
State Impact Environmental Interests	−.14**	.14	−.13**	.77	−.14**	.14	−.11**	.53
Capacity	−.01	.13			−.01	.53	−.02	.95
Business Climate	.01	.46			.01	.48		
Legislative Professionalism	−.02	.35			−.01	.35		
Public Opinion-Partisanship	.07	.42	.09**	.76	.06	.42		
Public Opinion-Ideology	−.03	.16			−.03	.15		
Moralistic Culture	.05	.36			.04	.36	.09**	.72
Individualistic Culture	.002	.35			−.01	.37		
Constant	−.32		−.25		−.35		−.23	
Adj R Sqr.	.28		.28		.27		.28	
F-Ratio	9.63**		27.78**		9.56**		28.12**	
Standard Error of Estimate	.61		.62		.61		.62	
N of Cases	401		405		402		406	

NOTES:

[1]Cell entries are regression coefficients based on standardized normal distributions. Missing data and deletion of cases with significant outliers resulted in the number of cases used in the analysis.

**p < .01   *p < .05

FIGURE 7.2   Summary of City-Level Findings (based on reduced equations

Environmental Harm	Race Inequity	Class Inequity	Political Mobilization	Other Explanations*
Total TRI Releases	Black (yes) Hispanic (no)	Yes	No	*Pollution Potential, Council-Manager, Environmental Interests,* Business Climate, *Partisanship,* Ideology
Stack Air TRI Releases	Black (yes) Hispanic (no)	Yes	No	Sewer and Sanitation Expenditures, *Per Capita Revenues, Pollution Potential,* Population Density, *Council-Manager, Legislative Professionalism,* Partisanship
Fugitive Air TRI Releases	Black (yes) Hispanic (no)	Yes	No	*Pollution Potential, Population Density, Mayor-Council, Environmental Interests*
Lead TRI Releases	Black (yes) Hispanic (no)	Yes	No	*Pollution Potential,* Mayor-Council, *Environmental Interests, Partisanship,* Moralistic Culture

NOTE: *Other variables included in either or both reduced equations. Entries that are italicized evidenced the hypothesized relationship.

based environmental injustice. We also found solid evidence, based on the simple analysis, to confirm both class-based environmental injustice and the role played by political mobilization in reducing TRI releases.

We developed a more complex test to assess the race, class, and political mobilization effects (the core concepts in the environmental injustice literature) on environmental hazards by adding a pool of explanations from the existing literature. The findings from this analysis are arrayed in Figure 7.2. The results indicate that political mobilization played no role in explaining toxic releases in U.S. cities. Additionally, our results for the Hispanic population reveal no evidence of race-based injustice. The class measure evidenced uniform results: Higher social class resulted in lower levels of TRI releases for all equations. The race-based findings for the percent black equations produced uniformly consistent results across all four TRI measures: Cities with increasing percentages of black populations also have higher levels of the type of toxic releases studied in this chapter.

Once again, we report consistent results for our pollution potential measure—this measure was related to all indicators of toxic releases in the hypothesized fashion. The consistent performance of this measure means that this key concept must be included in any future environmental injustice research.

Notes

1. Elimination of extreme outliers, to correct the skewed distribution of total TRI releases, was partially achieved by recoding data on nineteen out of 466 cities. The cities that were recoded are: Omaha, Nebraska, 334342.4 to 17926.4; Beaumont, Texas, 47361.0 to 17926.3; Warden, Ohio, 42927.6 to 17926.2; St. Louis, Missouri, 40806.9 to 17926.1; Dearborn, Michigan, 40792.9 to 17926.0; Houston, Texas, 36995.2 to 17925.9; Detroit, Michigan, 32214.4 to 17924.8; Baton Rouge, Louisiana, 30392.4 to 17924.7; Victoria, Texas, 29789.2 to 17924.6; Louisville, Kentucky, 26952.8 to 17924.5; Chicago, Illinois, 26233.8 to 17924.4; Cleveland, Ohio, 26031.6 to 17924.3; Canton, Ohio, 25547.0 to 17924.2; Indianapolis, Indiana, 23482.3 to 17924.1; Cheyenne, Wyoming, 21641.1 to 17924.0; Fort Wayne, Indiana, 20923.4 to 17923.9; Milwaukee, Wisconsin, 20594.1 to 17923.8; Muncie, Indiana, 202215.2 to 17923.7; and Phoenix, Arizona, 19009.5 to 17923.6. Once recoded, the values were subjected to a square root transformation (with the resultant values multiplied by ten to restore variance) in order to normalize—insofar as possible—the univariate distribution of this measure. The descriptive statistics for the original and recoded/transformed values of total TRI releases are shown below:

	Mean	Std. D.	Skewness	Kutosis	Variance	CV
Original	4001.6	16640.7	17.03	332.07	.276915E+.09	4.15
Recode	2873.6	4560.0	2.17	3.92	.207942E+.08	1.58
Transformed	401.6	355.4	1.18	.59	126341.1	.88
Standardized	.00	1.00	1.18	.59	1.00	.380209E+.15

2. Elimination of extreme outliers, to correct the skewed distributions for stack air and for fugitive air TRI releases in 1,000 pounts, was partially achieved by recoding data. For stack air, nine out of 466 cities were recoded: Richmond, Virginia, 3302.6 to 3124.6; Savannah, Georgia, 3340.8 to 3124.7; Baton Rouge, Louisiana, 3403.4 to 3124.8; Mobile, Alabama, 3931.2 to 3124.9; Chicago, Illinois, 4028.6 to 2125.0; Beaumont, Texas, 4633.9 to 3125.1; Grand Rapids, Michigan, 5124.2 to 3125.2; Louisville, Kentucky, 6859.8 to 3125.3; Rochester, New York, 7531.2 to 3125.4. For fugitive air TRI releases, a total of 38 out of 466 cities were recoded: Riverside, California, 725 to 669.1; Detroit, Michigan, 752.5 to 669.2; Cincinnati, Ohio, 780.9 to 669.3; Highpoint, North Carolina, 803.2 to 669.4; Toledo, Ohio, 804.9 to 669.5; Lincoln, Nebraska, 801.1 to 669.6; Cleveland, Ohio, 819.1 to 669.7; Mobile, Alabama, 870.7 to 669.8; Dallas, Texas, 879.9 to 669.9; Los Angeles, California, 898.0 to 670.0; Corpus Christi, Texas, 905.8 to 670.1; Decatur, Illinois, 905.9 to 670.2; Rochester, New York, 914.2 to 670.3; Antioch, California, 925.9 to 670.4; Portland, Oregon, 980.7 to 670.5; Wilmington, North Carolina, 1135.7 to 670.6; North Charleston, South Carolina, 1187.7 to 670.7; Indianapolis, Indiana, 1198.8 to 670.8; Columbus, Ohio, 1336.4 to 670.9; St. Louis, Missouri, 1423.0 to 671.0; Wichita Falls, Texas, 1462.1 to 671.1; Chicago, Illinois, 1620.2 to 671.2; Odessa, Texas, 1790.0 to 671.3; Birmingham, Alabama, 1997.8 to 671.4; Tulsa, Oklahoma, 1878.7 to 671.5; Wichita, Kansas, 2391.0 to 671.6; Port Arthur, Texas, 2412.8 to 671.7; Philadelphia, Pennsylvania, 2415.0 to 671.8; Richmond, Virginia, 2417.6 to 671.9; Longview, Texas, 2502.5 to 672.0; Baton Rouge, Louisiana, 2538.1 to 672.2; Baytown, Texas, 2701.6 to 672.2; Memphis, Tennessee, 2933.8 to 672.3; Louisville, Kentucky, 3572.8 to 672.4; West Allis, Wisconsin, 3715.0 to 672.5; Beaumont, Texas, 2701.6 to 672.6; Gary, Indiana, 4718.1 to 672.7; Houston, Texas, 5798.8 to 672.8. Once recoded, the values for each measure were subjected to square root transformations (with the resultant values multiplied by ten to restore variance) in order to normalized—insofar as possible—the univari-

ate distributions of each measure. The descriptive statistics for the original and recoded/transformed values for stack air and fugitive air TRI releases in 1,000 pounds are shown below.

Stack Air TRI Releases in 1,000 Pounds

	Mean	Std. D.	Skewness	Kutosis	Variance	CV
Original	456.08	864.23	3.83	19.9	746896.2	1.91
Recode	421.9	704.2	2.38	5.26	495948.1	1.66
Transformed	149.0	141.4	1.21	.82	20011.8	.94
Standardized	.00	1.00	1.21	.82	1.00	.106961E+16

Fugitive Air TRI Releases in 1,000 Pounds

	Mean	Std. D.	Skewness	Kutosis	Variance	CV
Original	259.6	605.5	5.00	30.71	366067.08	2.33
Recode	164.3	210.6	1.38	.64	44386.4	1.28
Transformed	100.0	80.3	.65	−.74	6462.5	.80
Standardized	.00	1.00	.65	−.74	1.00	−.301751E+16

3. Elimination of extreme outliers, to correct the skewed distribution for lead TRI releases to air, land, and water in pounds, was partially achieved by recoding scores for either out of 463 cities: Saginaw, Michigan, 185000 to 15998; Baton Rouge, Louisiana, 114091 to 15977; Peoria, Illinois, 46350 to 15996; Omaha, Nebraska, 40564 to 15995; Winchester, Massachusetts, 37673 to 15994; Knoxville, Tennessee, 24600 to 15993; El Paso, Texas, 22218 to 15992; Atlanta, Georgia, 19131 to 15991. The recoded values on this measure were subjected to a square root transformation (with the resultant values multiplied by ten to restore variance) in order to normalize—insofar as possible—the univariate distribution of the measure. The descriptive statistics for the original and recoded/transformed values for lead TRI releases to air, land, and water are shown below.

	Mean	Std. D.	Skewness	Kutosis	Variance	CV
Original	1797.6	10944.0	12.87	192.68	.119773E+.09	6.08
Recode	1016.4	3113.9	3.76	13.54	9696498.78	3.08
Transformed	6.58	9.48	1.44	1.10	96.97	1.49
Standardized	.00	1.00	1.44	1.10	1.00	.147557E+16

4. Our initial analysis revealed six cities with statistically significant residual outliers. The corresponding cases that contributed these outliers were deleted and the analysis redone. The second analysis revealed a new set of residual outliers that was subsequently deleted and the process repeated. This condition existed until approximately 100 cases had been deleted—and even at this point each subsequent analysis revealed another set of statistically significant residual outliers. Since we could see no end in sight, we report the results of the initial analysis—noting that all equations in Tables 7.4 and 7.5 are based on six significant residual outliers. The six cities with significant residual outliers are: Antioch, California; Baytown, Texas; West Allis, Wisconsin; Cheyenne, Wyoming; Chula Vista, California; and, Orange, California.

8

Summary and Conclusions from the Multilevel Analyses

In this chapter, we review the findings for Chapters 5–7 as they address the question posed at the beginning of the book: When other explanations are taken into account, does race, class, and political mobilization matter with regard to the severity of environmental harms? To aid the reader in keeping track of the results from these chapters, Figure 8.1 arrays the findings for the various race, class, and mobilization measures at the state, county, and city levels. Once again, to simplify the reader's task, the reported results focus only on the reduced equations in the state, county, and city analyses.

Summary of Race, Class, and Political-Mobilization Findings

Political Mobilization

The most consistently null findings from the multilevel analysis indicates that there was either no relationship between political mobilization and environmental harms or that the relationship was opposite to the initial hypothesis for thirteen out of the fourteen dependent variables studied. This finding stands in stark contrast to the idea that politically mobilized communities capture the attention of decisionmakers and, thus, increased political mobilization has the effect of minimizing environmental harms. Indeed, some previous studies had included this concept (Allen, 2001; Allen, Lester, and Hill, 1995; Crews-Meyer, 1994; Hird, 1993, 1994; Hird and Reese, 1998; Hamilton, 1993, 1995; Lester, Allen, and Lauer, 1994; Lester and Allen, 1996; Ringquist, 1995, 1996, 1997); however, only a few studies had confirmed that political mobilization reduced the level of environmental hazards in a community (Hamilton, 1993, 1995; Lester, Allen, and Lauer, 1994).

FIGURE 8.1   Summary of Race, Class, and Political Mobilization Findings for State-, County-, and City-Level Analyses—Reduced Equations[1]

Level of Analysis and Environmental Harm	Black Population	Hispanic Population	Social Class Black	Social Class Hispanic	Mobilization Black	Mobilization Hispanic
State Level Analysis						
Ozone Depletion and Toxic Chemicals to Air	Yes	No	Yes	No	No	No
Nitrogen Oxide and Sulphur Dioxide to Air	Yes*	No	No	No	No	No
Hazardous Waste	Yes*	Yes	No	No	No	No
Solid Waste	No	No	No	No	No	No
Toxic Waste	Yes	Yes*	No	No	No	No
Degree of Water System Violation	No	Yes*	No	No	No	No
Toxic and Chemical Pollution of Water	Yes	Yes*	No	No	No	No
County Level Analysis						
Total Toxic Releases	Yes*	Yes*	No	Yes*	No	No
Stack Air Toxic Releases	Yes*	Yes*	No	Yes*	No	No
Fugitive Air Toxic Releases	Yes*	Yes*	No	Yes*	No	Yes
City Level Analysis						
Total Toxic Releases	Yes	No	Yes	Yes	No	No
Stack Air Toxic Releases	Yes	No	Yes	Yes	No	No
Fugitive Air Toxic Releases	Yes	No	Yes	Yes	No	No
Lead Toxic Releases	Yes	No	Yes	Yes	No	No
Positive Findings	12/14	7/14	5/14	7/14	0/14	1/14
Percent Positive Findings	85.7	50.0	35.7	50.0	0.00	7.1

NOTES:

[1]Separate equations were constructed for the percent black and percent Hispanic measures. As a consequence, the social class and political mobilization results for the corresponding equations are reported in separate columns.

KEY: "Yes" = positive relationship, i.e., evidence of environmental injustice.
"No" = either no relationship or a relationship that contradicts the initial hypothesis.
* = conditional relationship.

The political-mobilization findings in this book—spanning multiple levels of analysis, different time periods, and multiple environmental harms—are consistent with the majority of the cited literature that reports little in the way of support for the political-mobilization dimension of the environmental injustice model.[1]

Although this chapter is concerned with summarizing the results from the reduced complex tests, the nature of our political-mobilization finding does require us to compare the simple tripartite model and the more complex test results. The results from the simple tripartite model revealed support for the political-mobilization aspect of the model, albeit the nature of the findings varied across the three levels of analysis. For the black and Hispanic populations, the state-level simple equations' support for the political mobilization hypothesis was scattered, that is, only three out of the fourteen equations supported the hypothesis. However, the county-level simple-model findings did show a consistent pattern, with six out of six equations supporting the hypothesis. Findings similar to the county-level simple-model test were replicated by the simple city-level test in that eight out of eight equations supported the political-mobilization dimension of the environmental injustice thesis. Yet when placed in the complex model, only one of the complex equations confirmed a relationship between the level of political mobilization and the level of the environmental hazards that were studied. Under these conditions, we conclude that the results from the test of the simple model were spurious.

Social Class

The social-class findings from the multilevel complex tests are somewhat more robust than the political-mobilization findings, yet they are still mixed. At the state level, only one instance of class-based environmental injustice was present—that for the air-pollution measure of ozone depletion and toxic chemicals released to the atmosphere that focused on the black population.

All other evidence of class-based environmental injustice appears in different equations at only the county and city levels. Thus, the first conclusion regarding the social-class findings is that some of the results—roughly 35–50 percent—support the class dimension of the environmental injustice thesis. As a consequence, some of our class-based findings are consistent with previous research (Allen, 2001; Anderton, et al., 1994a; Asch and Seneca, 1978; Berry, 1977; Bullard, 1983, 1990a; Burch, 1976; Cutter, 1994; Freeman, 1972; Gelobter, 1987; Gould, 1986; Greenberg, 1993, 1994; Hamilton, 1995; Handy, 1977; Harrison, 1975; Hird, 1993, 1994; Hird and Reese, 1998; Krieg, 1995, 1998; Lavelle and Coyle, 1992; Lester, Allen, and Lauer, 1994; Mohai and Bryant, 1992; Perlin, et al., 1995; Polloch and Vittas, 1995; Ringquist, 1995, 1996, 1997; Shaikh, 1995; Shaikh and Loomis, 1998; United Church of Christ, 1987; U.S. Council on Environmental Quality, 1971; U.S. General Accounting Office, 1983; Zimmerman, 1993; Zupan, 1973). Yet the class findings reported herein also provide some support for that body of literature that reports no relationship between class and a variety of environmental harms (Adeola, 1994; Allen, Lester, and Hill, 1995; Bowman and Crews-Meyer, 1995; Gianessi, Peskin, and Wolfe, 1979; Lester and Allen, 1996; West, 1992).

Even with these mixed findings, we do find something quite different from previous research. A conditional relationship is present between social class and the Hispanic population for two county-level environmental harms: stack air and fugitive air toxic releases. This finding, exploratory as it may be, is different from results reported in existing literature and indicates that in counties scoring relatively low on social class Hispanics are marginally more exposed to toxic air pollution.

Race/Ethnicity

The race/ethnicity findings present a divergent pattern. This section first discusses the results from the analysis focusing on the black population, then turns to a discussion of the results from the analysis of the Hispanic population.

Percent Black Population.   Evidence of race-based environmental injustice is evident, in one form of another, in nearly 86 percent of the equations that focus on the percent black population. For seven out of the fourteen equations that focus on the percent black population, the relationship conforms to the linear pattern set forth in the initial hypothesis, that is, as the percent black population increases, so does the level of two out of seven state-level environmental harms and four out of four city-level environmental harms. These findings are consistent with results reported in pre-1992 literature (Asch and Seneca, 1978; Attah, 1992; Berry, 1975; Bullard, 1983, 1990a; Burch, 1976; Clean Sites, Inc., 1990; Colquette and Robertson, 1991; Costner and Thornton, 1990; Davies, 1972; Dorfman, 1979; Fitton, 1992; Freeman, 1972; Gelobter, 1987; Gianessi and Peskin, 1980; Gianessi, Peskin, and Wolfe, 1979; Gould, 1986; Kohlhase, 1991; United Church of Christ, 1987; West, 1992; White, 1992) and post-1992 literature (Adeola, 1994; Been, 1994, 1995; Boerner and Lambert, 1995; Bowman and Crews-Meyer, 1995, 1997; Burke, 1993; Crews-Meyer, 1994; Cutter, 1994; Greenberg, 1993, 1994; Hird, 1993, 1994; Hird and Reese, 1998; Holm, 1994; Lester, Allen, and Lauer, 1994; Perlin, et al., 1995; Polloch and Vittas, 1995; Ringquist, 1995, 1996, 1997; Szasz, et al., 1992; Zimmerman, 1993, 1994).

In addition, five conditional relationships are also present in the percent black population analysis, and the outcome of this analysis is puzzling. For the state-level analysis, the results indicate that increasing levels of the black population in states outside the Sunbelt are exposed to higher levels of both nitrogen oxide, carbon dioxide, and sulphur dioxide air pollutants and hazardous waste. Yet the county-level analysis reveals that the black populations within Sunbelt counties are exposed to higher levels of total toxic releases and airborne toxic pollutants. The county-level findings make intuitive sense: high percentages of the nation's black population reside in the Sunbelt—and, further, Sunbelt counties have been home to rapidly expanding industrial development. As a consequence, it is logical to assume that the county-level conditional findings reflect this condition. However, the state-level findings are counterintuitive: The strongest relationship between the black population and a measure of air pollution and hazardous waste is evident outside the Sunbelt.

These divergent findings at the regional level could result from several sources. First, the different findings are for different levels of analysis. Second, the findings at the different levels are tied to different types of environmental harms, and the measures used to represent these harms are substantially different. The two state-level measures are factor scales that subsume, respectively, nine different measures of air pollution and nine different measures of hazardous waste. Contrarily, the county-level measures consist of a four-item factor scale that measures land, air, and water toxic releases, plus two additional measures of toxic releases via stack and fugitive air. Furthermore, the analyses for these different levels were performed on data drawn from two different time periods: State-level data are prior to 1990, county-level data as of 1995. Quite possibly, these different conditional findings result from a phenomena that Susan Cutter (1995) noted, that is, environmental injustice findings often differ given different levels of analysis, different time periods, different target populations, and different measures of environmental harms.

Cutter's (1995) claim is given additional support when the absence of conditional relationships in city-level percent black equations is considered. The environmental harms in the city-level analysis—although constructed from Toxic Release Inventory data similar to that used in the county-level analysis—are based on the 1993 Toxic Release Inventory. No conditional relationships are evident in the city-level results for the percent black equations.

Some may question why all our measurements were not taken from an identical time period and for identical hazards. The answer is simple: The design of our study consciously sought to assess multiple harms at different levels of analysis and for different time periods in order to determine whether comparable results would be forthcoming. If similar results were forthcoming, based on this skein of differences, then a higher degree of confidence could be placed in more discrete findings. Thus, at present, the conclusion that can be drawn from the percent black equations does tend to support a claim of environmental injustice for this sector of the population—but not in the manner set forth by previous literature. In three out of seven state-level analyses, circa 1990, incidences of environmental injustice of the simple positive linear form are evident for the black population. An additional two incidences of state-level environmental injustice based on conditional relationships are also present for the same sector of the population. Furthermore, in three out of three county-level analyses, incidences of environmental justice associated with toxic releases are reported; however, these findings are conditional and indicate that in 1995 the relationship between the percent black population and the three measures of toxic releases was stronger in the Sunbelt. Finally, in four out of four city-level analyses, incidences of environmental justice for the percent black population were present with regard to 1993 levels of total toxic releases, stack and fugitive air, and a global measure of lead toxic releases.

Percent Hispanic Population. This final section of the summary focuses on incidents of environmental injustice in relation to the Hispanic population. Unlike the evidence from the percent black analysis, incidents of environmental injustice are evident in only 50 percent of the percent Hispanic equations. We begin with the most consistently negative findings. The city-level analysis reveals that the percent Hispanic measure is related in negative fashion to all four measures of toxic releases. In sum, and contrary to the initial hypothesis, the results from the current analysis of 1993 TRI data indicate that cities with smaller percentages of Hispanics have the highest level of total toxic releases, stack and fugitive toxic releases, and lead releases. This set of findings stands in opposition to both the pre- and post-1992 literature cited earlier in this summary chapter.

Yet the 1995 county-level results indicate a complex and consistent pattern of relationships between the Hispanic population, total toxic releases, and stack and fugitive air toxic releases. The relationship between the Hispanic population and the three county-level measures of toxic releases is strongest in lower social class counties, western counties, and in counties with low fiscal capacity. In sum, in poorer western counties with low fiscal capacity, Hispanics are most likely to be confronted with incidences of environmental injustice. This is a pattern that is far more complex than that reported in existing literature.

The state-level analysis also provides evidence of four instances of environmental injustice for the Hispanic population: hazardous waste, toxic waste, water-system violations, and toxic and chemical pollution of groundwater. Yet in relation to three other state-level environmental harms, no support for a claim of race-based environmental injustice is present for the Hispanic population. For nitrogen oxide, carbon dioxide, and sulphur dioxide released to the atmosphere and solid waste, no race-based relationship was evident for the Hispanic population. For the final measure of air pollution—ozone-depleting and toxic chemicals released to the atmosphere—the relationship was negative, that is, states with lower percentages of the Hispanic population were related to higher levels of this environmental harm. The findings on air pollution from this section of the analysis stand in stark contrast to existing literature on environmental injustice and air pollution—a body of literature that consistently reported the existence of incidences of environmental injustice for this type of environmental harm.

However, the four positive results from the state-level Hispanic equation evidence a complex pattern. The relationship between the Hispanic population and hazardous waste fits the initial hypothesis: States with higher percentages of this ethnic group have higher levels of hazardous waste—a finding that is consistent with the United Church of Christ (1987) study. Further, we find that for toxic waste and one measure of water pollution—toxic and chemical pollution of surface water and groundwater—Hispanics living in western states are faced with higher incidences of environmental injustice. Finally, Hispanics residing outside western states are exposed to higher incidences of water-system violations. Two of these conditional findings—toxic waste and toxic chemical water pollution—support the claims of Hispanic activists that the western population of this ethnic group is faced with higher incidences of environmental injustice than is evident elsewhere in the nation. Yet the final result—dealing with water-system violations—indicates that for this type of harm the West is not the sole geographic area of concern.

Summary of Supplemental Findings

As a closing summary, several additional comments are in order. The initial research question posed by the book was this: When other explanations are taken into account, does race, class, and political mobilization matter with regard to severity of environmental harms? This chapter has focused on this primary concern and summarized the multilevel race, class, and political-mobilization findings. However, the battery of additional explanations used in the complex test do deserve some comment—if for no other purpose than to provide guidance for future researchers. The following paragraphs undertake this task in brief form.

First, pollution potential was a consistent explanation for the level of environmental harms in our state-, county-, and city-level analyses. This finding conforms nicely to existing research that has made use of some or all four of the components collected in this measure, that is, number of manufacturing establishments and employees, total population, and population density (Allen, 2001; Allen, Lester, and Hill, 1995; Anderton, et al., 1994a; Been, 1994; Bowman and Crews-Meyer, 1995, 1997; Burke, 1993; Cutter, 1994; Hird, 1993, 1994; Hird and Reese, 1998; Holm, 1994; Krieg, 1998; Ringquist, 1995, 1996, 1997; Zimmerman, 1994). With regard to toxic releases, this finding is not surprising in that toxic releases are a function of currently industrialized areas (Krieg, 1998). However, the utility of the pollution-potential measures spanned all equations. Thus, future research that focuses on environmental injustice should take this concept into account in order to completely specify any equation.

Beyond the consistent pollution-potential findings, the remaining control variables produced mixed results. However, some of these measures should be considered for inclusion in any future research. For example, the state-fiscal-capacity and environmental-interests measures showed their utility across all three levels of analysis and for many of the toxic-pollutant measures. Future researchers should include these measures when studying this form of pollution. Furthermore, controls for such regions as the Sunbelt and the West, in the form of conditional terms, were also important. Land area—with regard to county-level analysis—should also be considered when studying environmental injustice, and the form of city government should, of necessity, be taken into account when pursuing the inquiry at the city level of analysis. Still, measures such as state business climate, legislative professionalism, and public opinion and political culture either performed poorly or in a manner inconsistent with our initial hypotheses. Thus, future researchers may need to reformulate the arguments associated with these concepts or dispense with them altogether when studying environmental injustice.

Conclusion

The major conclusions from the state-, county-, and city-level analyses can provide meaningful guidance for policy formulation in this area. In general, the results from the three levels of analysis provided almost no support for the political-mobilization hypothesis. This measure evidenced support for the hypothesized relationship in only one instance: county toxic fugitive air releases. In two other instances, the relationship was other than hypothesized, and in all other instances of the state-, county-, and city-level analyses no relationship was evident for political mobilization, as it has been measured in this research, and the other environmental harms studied. Thus, we see no reason to argue that enhancing political mobilization will remedy instances of environmental injustice.

The social-class findings were definitely more robust than the political-mobilization findings but less so than the race/ethnicity findings. Social class was important in the county- and city-level findings on the Hispanic population. However, this concept's utility was useful only in conjunction with the city-level findings for the black population. Possibly, policy design needs to be concerned with aspects of social class only when dealing with the Hispanic population in substate areas and with the black population within U.S. cities.

Finally, the findings from the state-, county-, and city-level analyses do point to incidences of environmental injustice for black and Hispanic Americans. Both scattered and uniform findings were evident for these two groups at the state, county, and city levels. These findings will guide our analyses of existing policies and our formulation of alternative policy recommendations in the remainder of this book. Specifically, Chapter 9 will review existing policies in this area at the national and subnational levels. Chapter 10 will then offer several alternative policy designs for dealing with environmental injustice in the future.

Note

1. As noted in Chapter 4, we are not entirely satisfied with our city-level measure of political mobilization, i.e., median value of owner-occupied housing. However, no other measure was readily available, and we did not want to run the risk of mis-specifying the model. As a consequence, we were left with an indirect surrogate of the political-mobilization concept at the city level. The measure used is an indirect surrogate of the concept because the measure implies that the higher the value of owner-occupied housing, the greater the stake in the community and, therefore, the more likely a high level of political mobilization will eventuate. We justified the use of this measure on several grounds. First, median value of owner-occupied housing has been used to represent political mobilization in previous environmental injustice literature (Hird, 1993, 1994; Hird and Reese, 1998; Lester and Allen, 1996). Second, a more direct measure of mobilization, i.e., local elections, was inadequate in that there is no agency that systematically collects local election results and, further, local elections are held at different times. Third, some city-level presidential election results are reported for different geographic entities, making comparable measures difficult. We would be troubled by the city-level political-mobilization results were it not for two points. First, the city-level results track nicely with the remaining findings about this concept for our other levels of analysis—levels at which the concept was more directly measured. Second, work by Hird (1993, 1994) and Hird and Reese (1998)—which used the same measure for county-level environmental injustice analysis—also reports no relationship between mobilization and environmental harms.

9

Existing Federal and State Policies for Environmental Justice: Problems and Prospects

For several reasons, the twenty-first century is a particularly exciting time to examine environmental politics and policy at the federal and state levels. First, the 1980s were a period of implementation of federal environmental policies enacted during the two previous decades: the Clean Air Act and Amendments of 1970 and 1977, the Federal Water Pollution Control Act and Amendments of 1972, the Resource Conservation and Recovery Act of 1976, the Safe Drinking Water Act of 1974, the Surface Mining Control and Reclamation Act of 1977, the Federal Land Management Act of 1978, the Comprehensive Environmental Response, Compensation, and Liability Act of 1980, the Hazardous and Solid Waste Act Amendments of 1984, the Superfund Amendments and Reauthorization Act of 1986, and the Oil Pollution Act of 1990. Like the 1980s and the 1990s (Lester and Lombard, 1990), the 2000s will be an "implementation era" in environmental policy, as well as in other areas of public policy.

Second, intergovernmental relations have recently taken on greater significance than ever. During the 1980s, the doctrine of new federalism stressed devolution of authority from the federal level to the state and local levels in many areas of public policy. As part of the legacy of the Reagan, Bush, and Clinton presidencies, states and local communities are taking on many responsibilities for protecting the environment that were previously the province of the federal government. Indeed, the head of Vermont's environmental agency, Jonathan Lash, has said that the most important innovations in environmental protection are now occurring at the state level and many others agree with this assessment.

Finally, since 1970, the states themselves have undergone a number of important transformations in terms of their institutional capacities for implementing federal programs. For example, states have improved revenue systems, strengthened the governor's office, professionalized legislatures, reformed courts, and consolidated bureaucracies (Bowman and Kearney, 1986). Presumably, states are no longer the weak link in the intergovernmental system of the United States. These enormous changes are so far-reaching as to constitute a "definite break with the past" (Bowman and Kearney, 1986). Scholars thus will likely be engaged in the study of intergovernmental relations (and especially federal-state relations) as they affect the formulation, implementation, and impact of public policies (Benton and Morgan, 1986). These future investigators are likely to be concerned with the extent to which U.S. states and cities are providing leadership in the environmental area or, conversely, the extent to which they are not effectively implementing federal laws dealing with pollution.

This chapter reviews and discusses federal and state initiatives in the area of environmental justice. We also examine the problems and prospects presented by these initiatives in an era of regulatory federalism, which characterizes the contemporary period of intergovernmental relations, in order to make some basic recommendations regarding how federalism should be viewed as it pertains to environmental justice.

The Executive Branch and Environmental Justice

As we discussed in Chapter 3, in the early 1990s the environmental justice movement began to significantly affect national policy. Two major environmental justice conferences were held during 1990–1991, including the University of Michigan's Conference on Race and the Incidence of Environmental Hazards, and the Environmental Leadership Summit in Washington, D.C. An outcome of these conferences was the formation of the Michigan Coalition, a group of social scientists, civil rights leaders, and environmentalists interested in making environmental justice a national policy issue. In response to concerns of the U.S. Congressional Black Caucus and the Michigan Coalition, the EPA formed the Environmental Equity Workgroup, whose findings were reported in a two-volume report (U.S. Environmental Protection Agency, 1992a). Shortly thereafter, in November 1992, the Office of Environmental Equity was established within the Environmental Protection Agency.

Executive Order No. 12898

On February 11, 1994, President Clinton signed Executive Order No. 12898, which requires every federal agency to achieve the principle of environmental justice by addressing and ameliorating the human health and environmental effects of the agency's programs, policies, and activities on minority and low-income populations in the United States (Cushman, 1993, 1994). Two fundamental components of environmental justice were incorporated into the order: (1) that there be consideration of human health and socioeconomic factors and a valid incorporation of public sentiment into federal decisionmaking; and (2) that there be associated public education and outreach activities sponsored by each federal agency to obtain this input (National Conference of State Legislatures, 1995: 10). Essentially, all adverse effects on the health and environment of minority and low-income populations should be identified and scrutinized before decisions are made to site facilities. In compliance with this executive order, the Departments of Defense, Health and Human Services, Housing and Urban Development, Labor, Agriculture, Transportation, Justice, Interior, Commerce, and Energy, as well as the Nuclear Regulatory Commission, the National Aeronautics and Space Administration, and the Environmental Protection Agency, were directed to design and implement environmental justice plans (National Conference of State Legislatures, 1995:10).

During the second term of the Clinton administration, direct presidential action has been notably absent. Several possible explanations may account for this. First, having signed Executive Order No. 12898, which designated the Environmental Protection Agency as the lead agency, and having created the Office of Environmental Justice within the Environmental Protection Agency to deal with the day-to-day management of federal involvement with the issue of environmental justice, President Clinton may feel that the issue has an institutional locus and that agency action in dealing with the problem is best handled outside the Oval Office.

Second, in a eerie replay of the Nixon Watergate years—when inner-city environmental concerns first surface and then disappeared from the agenda—President Clinton may also have found himself continuously distracted from the environmental justice issue by the need to react to special prosecutors and congressional action on impeachment.

A third plausible explanation was alluded to in Chapter 3. During certain periods in the agenda-setting process, environmental justice entrepreneurs did not speak with a single voice. Possibly, the perception of multiple approaches to environmental justice caused the president to withdraw from the issue in order to allow the Interagency Working Group to resolve any conflicting claims before the president reengaged the topic.

A final plausible explanation for presidential silence during the period from 1995 to 1999 may be attributed to the nature of presidential and congressional relations. High-profile issues such as tax cuts, budget appropriations, and a variety of foreign policy controversies from 1995 on—all within the context of split party control of the executive branch and Congress—

may have made it politically not feasible for the president to push an environmental justice agenda. This is exceedingly possible given environmental policy actions within the Republican-dominated Congress. For example, the 103rd and 104th Congresses considered several environmental proposals in the complex area of environmental management. The Safe Drinking Water Act amendments, the Small Business Regulatory Fairness Act, and the Unfunded Mandates Reform Act can all be read as clear signs of congressional concern about the lack of sufficient economic consideration in environmental management (Morgenstern, 1999: 124–125). Indeed, the Unfunded Mandates Reform Act—designed to curb the practice of imposing so-called unfunded federal mandates on state and local government (Morgenstern, 1999:125)—would certainly have served as a sign that any federal strategy that planned to impose environmental justice mandates on state and local instrumentalities might meet with serious opposition. And given these considerations, possibly President Clinton decided not to enter the fray on the issue of environmental justice when he needed to carefully expend limited political capital on other high-profile issues.

Agency Action

The signing of Executive Order No. 12898, with its accompanying memorandum indicating that Title 6 of the Civil Rights Act of 1964 could be used as an enforcement tool, the designation of the U.S. Environmental Protection Agency as the lead agency to assist other instrumentalities of the executive branch in implementing the executive order, and the creation of the Office of Environmental Justice—formerly the Office of Environmental Equity—gave rise to an additional series of environmental justice actions on the part of the federal government.

For example, in 1994 EPA was designated as the lead agency to assist other federal agencies in implementing the executive order and addressing the problems that confront minority and low-income populations. EPA Administrator Carole Browner chairs the Interagency Working Group on Environmental Justice under the executive order. The Office of Environmental Justice coordinates EPA efforts to develop and implement environmental justice initiatives (National Conference of State Legislatures, 1995: 11). Since the executive order was issued, the EPA has established the Environmental Justice Steering Committee and Policy Work Group; it has formed the National Environmental Justice Advisory Council; and it has held the EPA National Goals Project since 1993 to identify major environmental priorities, including environmental justice issues (National Conference of State Legislatures, 1995: 11). In addition, EPA administers a number of environmental justice grant programs, including the State and Tribal En-

FIGURE 9.1   Summary of Waste Programs Environmental Justice Accomplishments[1]

Agency-wide efforts to coordinate and develop scientifically valid standards for measuring cumulative risks, synergistic effects, and multiple pathways that may result from exposure to a single contaminant or multiple contaminants from one or more sources. Use of GIS to assess these risks and Region 9 RCRA staff conducting assessment of cumulative risks.

EPA Region 5 using LandView II software to identify demographic, including minority and low-income populations, surrounding Superfund sites.

Conducting a series of outreach, communications, and partnerships to deal with environmental justice, including activities with the Office of Emergency and Remedial Response, public dialogues on brown fields and urban revitalization, and partnerships with states—such as the Massachusetts Department of Environmental Protection.

Economic redevelopment, jobs, and worker training in communities with environmental justice concerns.

Including environmental justice initiatives into grants and cooperating agreements with Tribal-led environmental programs, minority business enterprises, women's business enterprises, and Superfund cleanup grants.

Developed federal interagency cooperation with the Agency for Toxic Substance and Disease Registry, U.S. Department of Justice, the National Institute of Environmental Health Services, Department of Housing and Urban Development, Department of Agriculture, and Department of the Interior.

Expand public involvement in Resource Conservation and Recovery Act permitting procedures, actions under Comprehensive Environmental Response, Compensation, and Liability Act, the Oil Pollution Act, and the Spill Prevention and Countermeasures Program.

NOTE:

[1]Compiled by the authors from U.S. Environmental Protection Agency, 1996, *Waste Programs Environmental Justice Accomplishments Report,* http://www.epa.gov/swerosps/ej/ejaa96/execsum.htm.

vironmental Justice Grants Program. Finally, each EPA regional office has also begun to collect data on exposure to environmental pollutants by race and income categories.

Since the date of the creation of the Office of Environmental Equity, a series of additional efforts has transpired. A partial list of the activities—designed to give the reader a feel for the scope and complexity of agency actions—is arrayed in Figure 9.1.

EPA's Environmental Justice Strategy

In late 1994 and early 1995, EPA produced a draft proposal for an environmental justice plan. This plan has several key points: public participation, accountability, partnerships, outreach, and communication with stakeholders; health and environmental research; data collection, analysis, and stakeholder access to public participation; American Indian and indigenous environmental protection; and enforcement, compliance, assurance, and regulatory review (National Conference of State Legislatures, 1995: 11).

Title 6 of the Civil Rights Act of 1964

The presidential memorandum issued with Executive Order No. 12898 emphasizes that Title 6 of the Civil Rights Act of 1964 provides an opportunity for federal agencies to address environmental hazards in minority and low-income communities. Title 6 prohibits discrimination on the basis of race, color, and national origin in all federally assisted programs. Under Title 6, an environmental justice matter is any civil or criminal matter where a conduct or action involves a disproportionate and adverse environmental or human health effect on an identifiable low-income or minority community or federally recognized tribe (National Conference of State Legislatures, 1995: 11).

Although Title 6 has been used in some instances, recurring enforcement problems have not made this a first choice for resolving issues associated with environmental justice. Indeed, Title 6 action has been avoided at some Brownfield Pilot Project sites (U.S. Environmental Protection Agency, Office of Environmental Justice, 1999: 13). However, in some locales there are active Title 6 complaints and environmental justice concerns. In Camden, New Jersey, community members have filed a class-action lawsuit against the County Municipal Authority and the New Jersey Department of Environmental Protection Agency for disparate impacts related to a sewage treatment plant. Furthermore, Title 6 suits could develop in Detroit—regarding violation of the Safe Drinking Water Act—and in Miami-Dade County, Florida, as well as Tallahassee and Broward Counties, Florida, with regard to incinerators (U.S. Environmental Protection Agency, Office of Environmental Justice, 1999:14).

The States and Environmental Justice

During the 1990s, state-level responses to environmental justice followed an upward curve. Generally speaking, some state action in this area often outstripped actions of the federal government; other states took no action. As noted in Figure 9.2, twenty-two states have apparently not engaged in any environmental justice activity. The remaining twenty-eight states have either attempted or succeeded in a range of efforts.

In the area of attempted or successful action, eighteen states have taken some action, usually in the form of trying to pass environmental justice legislation that would incorporate considerations of race and class into the environmental decisionmaking process. Additionally, fourteen states have either commissioned a study assessing environmental injustice within their boundaries or have established a study commission to evaluate the nature and scope of the problem. Eleven other states have established boards or commissions that are to direct state activities in the environmental justice area. Finally, seven states have passed some form of environmental justice legislation; however, as noted in Figure 9.2, Michigan's legislative solution was simply to "memorialize" the U.S. Congress—requesting Congress to adopt environmental justice legislation. The remaining six states that have passed legislation have taken a range of approaches:[1]

North Carolina: N.C. Gen. Stat. Art. 160-A–325(a)(1994) requires analysis of socioeconomic and demographic data as a prerequisite for siting approval.

Georgia: Ga. Code Ann. Art. 12–8–25.4 (1996) acknowledges environmental justice considerations in siting provisions and permit approval.

Alabama: Ala. Code Art. 22–3–5.1 (1990) includes environmental justice concerns in duties of the state health office.

Louisiana: La. Rev. Stat. Ann. Art. R.S. 30:2011.2 requires study of the relationship between air-pollution emissions and waste discharges and the location of residential areas.

New York: AB 7140 (1994) requires new facility permit applicants to include an economic development strategy with the application and promotes more equitable location of environmental facilities.

Arkansas: Ark. Code. Ann. Art. 86–1501 to 8–6 1504 creates a "rebuttable presumption against" citing high-impact solid waste management facilities within twelve miles of one another and allows a project to proceed if specific benefits are provided to host communities, such as fees, infrastructure improvements, community management sites, and dedicated waste handling facilities.

Although the descriptive information in Figure 9.2 provides the basic profile of state action, it must be noted that the states vary dramatically with regard to their overall commitment to environmental concerns (Lester and Stewart, 2000: 235). This phenomenon has resulted in states being classified as "progressives," "strugglers," "delayers," and "regressives" (Lester, 1994: 63–65).

Progressive states have a high commitment to environmental protection coupled with a strong institutional capacity. In the 1990s, this set of ten

FIGURE 9.2   Summary Description of State Activities to Achieve Environmental Justice, 1992–1999[1]

States[2]/Items	Attempt[3]	Study[4]	Board[5]	Legislation[6]
North Carolina	yes	yes	yes	yes
Georgia	yes		yes	yes
Minnesota	yes	yes	yes	
Tennessee	yes	yes	yes	
Texas	yes	yes	yes	
Alabama	yes			yes
Colorado	yes	yes		
Connecticut	yes		yes	
Louisiana		yes		yes
Maryland		yes	yes	
Massachusetts	yes	yes		
Michigan	yes			yes[7]
New York	yes[8]			yes
South Carolina	yes	yes		
Washington	yes	yes		
Wisconsin	yes		yes	
Arkansas				yes
Florida			yes	
Missouri		yes		
New Hampshire		yes		
New Jersey			yes	
Oregon		yes		
Vermont			yes	
Virginia		yes		
California	yes			
Illinois	yes			
Mississippi	yes			
Pennsylvania	yes			
Total	18	14	11	7

NOTES:

[1]Compiled by the authors from existing sources: K. Sexton and R. Zimmerman, "The Emerging Role of Environmental Justice in Decision Making." In K. Sexton, et al., *Better Environmental Decisions.* Washington, D.C.: Island Press, 1999; National Conference of State Legislatures, *Environmental Justice: A Matter of Perspective.* Denver: National Conference of State Legislatures, 1995; and other information available to the authors.

[2]States that have not taken any action in the four categories summarized in this figure: Alaska, Arizona, Delaware, Hawaii, Idaho, Indiana, Iowa, Kansas, Kentucky, Maine, Montana, Nebraska, Nevada, New Mexico, North Dakota, Ohio, Oklahoma, Rhode Island, South Dakota, Utah, West Virginia, Wyoming.

[3]"Yes" means attempted to pass legislation at one time or another but the legislation either died in committee or is still pending.

[4]Refers to either completing a study or creating a commission to study environmental justice.

[5]Created a board or commission with authority to take action in the area of environmental justice.

[6]Passed legislation or rule change to effect some aspect of environmental justice that was not a study or creation of a board or commission.

[7]Michigan's legislature "memorialized" the U.S. Congress to pass environmental justice legislation.

[8]New York passed legislation in 1994 indexing facilities to promote an equitable distribution of facilities. It has also, since 1994, attempted to pass legislation to conduct studies of the problem, to establish a commission, as well as other legislation designed to achieve environmental justice.

states had made substantial improvements in the implementation of federal and state legislation and in the quality of the environment.[2] As their environmental quality gets better, these states may adopt policies independent of federal mandates (Lester and Stewart, 2000: 235). As such, we would expect that environmental justice initiatives would be most pronounced in the progressive states.

Fifteen struggler states have a strong commitment to environmental protection but limited institutional capacity.[3] These states do not have the fiscal and institutional resources to pursue aggressive environmental protection policies. Progress can be made in these states but at a pace that is slower and possibly less innovative than in the progressive states (Lester, 1994:63–64). Struggler states will probably do the best they can in the area of environmental justice given existing constraints.

Fifteen delayer states have a strong institutional capacity but a limited commitment to environmental protection.[4] Delayer states maintain the status quo on the environment, and whatever progress is made will be painstakingly slow. Apathetic state bureaucracies are the major concern in this group of states (Lester, 1994: 64).

Ten regressive states have weak institutional capacities and a weak commitment to environmental protection.[5] Because of limited capacity and commitment, regressive states are unlikely to take independent actions, such as dealing with environmental justice issues, and the quality of life may deteriorate. Dirty industries may continue to move to these states, and these states will continue to promote economic development at the expense of environmental quality (Lester, 1994:64–65).

We compare what we know about state environmental justice actions—passing legislation, creating a board, commission, or agency, conducting a study, or attempting some other action—to the progressive, struggler, delayer, and regressive states typology. The results of this comparison are shown in Table 9.1.

The first thing that stands out on Table 9.1 is the almost total lack of activity in the regressive states. Only one state, Mississippi, attempted to pass environmental justice legislation. The remaining nine states in this category conform exactly to the expectations of their regressive classification; indeed, all ten states in this category exemplify the condition of being unlikely to take any independent actions in the area of environmental justice.

The remaining three categories of states—progressive, struggler, and delayer—present an interesting picture. Although 20 percent of the progressive states passed legislation to deal with environmental injustice, 26.7 percent of the delayer states engaged in this action. However, 40 percent of the progressive states have created a board, commission, or agency to deal with environmental justice concerns, whereas only 26.7 percent of the delayer states completed this task. Equally true, 40 percent of the progressive states

TABLE 9.1   Summary of Major Environmental Justice Actions in Progressive, Struggler, Delayer, and Regressive States[1]

Item/State	Progressive States	Struggler States	Delayer States	Regressive States	Row Total[2]
Passed Legislation or Rule Change[3]	20% (2/10)	6.6% (1/15)	26.7% (4/15)	0% (0/10)	14% (7/50)
Created Board, Commission, or Agency[4]	40% (4/10)	20% (3/15)	13.3% (2/15)	0% (0/10)	18% (9/50)
Conducted Study[5]	40% (4/10)	20% (3/15)	40% (6/16)	0% (1/10)	28% (14/50)
Proposed Some Action[6]	50% (5/10)	26.7% (4/15)	46.7% (7/15)	10% (1/10)	34% (17/50)

NOTES:

[1]Compiled by the authors from a variety of existing sources: K. Sexton and R. Zimmerman. "The Emerging Role of Environmental Justice in Decision Making." In K. Sexton, et al., *Better Environmental Decisions.* Washington, D.C.: Island Press, 1999; National Conference of State Legislatures, *Environmental Justice: A Matter of Perspective,* Denver: National Conference of State Legislatures, 1995; and other information available to the authors. Classification of states as progressive, struggler, delayer, and regression in accordance with James P. Lester, "A New Federalism: Environmental Policy in the States," in Norman J. Vig and Michael E. Kraft (eds.), *Environmental Policy in the 1990s,* 2nd ed. Washington, D.C.: C.Q. Press, 1994. States within each classification are: (1) Progressive States: California, Florida, Maryland, Massachusetts, Michigan, New Jersey, New York, Oregon, Washington, Wisconsin; (2) Struggler States: Colorado, Connecticut, Delaware, Hawaii, Idaho, Iowa, Maine, Minnesota, Montana, Nevada, New Hampshire, North Carolina, North Dakota, Rhode Island, and Vermont; (3) Delayer States: Alabama, Alaska, Arkansas, Georgia, Illinois, Louisiana, Missouri, Ohio, Oklahoma, Pennsylvania, South Carolina, Tennessee, Texas, Virginia, West Virginia; (4) Regressive States: Arizona, Indiana, Kansas, Kentucky, Mississippi, Nebraska, New Mexico, South Dakota, Utah, Wyoming.

[2]Read all entries across row. Columns cannot be totaled because some states in each category may have accomplished more than one item in each category.

[3]Items in this category do not include legislation that created a board, commission, or agency or that authorized or commissioned a study.

[4]Items in this category do not include the creation of a study commission.

[5]Items in this category refer either to a study that was commissioned or the creation of a board or commission that was tasked with studying the problem.

[6]Refers to some type of action that would fit into one of the previous categories that never reached fruition.

and 40 percent of the delayer states established some mechanism to assess the level of environmental justice concerns within their respective geographic boundaries. It remains to be seen if this common portrait of progressive and delayer states will result in equal progress on the issue of environmental justice or whether the higher level of commitment and capacity inherent in the progressive states will turn the current situation into a more formidable array of state responsiveness.

Fitting between the progressive and delayer states—which have made some progress in the area of environmental justice—and the regressive states—which have remained inactive on this subject—are the struggler states. The struggler states have a strong commitment to environmental protection but limited institutional capacity. The typology predicts that some progress might be made in these states but at a pace that is slower and possibly less innovative than in the progressive states. This is indeed the case. The struggler-states category in Table 9.1 shows about half or less than half of the activity evidenced by progressive states. For example, 20 percent of the progressive states passed legislation or made rule changes; only roughly 6 percent of the struggler states accomplished the same task. Furthermore, 40 percent of the progressive states established boards, commissions, or agencies and conducted studies; only 20 percent of the struggler states accomplished similar objectives. The same pattern is evident for attempting some action. Apparently—in comparison to progressive states—struggler states are doing the best they can given existing constraints.

However, an interesting contradiction in Table 9.1 is the unusual difference between struggler and delayer states. Delayer states outperformed struggler states in almost all the categories listed in Table 9.1. More delayer states passed legislation or rule changes than is the case for struggler states, 26.7 percent versus 6.6 percent, respectively. Twice as many delayer states completed studies as compared to struggler states, 40 percent versus 20 percent, respectively, and there is a gap in attempted actions as well: 46.7 percent of the delayer states attempted some activity as opposed to only 26.7 percent of struggler states. Only in the area of boards, commissions, and agencies do struggler states outperform delayer states, and this is a narrow gap: 20 percent versus 13.3 percent, respectively.

One possible explanation for these findings may be community forces. A large proportion of delayer states, when compared to struggler states, contains increasingly large percentages of the nation's minority populations. Possibly, the presence of minority groups in delayer states is encouraging a higher level of activity as compared to struggler states.

Assessing Federal and State Initiatives: Problems and Prospects

One of several strategies that the Environmental Protection Agency is considering focuses on the imposition of environmental justice mandates on all states. Yet as we have seen, states vary significantly in terms of the extent to which they impose health risks on their populations and the extent of their responsiveness to environmental problems. In other words, the degree of inequality in exposure to environmental health risks varies significantly across states. Moreover, states vary significantly in the extent of their overall commitment to environmental protection and their institutional capacity to remedy pollution problems when they occur (Lester, 1994: 51). The essential problem for the federal government and the states is to realize that not all states are equal in terms of their commitment toward environmental protection and in their institutional and fiscal capabilities to deal with pollution problems when they occur. Thus, some states will require more assistance from the federal government (e.g., Mississippi) than will others (e.g., California). Some scholars have suggested that a program of "selective decentralization" by the federal government will work best, in that some states would be given more leeway (or assistance) than others (Lester and Stewart, 2000: 242).

As we note above, some of the states are laggards in the area of environmental justice, whereas others are more progressive. Thus, although some state governments have made some progress, much remains to be done. We can identify several areas where states can become more engaged in the study of environmental injustice. First, additional research is needed within each state to assess the current capability of state environmental protection agencies in the implementation of state environmental protection programs. There is a strong need for this type of research, because the federal government has, since the early 1970s, been turning more environmental programs over to the states under the twin rubrics of new federalism and the devolution revolution. Thus, the driving forces for this research inquiry are the following: (1) We need to more fully understand the impacts of federal devolution on state efforts to protect the environment; (2) we need to relate the various state responses to environmental injustice during this period of devolution to political, geographical, demographic, ethnic, and socioeconomic data; (3) we need to provide ways to allocate government funds more equitably and more efficiently in this area; and (4) we need to better understand state capacities for environmental management in order to improve conditions for people who might be disadvantaged due to a lack of state institutional capability to effectively implement environmental protection programs under the era of New Federalism during the 1970s–1990s. Moreover, these studies need to be conducted at the state, county, city, and ZIP code levels, using multiple health risks as the dependent variables.

Second, the formation of advisory boards and commissions to discuss potential problems of environmental injustice (and how to deal with it) is a useful strategy from the standpoint of community outreach activities. Moreover, establishing separate agencies for dealing with environmental injustice within the state environmental bureaucracy is a constructive approach in that it provides a focal point for citizen contact and for promulgating and enforcing existing and new regulations on this topic.

Finally, state legislation could be enacted to address potential problems of environmental injustice, but this legislation needs to carefully consider the exact nature of the problem in a specific geographic area before the policies are finally designed. In other words, it is essential that the driving force behind legislation be addressed and carefully considered so that the remedy is based on an understanding of the problem and that the policy that is delivered is both equitable and efficient. This legislation could potentially be based on race, class, or politics as the driving force; alternatively, it could be based on the severity of the health risks presented by various toxins.

In Chapter 10, we return to precisely this point and base our policy recommendations on a rational understanding of the problem as well as the utilization of equity and efficiency as key criteria for evaluating the most desirable policy.

Summary and Conclusion

In this chapter, we have discussed federal and state initiatives in the area of environmental justice and identified some of the potential problems therein. In Chapter 10, we suggest several alternative policy designs for both the federal government and the states to consider and evaluate as they design legislation to remedy this public policy problem. In doing so, we offer a policy recommendation to decisionmakers based on our analyses in Chapters 5–7, as well as the analyses of other scholars who have preceded us.

Notes

1. The following list of legislative actions was adopted from Sexton and Zimmerman (1999), the National Conference of State Legislatures (1995), and contacts established by the authors over the duration of the project.

2. Progressive states are California, Florida, Maryland, Massachusetts, Michigan, New Jersey, New York, Oregon, Washington, and Wisconsin.

3. Struggler states are Colorado, Connecticut, Delaware, Hawaii, Idaho, Iowa, Maine, Minnesota, Montana, Nevada, New Hampshire, North Carolina, North Dakota, Rhode Island, and Vermont.

4. Delayer states are Alabama, Alaska, Arkansas, Georgia, Illinois, Louisiana, Missouri, Ohio, Oklahoma, Pennsylvania, South Carolina, Tennessee, Texas, Virginia, and West Virginia.

5. Regressive states are Arizona, Indiana, Kansas, Kentucky, Mississippi, Nebraska, New Mexico, South Dakota, Utah, and Wyoming.

10

Designing an Effective Policy for Environmental Justice: Implications and Recommendations

===============================

In this final chapter, we make use of the findings from the multilevel analysis to formulate an effective policy for environmental justice. However, simply using the statistical results in the absence of some overarching set of premises to assess any policy recommendation may lead to an erroneous policy design. In this chapter, we present a design for what we believe to be a rational, equitable, and efficient policy for dealing with environmental justice issues. First, we discuss the criteria by which we arrived at our policy proposal. We then develop detailed arguments. This complete picture is necessary because, as the late Aaron Wildavsky once remarked:

> policy analysis must create problems that decision-makers are able to handle with the variables under their control and in the time available. Only by specifying a desired relationship between manipulable means and obtainable objectives can analysis make the essential distinction between a puzzle that can be solved definitively ... and a problem for which there may not be a programmatic solution. (Wildavsky, 1979: 16)

Traditionally, the primary focus of the policy analyst's work has been the generation of policy alternatives and options for consideration by decision-makers (Brewer and deLeon, 1983: 61). Policy analysis, then, refers to the determination of which of various alternative policies, decisions, or means are best for achieving a given set of goals in light of the relations between the alternative policies and the goals (Dunn, 1994: 62; Nagel, 1984: 3).

Some Criteria for Alternative Policy Designs

The first step in developing a policy solution involves moving from very general goals to very specific criteria for evaluating the desirability of alternative policies. The cardinal rule for selecting criteria should be that "the set of criteria should capture all the important dimensions of the relevant goals" (Weimer and Vining, 1992: 223–225). There are several criteria for policy design that could be adopted for the purposes of this analysis. Decision criteria are normally of six main types: effectiveness, efficiency, adequacy, equity, responsiveness, and appropriateness (Dunn, 1994: 282).

Following these guidelines, we have selected three criteria to guide our discussion of alternative policy designs. These three criteria—that the recommended policy be a product of rational choice, that it be equitable, and that it be efficient—seem to fit the problem to be solved.[1] We first define the three criteria and indicate their applicability to the problem at hand before proceeding farther.

Rationality in Policy Design

"Rationality" means that the most desirable policy should be one that has approached the "rational-comprehensive model" (Dye, 1995: 29), that is, the decisionmaker has made a decision on the basis of a calculation of costs and benefits. More specifically, as outlined by James Lester and Joseph Stewart (2000:91), this model includes six basic components. We list the components and then provide a set of comments that justify the consideration of the component with regard to the policy design problem that we face.

The first component of the rational-comprehensive model maintains that the decisionmaker is confronted with a given problem that can be separate from other problems or at least considered meaningfully in comparison with them. In this instance, the problem is defined as assuring that no definable group in society is exposed to a disproportionate burden of environmental hazards. We do not conceive of the problem as one of affirmative action in either hazard siting or in exposure to existing hazards. The task is not to ensure that all definable groups in society are faced with equally mounting hazards. Rather, the idea contained within the ethos of environmentalism is to assure that we constrain, within a realistic set of boundaries, increases in environmental hazards—and hopefully find a way to decrease the burgeoning problem faced in the United States.

We take a realistic approach in this regard. We cannot, in good conscience, subscribe to a utopian proposition that seeks zero tolerance for environmental hazards. Instead, we face the paradox of a modern industrial society:

Everyone wants the goods supplied by a technologically advanced community yet no one wants the by-products of society's industrial capacity—pollution. To live within the paradox requires realization that there is no "away" when we throw things away. Every "away" is someone's backyard. We therefore accept the premise that siting of new industries, landfills, and other hazardous waste facilities must take into account preexisting facilities and that levels of pollution must be managed in such a way as to reduce—not exacerbate—its impact on current life.

The second component of the rational comprehensive model maintains that goals, values, or objectives that guide the decisionmaker are clarified and ranked according to their importance. The items under this component flow from the first component—that no definable group in society is exposed to a disproportionate share of environmental harms—either in terms of new siting decisions or in terms of exposure to higher levels of the by-products of industrial society.[2]

The third component of the rational comprehensive model is that a complete set of alternative policies for the problem is prepared. The alternate policies that derive from the environmental injustice literature appear to be four in number: a political-based solution; a class-based solution; a race-based solution; and a risk-based solution. The political-, class-, and race-based solutions conform to the items included in our simple tripartite model. The risk-based solution has its origins in several forums—including our own research. For example, Benjamin Chavis—an environmental justice entrepreneur—first suggested a variation of the risk-based solution in his February 25, 1992, testimony before a congressional subcommittee.[3] Another author (Foreman, 1998: 117) maintains that we should—within the confines of environmental justice—begin to think in terms of risk priorities such that our attention is focused on ranking hazards in terms of most serious to most trivial, and then concentrate on the most serious hazards first. The same worst-first strategy has been recommended by other researchers as well—although not necessarily within the body of literature collected under the rubric of environmental justice (see, e.g., Andrews, 1998; Kraft and Scheberle, 1995: 113–121).

The fourth, fifth, and sixth components of the rational comprehensive model maintain that the consequences—costs and benefits, advantages and disadvantages—that would follow from the selection of each alternative are investigated; each alternative, and its attendant consequences, can be calculated and compared with other alternatives; and the decisionmaker chooses the alternative that maximizes attainment of goals, values, and objectives. Assessing these three components requires us to turn to the specifics of the four policy alternatives that have been isolated: politics, class, race, and severity. We do this in a later section of this chapter.

Equity in Policy Design

Our second criterion is equity in policy design, meaning that the policy selected should be one that meets stringent criteria for justice and fairness to
all groups in society (Dunn, 1994: 286; Nagel, 1984: 69). "Equity" is normally defined in terms of equality across groups. More specifically, it refers
to providing benefits (or detriments) equally to groups that are alike on
whatever characteristics society defines as being relevant to one's worthiness
in receiving benefits or detriments (Nagel, 1984: 42). Sometimes it also
means that two or more places, groups, or people receive proportionate
equality. In other words, the benefits would be distributed in a manner that
recognizes the scale of the problem for each group (Nagel, 1984: 69). We
would hope that the ultimate policy selected would distribute benefits in an
equal manner to all affected groups, meaning the poor, the affluent, minorities, and nonminorities. In other words, we are opposed to preferential
treatment policies that distribute benefits only to selected groups but ignore
other groups with serious pollution problems. Such policies would not, in
our view, be equitable because they would ignore serious problems for some
groups.

The policy we focus on as the best alternative—a risk-based solution—
appears to meet equity concerns in that it has the potential for assuring that
the benefits of a livable environment are available to all equally—meaning
the poor and the nonpoor and minorities and nonminorities alike.

Efficiency in Policy Design

The final criterion we have selected is efficiency, or the amount of effort required to produce a given level of effectiveness (Dunn, 1994: 283). It normally means that the selected policy should be one that combines cost-
effectiveness and goal achievement (Nagel, 1984: 42–44; Weimer and Vining,
1992: 221–222). Policies that achieve the greatest effectiveness at the least
cost are said to be efficient (Dunn, 1994: 283). Thus, we are seeking a policy
that is a combination of outcome desirability (rational, comprehensive, and
equitable) and output costliness. In other words, we desire a policy that provides the best possible outcome at the least possible cost.

Under cost considerations, two caveats are in order. First, we adopt the
position that financial and other necessary resources are not unlimited. In
brief, environmental protection—albeit an important societal concern—is
one among many concerns on the governmental agenda: education, health,
defense, and the like, all of which compete for a share of the pie. As such,
when resources—money, the attention of decisionmakers, technical competence, information—are scarce, any policy alternative must make do with
the resources that are available. And these limited resources cannot be obli-

gated on the basis of decisions that show little chance of success or, in the alternative, that will produce results that are the exact opposite of the original intent.

The second caveat regarding cost-effectiveness is that any policy that requires more than simply filling in forms is going to cost money. Although siting decisions for new facilities will basically entail information costs, reducing pollution at existing sites or cleaning up abandoned sites represent another consideration. Pollution reduction and cleanup are expensive problems—and although we are mindful of cost-effectiveness as a guiding factor, policymakers, at the outset, must be mindful that dollars will have to be spent. In short, "efficiency" and "cost-effectiveness" are not synonyms for "cheap."

The Alternative Policy Designs Evaluated

The existing alternatives advanced as a means of achieving environmental justice consist of a political-based solution, a class-based solution, a race-based solution, and a risk-based solution. The following sections analyze each alternative in light of our selected criteria: rationality, equity, and efficiency. To aid the reader, we have prepared Figure 10.1, which summarizes the results for each policy in light of these three criteria.

A Political-Based Solution

We begin with this policy solution because we think it is the weakest of the four alternatives. In this policy design, decisions on siting new facilities and cleanup of existing sites would be based primarily on political considerations. In other words, decisions under this policy alternative would be driven largely by active and vocal groups (or possibly even partisan demands), whether minority or nonminority, affluent or nonaffluent, supportive or not of incumbent administrations.

This solution fails to take into account many of our criteria and, furthermore, does not fit either the analysis that resulted from Chapters 5–7 or the historical record. We begin by analyzing this solution under our three criteria and weave in, as applicable, the evidence from our analysis and the historical record as well.

Rationality and the Political-Based Solution. The political-based solution does not appear to meet any of the components of the rational comprehensive model. First, trying to separate the vocal demands of multiple constituencies—minority and nonminorities, affluent and nonaffluent, all mixed within the confines of supporters and nonsupporters of incumbent administrations—is an impossible task. Under these conditions, claims of

FIGURE 10.1   Summary of the Utility of Alternative Policy Solutions
Based on the Selected Criteria of Rationality, Equity, and Efficiency

Criteria/Alternate Policies	Politically Based Solution	Class Based Solultion	Race Based Solution	Risk Based Solution
Rationality				
Given Problem is Separable/Comparable	No	Yes	Yes	Yes
Goals, values, or objectives can be clarified and ranked	No	Yes	Yes	Yes
A complete list of alternate policies are compared	No	No	No	Yes
Consequences of alternate policies are compared	No	No	No	Yes
Consequences can be calculated and compared	No	No	No	Yes
Selected alternate maximized goals/values/objectives	No	No	No	Yes
Equity: Solution is Equitable for all Groups	No	No	Yes-Black Population Marginal-Hispanic Population	Yes
Efficiency: Solution is cost effective	No	No	No	Yes
Total Positive Evaluations[1]	0	2	3	8

Source: Compiled by the authors.
Notes:
[1]The score in this row results from adding one point for each "yes" entry in the various cells.

affluent mainstream groups, which are well positioned within incumbent administrations, would receive the highest priority. Given the track record and results of our analysis in Chapter 3—wherein we demonstrate that environmental justice has tried to obtain and maintain a position on the policy agenda for some three decades with only marginal success—we feel a political-based solution would result in predominately poor and minority communities continuing to be the prime sites of environmental hazards.

This solution would also ensure that goals, values, and objectives that guide decisionmakers are not clarified and ranked according to importance.

First, under the political-based solution, the well-financed squeaky wheel gets the grease. This consideration, by definition, would exclude the claims of poorer communities. Second, in a world of competing claims, decision-makers begin to assign importance, not on the basis of objective criteria associated with the problem to be solved but rather on the basis of the largest constituency; minorities, by definition, cannot be classified as the largest or most important constituency because in the competition for votes and campaign contributions they simply lack the requisite resources necessary to ensure continued dominance over the political agenda. In short, under this component goals, values, and objectives are transformed from environmental protection for all to environmental protection for the affluent mainstream and favored few.

The third criteria in the rational comprehensive model is that a complete set of alternate policies is prepared. Under the political-based solution, a complete set of alternatives would not be prepared. Instead, only the alternatives prepared by the favored few would be considered. If this situation eventuated—as we assume would be the case—the remaining components of the rational comprehensive model could not be used in that costs-benefits, advantages-disadvantages, and attendant consequences of policy outcomes would be skewed away from concerns about environmental justice.

Equity and the Political-Based Solution. Equity in policy design means that the policy selected would be one that meets stringent criteria for justice and fairness to all groups in society. We feel that the political-based solution would not meet equity considerations on several grounds. According to our analyses in Chapters 5–7, the burden of environmental hazards has not been distributed in an equitable fashion. Our analysis finds consistent evidence of environmental injustice for African Americans at the state, county, and city levels. We also found some degree of environmental injustice affecting Hispanics and the less affluent. Our conclusions from this analysis is that whether by accident, design, or a massive fit of political inattentiveness the activities of active and vocal groups working within the skein of existing political relationships have not resulted in an equitable situation. Further, one of our key findings—highlighted in Chapter 8—was the failure of the political-mobilization concept to perform as hypothesized. Under these conditions, we would not expect a political-based solution to produce an equitable policy outcome.

Efficiency and the Political-Based Solution. It is our view that the political-based solution would not combine cost-effectiveness and goal achievement—that is, this solution would not provide the best possible outcome at the least possible cost.

Decisions based on politics blow with the prevailing winds, that is, as administrations change or new vocal and active groups make their claims on existing finite resources, the allocation of priorities is often altered dramatically. Under these conditions, last year's decisions on resource allocation to solve problems often slide to the bottom of the spending ladder and new allocations (based on new priorities) come to the fore. This shift means that old but needed projects wind up starved for funds at crucial stages while new projects consume a disproportionate share of resources for start-up costs. This well-known feature of political policymaking leads to large expenditures, low returns on investment, and myriad projects that never quite reach completion.

A Summary of the Political-Based Solution. Our analysis of the political-based solution—given the criteria of rationality, equity, and efficiency—indicates that this is the least favored of the four alternatives. It does not lead to a rational, equitable, or efficient policy outcome. Indeed, from all indications it would result in a continuation—as opposed to a cessation—of environmental injustice.

A Class-Based Solution

Under this alternative, the actions governing siting and cleanup decisions would be based primarily on class characteristics. In other words, action would be driven by the needs of geopolitical units with poorer—as opposed to more affluent—populations.

Rationality and the Class-Based Solution. The class-based solution would be amenable to some of the components of the rational comprehensive model. First, decisionmakers would be confronted with a given problem that was separable from other problems or at least could be considered in meaningful fashion in comparison to other problems, that is, locating poor communities and assessing their level of existing environmental hazards are entirely feasible undertakings in that definitions of poverty exist and information about existing environmental hazards is readily available. Second, goals, values, and objectives that guide decisionmaking can be clarified and ranked according to importance under this alternate solution.

However, the third component of the rational comprehensive model does present a problem. Focusing solely on poverty as the source of the problem results in alternate policy solutions being discounted. Although we feel that our previous analysis of the political-based solution had eliminated all alternative policy choices, a focus on poverty precludes consideration of alternatives based on race or risk. As such, the class-based solution immediately limits the range of alternatives that a decisionmaker might consider. Furthermore, because of the limiting feature of poverty, the fourth, fifth, and sixth components of the rational comprehensive model would be exceedingly limited in that only costs-benefits and advantages-disadvantages of policy decisions based on poverty would be considered as being viable policy designs.

Equity and the Class-Based Solution.   An equitably designed policy would meet stringent criteria for justice and fairness to all groups in society. A class-based solution to the problems of siting new facilities or abating existing pollution would not meet stringent equity considerations. First, focusing solely on poor communities excludes nonpoor communities from the solution agenda. Second, consider the following class-based paradox. Assume the existence of two adjacent communities—one affluent and the other not. Polluting facilities exist in the affluent community, however, prevailing wind conditions disperse pollutants to the less-affluent geopolitical unit. A class-based solution would result in the assignment of a low priority for cleanup to the affluent community because this geopolitical unit did not meet the decision criteria of being poor. The outcome of this scenario is that the class-based policy would preclude or delay pollution abatement in the affluent community, and the less affluent area would still be faced with a class-based inequity that the policy was powerless to address.

Efficiency and the Class-Based Solution.   "Efficiency" means that the policy alternative should achieve the greatest effectiveness at the least cost. The class-based solution would not be efficient. Chapters 5–7 indicate that social class was associated with 35–50 percent of the environmental harms in our equations. Thus, social class is unrelated to many environmental harms across the multiple levels of analysis in our inquiry. Basing a policy on social class would therefore not be efficient in that this concept is not tied to all environmental harms within all geopolitical locales. As such, a class-based solution would, by definition, be unable to achieve the greatest effectiveness at the lowest possible cost.

A Summary of the Class-Based Solution.   Our analysis of the class-based solution indicates that this policy alternative meets two of our rationality concerns—a problem that is separable and comparable and that the goals, values, or objectives can be clarified and ranked. Yet as shown in Figure 10.1, the analysis of the class-based solution does not fare well in comparison with the remaining four rationality components and also fails to meet equity and effectiveness considerations. Thus, although this policy alternative is somewhat superior to the political-based solution, it is still far from optimal.

A Race-Based Solution

In this policy design, siting decisions and appropriations for cleanup resources for existing environmental hazards would be based on racial characteristics; accordingly, geopolitical units with increasing proportions of black and/or Hispanic populations would receive the highest consideration for cleanup funds.

Rationality and the Race-Based Solution. A race-based solution would be amenable to some of the components of the rational comprehensive model. First, the decisionmaker would be confronted with a given problem that was separable from other problems or at least comparable to other problems. In other words, locating predominately minority communities and assessing the level of existing environmental hazards is an entirely feasible undertaking in that race-based demographic portraits of communities exist and information about existing environmental hazards is available. Second, goals, values, and objectives that guide decisionmaking can be clarified and ranked according to importance under this alternative solution. For example, our analyses in Chapters 5–7 indicate that race-based inequities for the black population were significantly higher in Sunbelt counties; the same type of inequity was visited upon Hispanics in western substate regions of the United States.

However, the third component of the rational comprehensive model does present a problem. Focusing solely on race as the driving force behind policy solutions results in alternative policy solutions being discounted. Furthermore, the fourth, fifth, and six components of the rational comprehensive model would be exceedingly limited in that only the cost-benefits and advantages-disadvantages of policy decisions based on the size of the proportion of minorities within a geopolitical unit would be considered as being the viable policy design.

Equity and the Race-Based Solution. A policy that meet our equity criteria would be one that provides justice and fairness to all groups in society—regardless of their proportionality to the total population in any geopolitical unit. A race-based solution to the problems of siting new facilities or abating existing levels of environmental hazards does not meet stringent equity considerations. First, focusing on predominantly minority communities (more than 50 percent minority) excludes consideration of minority communities with—for example—only 20 percent black and/or Hispanic populations. As such, the race-based solution, which looks to locales populated by large numbers of minorities, disadvantages geopolitical units where small percentages of minorities are present—regardless of the level of the environmental problem.[4]

A second equity consideration takes the following form. Assume the existence of two adjacent communities, one predominantly nonminority, the other—by comparison—predominantly minority. The polluting facilities exist in the predominantly nonminority community, but prevailing wind patterns result in the minority community being adversely affected by the facilities sited in the neighboring nonminority community. A race-based solution in this circumstance would result in the following combined inequity. The nonminority community would be assigned a low priority for abatement because it lacked a sufficiently large minority population. Concurrently, the adjacent minority community—the recipient of its neighbor's pollution—would get no funds because it had no polluting facilities. Under these conditions, both the predominantly minority and nonminority communities would continue to suffer.

Finally, the race-based solution would fail to meet stringent equity criteria based on the results in Chapters 5–7. In several instances, we found that the exposure of minorities to environmental harms had a regional component, with black communities in Sunbelt states and Hispanic communities in western states exposed to higher levels of pollution. A race-based solution that was driven solely by large population figures would not be able to deal with situations wherein regional considerations matter.

Efficiency and the Race-Based Solution.   "Efficiency" means that the policy achieves the greatest effectiveness at the least cost. We do not feel that a race-based policy would be efficient in all cases. The results in our earlier chapters did indicate that 85 percent of our equations reported race-based inequities for the black population. However, only 50 percent of our equations reported race-based inequities for the Hispanic population. Thus, although a race-based solution might be cost-effective when dealing with one minority population, adapting it for all minority populations might not achieve the intended results.

A Summary of the Race-Based Solution.   Our analysis of the race-based solution—which uses the criteria of rationality, equity, and efficiency—indicates that this policy alternative meets two of our rationality concerns: a problem that is separable and comparable and that goals, values, and objectives can be clarified and ranked. Yet as shown in Figure 10.1, the analysis of the race-based solution did not fare well in comparison to the remaining four rationality components. Furthermore, the race-based solution did not meet the stringent equity criteria for justice and fairness to all groups. Indeed, we found two instances wherein a race-based solution might create racial inequities for minority populations. Finally, although the race-based solution would be cost-effective for most of the black population in the United States, it would be cost-effective for only some Hispanic communities.

A Risk-Based Solution

In this instance, decisions on siting new facilities and abatement of existing environmental hazards would be driven by the severity of the pollution problem. In other words, siting decisions and allocations of cleanup funds would be driven by the threat or health risks posed by existing environmental hazards and, concurrently, what those hazards entail. Environmental degradation does not consist solely of aesthetic degradation, that is, we are not simply concerned with the consequences of unpleasant smells and diminished physical attractiveness of polluted areas. We are also concerned with the nature of the risks that pollution poses for human health.

Rationality and the Risk-Based Solution.   The risk-based solution appears to meet the requirements of all six components of the rational comprehensive model. First, the decisionmaker is dealing with a problem that can be separated from other problems or at least can be considered meaningfully in comparison to other problems. Pollution is measurable in many ways; the existence of active sites as well as abandoned sites can be considered. The nature of health risks posed by the sites is measurable. The predominance of existing sites can be cataloged in order to determine what additional siting decisions will do to the surrounding area; such decisions are relatively clear-cut and can be quantified.

Second, the goals, values, and objectives that guide decisionmaking can be clarified and ranked according to importance, and in ranking goals, values, and objectives the decisionmaker is presented with a plethora of options. For example, decisions can be clarified or ranked for such concerns as siting new facilities and the impact of the new sites on the surrounding areas. Furthermore, communities can be ranked by the number of abandoned sites or active sites and in terms of the level of pollution that is produced. Finally, the health risks posed by the synergistic effects of different combinations of specific pollutants can be considered. And although the latter ranking would be a complex task, its clarification under this component does not render the ranking insolvable. These are options that were not available to decisionmakers under the political-, class-, or race-based alternatives that were previously analyzed.

Third, because the goals, values, and objectives of the policy can be clarified and ranked according to importance, decisions could branch out to a set of alternate policies for the various siting, abatement, and health concerns. Previous policies had not allowed for a broadening of the policy; instead, previous solutions narrowed the range of alternatives available to the decisionmaker. Indeed, the previous solutions seem to have the same effect on the third component—imposing a tunnel-vision effect on what could be considered as a viable consideration.

Fourth, the cost-benefit and advantages-disadvantages of ranking various locales on siting, abatement, and health concerns could be investigated so that the attendant consequences of decisions could be calculated and compared. Finally, the risk-based solution allows decisionmakers to select a siting decision, cleanup priority, or health concern that maximizes the overall goals, values, and objectives of an environment that is more conducive to the total population. These components of the rational comprehensive model were not available for the previous three alternative solutions.

Equity and the Risk-Based Solution.   "Equity" in policy design means that the solution meets stringent criteria for justice and fairness to all groups in society. Additionally, it refers to providing benefits—or detriments—equally to all groups that are alike on whatever characteristic society defines as being relevant. Furthermore, equity recognizes that benefits would be distributed in a manner that recognizes the scale of the problem for each group.

A risk-based solution appears to meet the requirements of the equity criteria nicely. The poor, the affluent, minorities, and nonminorities would have equal access to benefits. For example, absence of financial resources and lack of political mobilization would not mean that poor and minority communities would be overlooked or shunted aside when considering siting of new facilities, cleanup of existing hazards, and health hazards associated with pollution. If the community, regardless of its demographic profile, faced a pollution problem, then funds and other resources would be directed toward solving the identified level of risk—uncontaminated by either racism or classism.

Second, the equity paradoxes noted in our examination of class- and race-based solutions would be vitiated. These paradoxes are combined and repeated for the reader's convenience. Assume the existence of two adjacent communities, one relatively affluent and predominantly nonminority, the other poor and predominantly minority. The first community has a high level of polluting industry, but prevailing wind conditions disperse the pollutants to the poorer, predominantly minority community. Under the risk-based solution, abatement funds would be directed to the relatively affluent nonminority community, because that is the site of the serious pollution problem. Concurrently, funds to deal with health risks could be directed toward the less-affluent, predominately minority community to deal with that problem. Neither outcome would have been possible under the class- and race-based solutions. Indeed, under the risk-based solution, communities that are widely different in terms of race and class—such as Toole, Utah (which is relatively affluent and predominately nonminority and consistently has the highest level of toxic releases in the nation) and the toxic doughnut in Chicago (a community that is poor and predominantly minority according to census data) would each be given equal consideration. Under the class- and race-based solutions, Toole would not be given consideration, even if the surrounding communities were predominantly poor or minority.

Efficiency and the Risk-Based Solution. "Efficiency" means that the policy achieves the greatest effectiveness at the least cost. Concentrating on the severity of the problem—be it conceptualized as improved siting decisions, pollution abatement, or alleviating health concerns arising from toxic pollutants—would allow for achievement of a broad range of solutions that could piggyback the costs of one problem upon another. Unlike the political-based solution, with its hypothesized continuously altered funding priorities, and the class- and race-based solutions, which did not always direct funds to the most serious problem, the risk-based solution directs funds to the most serious concerns first.

A Summary of the Risk-Based Solution. Our rationality, equity, and efficiency analysis of the risk-based solution points up the utility of adopting this approach to the problem of environment injustice. This solution fits well within the six components of the rational comprehensive model and allows for a broadening—not a narrowing—of options. It provides equity for all under circumstances that neither the class- nor race-based solutions could accomplish. Finally, this solution is efficient in that it allows for maximizing results in a cost-effective manner.

Although our analysis of the various alternative solutions has been different from those of other authors, we are pleased by the level of agreement between our conclusions and those of other authors who have recommended a similar method of handling the problem. For example, the results of our analysis for the risk-based solution mirror the ideas proposed by Benjamin Chavis in 1992 when he first proposed the 1992 Environmental Equity Act. Chavis proposed isolating the worst 100 geopolitical units in the country and allocating funds to handle the siting, abatement, and health-related problems associated with environmental degradation.

Furthermore, Christopher Foreman calls the solution we have selected a "rationalizing approach" (Foreman, 1998: 109–136), and he cites Albert Nichols (1994) in support of this particular solution:

> If we accept the argument that the existing [politicized] approach has paid insufficient attention to the health and environmental risks faced by minority communities, what does this say then about a risk-based alternative? A strategy that emphasized attacking the largest and most easily reduced risks first would appear to represent a major gain for minority communities. To the extent that such communities bear unusually high risks as a result of past discrimination or

other factors, a risk-based approach would direct more resources to these communities. Indeed, a risk-based approach would give highest priority to attacking precisely the kinds of problems that concern Bullard (Nichols, 1994: 268).

Other scholars have argued for setting meaningful priorities for risk reduction and cost-effective pollution control policies (Andrews, 1998; Helfand and Peyton, 1999; Portney, 1991). Still others argue for environmental policies that combine both equity and risk assessment (see, e.g., Kraft and Scheberle, 1995: 113–121; Sexton, Anderson, and Adgate, 1999). The uniformity of the call for a risk-based solution, based on different arguments and different methods of analysis, would seem to lend a high degree of credibility to our rationality-equity-efficiency analysis, which has also arrived at the same preferred risk-based solution selected by other policy analysts.

Conclusion

This book has covered a wide range of topics associated with the question of environmental justice in the United States. We started with the nature of the problem in Chapter 1, reviewed the existing evidence in Chapter 2, and outlined how the question arrived on the agenda in Chapter 3. In Chapters 4–8, we outlined a wide range of statistical analysis that clearly articulated the scope and nature of the problem confronting the nation. In Chapter 9, we outlined actions by the federal and state governments designed to deal with aspects of the problem. Finally, Chapter 10 assessed the arguments about how to deal with the problem in a far more systematic and coherent fashion that has been heretofore attempted. This long journey has allowed us to recommend future directions for policy development that are based on rationality, equity, and efficiency. In doing so, we have argued that a risk-based solution would be the most desirable policy option for dealing with the problem.

Thus, we will close with the admonition made by Aaron Wildavsky some years ago:

> Whatever the combination, speaking truth to power remains the ideal of analysts who hope they have truth, but realize they have not power. No one can do analysis without becoming aware that moral considerations are integral to the enterprise. After all, analysis is about what ought to be done, about making things better, not worse (Wildavsky, 1979: 12–13).

It is our fervent hope that this policy analysis will make the problem of environmental injustice much better and not worse. After all, policy analysis is about improvement—about improving governmental and citizen decisionmaking for the policies they have before them, about improving the environment that gave rise to the problem in the first place. If we have helped in this complex yet terribly important process, then our mission is completed, and our reward is the satisfaction that comes from the labor therein.

Notes

1. We are using the term "rationality" as a surrogate or substitute for the usual criteria of "responsiveness and appropriateness."

2. Our analysis of environmental injustice was based on the strategic choice to focus, wherever possible, on the *level* of pollution with geopolitical units. We made this choice because it is the pollution dispersed into the community that is the source point of the problem. Our analyses in Chapters 5–7 do not speak to siting of new facilities. However, siting new facilities is of concern, and thus we need to discuss this aspect of the problem when dealing with policy alternatives.

3. U.S. House of Representatives, Subcommittee on Health and the Environment, Committee on Energy and Commerce, 1992, Impact of Lead Poisoning on Low-Income and Minority Communities, 102nd Cong., 2nd Sess., February 25, 1992.

4. This is not an implausible situation. Indeed, the *Bean* case—discussed in Chapter 3—encountered this problem. The *Bean* case, a 1979 class-action lawsuit over hazardous waste against the city of Houston, Texas, and Houston-headquartered Brown Ferris Industries, was a major event in putting environmental racism on the policy agenda. The *Bean* case focused on opposition to a plan to site a municipal landfill near a suburban, middle-income neighborhood and a predominately African American high school. In their move for a preliminary injunction against the Texas Department of Health's disposal permit, the plaintiffs argued, in part, that the Texas Department of Health had engaged in a broader pattern of historical discrimination by allowing the siting of disposal facilities in minority communities. In support of their claim, the plaintiffs advanced statistical evidence compiled by Professor Robert Bullard that indicated that in Houston 82.4 percent of the seventeen disposal facilities in operation since 1978 were located in areas where the minority population was 50 percent or less. Of the total number of sites, 59 percent were in areas where the minority population was 25 percent or less. The trial court's opinion in *Bean* did not substantiate the claim of discrimination, noting that more than half of the sites were located in census tracts with minority populations of less than 25 percent. In sum, the *Bean* decision indicates that unless the minority population is large, regardless of the level of environmental hazards, official notice will not be taken of the problem of a race-based inequity. This is exactly the equity problem discussed in our hypothetical example.

References

Achen, C.H. 1982. *Interpreting and Using Regression*. Beverly Hills, Calif.: Sage Publications.

Adeola, Francis O. 1994. "Environmental Hazards, Health, and Racial Inequity in Hazardous Waste Distribution Commission." *Environment and Behavior* 26(1): 99–126.

Advisory on Intergovernmental Relations. 1984. *Regulatory Federalism: Policy, Process, Impact, and Reform*. Washington, D.C.: Advisory Commission on Intergovernmental Relations.

Aiken, L.S., and S.G. West. 1991. *Multiple Regression: Testing and Interpreting Interactions*. Newbury Park, Calif.: Sage Publications.

Allen, D.W. Forthcoming 2001. "Social Class, Race, and Toxic Releases in American Counties, 1995." *Social Science Journal*.

Allen, D.W., J.P. Lester, and K.M. Hill. 1995. "Prejudice, Profits, and Power: Assessing the Eco-Racism Thesis at the County Level." Paper prepared for the annual meeting of the Western Political Science Association, Portland, Oregon, March 16–18.

Almedia, P. 1994. "The Network for Environmental and Economic Justice in the Southwest: Interview with Richard M. Moore." *Capitalism, Nature, Socialism* 5(1): 21–54.

Anderton, D. L. 1996. "Methodological Issues in the Spatiotemporal Analysis of Environmental Equity." *Social Science Quarterly* 77(3): 508–515.

Anderton, D. L., A. Anderson, J. M. Oates, and M. Fraser. 1994a. "Hazardous Waste Facilities: Environmental Equity Issues in Metropolitan Areas." *Evaluation Review* 18(2): 123–140.

———. 1994b. "Environmental Equity: The Demographics of Dumping." *Demography* 31: 229–48

Andrews, C.J. 1998. "Public Policy and the Geography of the U.S. Environmentalism." *Social Science Quarterly* 79(1): 57–73.

Angel, B. 1992. *The Toxic Threat to Indian Lands: A Greenpeace Report*. San Francisco: Greenpeace.

Arora, S., and T.N. Carson. 1999. "Do Community Characteristics Influence Environmental Outcomes? Evidence from the Toxic Release Inventory." *Southern Economic Journal* 65(4) 691–716.

Asch, P., and J.J. Seneca. 1978. "Some Evidence on the Distribution of Air Quality." *Land Economics* 54(3): 278–297.

Attah, E.B. 1992. "Demographics and Siting Issues in Region IV." Proceedings of the Clark Atlanta and EPA Region IV Conference on Environmental Equity.

Austin R., and M. Shills. 1991. "Black, Brown, Poor, and Poisoned: Minority Grassroots Environmentalism and the Quest for Eco-Justice." *Kansas Journal of Law and Public Policy* (Summer): 69–82.

Baer, D.L., and D.A. Bositis. 1993. *Politics and Linkage in a Democratic Society*. Englewood Cliffs, N.J.: Prentice-Hall.

Banks, J., and B. Weingast. 1992. "The Political Control of Bureaucracies under Asymmetric Information." *American Journal of Political Science* 36(2): 509–524.

Barkenbus, J.N., J. Peretz, and J.D. Rubin. 1996. "More on the Agenda." *Social Science Quarterly* 77(3): 516–519.

Beasley, C. 1990a. "Of Pollution and Poverty: Reaping America's Unseemly Harvest." *Buzzworm* 2(3): 40–47.

_____. 1990b. "Of Pollution and Poverty: Keeping Watch in Cancer Alley." *Buzzworm* 2(4): 39–45.

Been, V. 1994. "Locally Undesirable Land Uses in Minority Neighborhoods: Disproportionate Siting or Market Dynamics." *Yale Law Journal* 103(6): 1383–1422.

_____. 1995. "Analyzing Evidence of Environmental Justice." *Journal of Land Use and Environmental Law* 11: 1–36.

Bentley, A. 1967. *The Process of Government*. Ed. Peter Odegrad. Cambridge, Mass.: Belknap Press of Harvard University [orig. publ. 1908].

Benton, J.E., and D.R. Morgan. 1986. *Intergovernmental Relations and Public Policy*. Westport, Conn.: Greenwood Press.

Bernstein, M. 1955. *Regulating Business by Independent Commissions*. Princeton: Princeton University Press.

Berry, B.J. 1977. *The Social Burdens of Environmental Pollution*. Cambridge, Mass.: Ballinger Publishing Company.

Boer, J.T., M. Pastor, Jr., J.L. Sadd, and L.D. Synder. 1997. "Is There Environmental Racism? The Demographics of Hazardous Waste in Los Angeles County." *Social Science Quarterly* 78(4): 793–810.

Boerner, C., and T. Lambert. 1995. "Environmental Justice in the City of St. Louis: The Economics of Siting Industrial and Waste Site Facilities." *Center for the Study of American Business*. Washington University, Campus Box 1208, One Brookings Drive, St. Louis, Missouri, 63130.

Bowen, W.M., M.J. Salling, K.E. Hayner, and E.J. Cryan. 1995. "Toward Environmental Justice: Spatial Equality in Ohio and Cleveland." *Annals of the Association of American Geographers* 85: 641–663.

Bowman, A. O'M. 1996. "Environmental (In)Equity: Race, Class and the Distribution of Environmental Bads." In S. Kamieniecki, G. Gonzales, and R.O. Vos, eds. *Flashpoints in Environmental Policy Making: Controversies in Achieving Sustainable Development*. Albany: State University of New York Press.

_____. 1995. "Locating Southern LULUs: Is It Race, Class, or Land?" Paper prepared for the annual meeting of the Western Political Science Association, Portland, Oregon, March 16–18.

Bowman, A. O'M., and K. Crews-Meyer. 1997. "Locating Southern LULUs: Race, Class, and Environmental Justice." *State and Local Government Review* 29: 110–119.

Bowman, A. O'M., and R.C. Kearney. 1986. *The Resurgence of the States*. Englewood Cliffs, N.J.: Prentice-Hall.

Brewer, G.D., and P. deLeon. 1983. *The Foundations of Policy Analysis*. Homewood, Ill.: Dorsey Press.

Brion, D.J. 1988. "An Essay on LULU, NIMBY, and the Problem of Distributive Justice." *Boston College Environmental Affairs Law Review* 15(3–4): 437–503.

Brown, A.L. 1992. "Environmental Justice: New Civil Rights Frontier." *Trial* 29(7): 48–54.

Brown, P., and S. Masterson-Allen. 1994. "The Toxic Waste Movement: A New Type of Activism." *Society and Natural Resources* 7: 269–287.

Bruce, C.E. 1993. "Environmentalism and Student Activism." *Black Collegian* 23(4): 52–57.

Bruce, C.E., and P. Mohai. 1992. *Race and the Incidence of Environmental Hazards: A Time for Discourse*. Boulder: Westview Press.

_____. 1992. "The Michigan Conference: A Turning Point." *EPA Journal* 18(1): 10.

Bryant, B. 1995. *Environmental Justice: Issues, Politics, and Solutions*. Washington, D.C.: Island Press.

Bulanowski, G.A. 1981. *The Impact of Science and Technology on the Decision-making Process in State Legislatures: The Issue of Solid and Hazardous Waste*. Denver: National Conference of State Legislatures.

Bullard, R.D. 1983. "Solid Waste Sites and the Black Houston Community." *Sociological Inquiry* 53: 273–288.

_____. 1990a. *Dumping in Dixie: Race, Class, and Environmental Quality*. Boulder: Westview Press.

_____. 1990b. "Ecological Inequities and the New South: Black Communities Under Siege." *Journal of Ethnic Studies* 17: 101–115.

_____. 1993a. "Waste and Racism: A Stacked Deck?" *Forum for Applied Research and Public Policy* 8: 29–45.

_____. 1993b. "The Threat of Environmental Racism." *Natural Resources and Environment* 7: 23–25, 55–56.

_____. 1994a. *Unequal Protection: Environmental Justice and Communities of Color*. San Francisco: Sierra Club Books.

_____. 1994b. "Overcoming Racism in Environmental Decision-making." *Environment* 36(4): 10–20, 39–44.

_____. 1994c. "Grassroots Flowering: The Environmental Justice Movement Comes of Age." *Amicus Journal* 16(1): 32–37.

Bullard, R.D., and B.H. Wright. 1992. "The Quest for Environmental Equity: Mobilizing the African-American Community for Social Change." In R. Dunlap and A. Mertig, eds. *American Environmentalism: The U.S. Environmental Movement, 1970–1990*. Philadelphia: Taylor and Francis.

Burch, W.R. 1976. "The Peregrine Falcon and the Urban Poor: Some Sociological Interrelations." In P. Richerson and J. McEvoy, eds. *Human Ecology: An Environmental Approach*. Belmont, Calif.: Duxbury Press.

Burke, L.M. 1993. "Race and Environmental Equity: A Geographic Analysis in Los Angeles." *Geo Info Systems* (October): 44–50.

Cable, S., and M. Benson. 1993. "Acting Locally: Environmental Injustice and the Emergence of Grass-Roots Environmental Organizations." *Social Problems* 40(4): 464–470.

Camacho, D.E. 1998. "The Environmental Justice Movement: A Political Framework." In D.E. Camacho, ed. *Environmental Injustice, Political Struggles: Race, Class, and the Environment*. Durham: Duke University Press.

Camia, C. 1993. "Poor, Minorities Want Voices in Environmental Choices." *Congressional Quarterly Weekly Report* 51(34): 121.

Capek, S.M. 1993. "The 'Environmental Justice' Frame: A Conceptual Discussion and an Application." *Social Problems* 40(1): 5–24.

Carroll, G. 1991. "When Pollution Hits Home." *National Wildlife* 29: 30–39.

Chamber, J. 1998. "Environmental Law." *National Law Review* (June 22): B6–B7.

Chase, A. 1992. "Assessing and Addressing Problems Posed by Environmental Racism." *Rutgers Law Review* 45: 335–369.

Chiro, G.D. 1992. "Defining Environmental Justice: Women's Voices and Grassroots Politics." *Socialist Review* 22(4): 93–121.

Clean Sites, Inc. 1990. *Hazardous Waste Sites and the Rural Poor*. Alexandria, Va.: Clean Sites, Inc.

Cohen, J., and P. Cohen. 1983. *Applied Multiple Regression/Correlation Analysis for the Behavioral Sciences*. 2nd ed. Hillsdale, N.J.: Lawrence Erlbaum Associates.

Cole, L.W. 1992a. "Empowerment as the Key to Environmental Protection: The News for Environmental Poverty Law." *Ecology Law Quarterly* 19(4): 619–683.

_____. 1992b. "Remedies for Environmental Racism: A View from the Field." *Michigan Law Review* 90(7): 1191–1197.

_____. 1994. "Environmental Justice Litigation: Another Stone in David's Sling." *Fordham Urban Law Review* 21(3): 523–545.

Coleman, L.A. 1993. "It's the Thought that Counts: The Intent Requirement in Environmental Racism Claims." *St. Mary's Law Journal* 25(1): 447–492.

Collin, R.W. 1992. "Environmental Equity: A Law and Planning Approach to Environmental Racism." *Virginia Environmental Law Journal* 11: 495–546.

_____. 1993. "Environmental Equity and the Need for Government Intervention." *Environment* 35(9): 41–43.

Colopy, J.H. 1994. "The Road Less Traveled: Pursuing Environmental Justice Through Title VI of the Civil Rights Act of 1964." *Stanford Environmental Law Journal* 13(1): 1039–1134.

Colquette, K.M., and E.H. Robertson. 1991. "Environmental Racism: The Causes, Consequences, and Commendations." *Tulane Environmental Law Journal* 5: 153–208.

Costner, P., and J. Thornton. 1990. *Playing with Fire: Hazardous Waste Incineration*. Washington, D.C.: Greenpeace.

Coyle, M. 1992. "Company Will Not Build Plant: Lawyers Hail Victory. *National Law Journal* 15(7) (October 19): 3.

Crews-Meyer, K. 1994. "Race and Hazardous Waste in South Carolina." Paper prepared for the annual meeting of the South Carolina Political Science Association, February 26.

Cushman, J.H. 1993. "U.S. to Weigh Black's Complaints About Pollution." *New York Times*, November 19, p. A1.

_____. 1994. "Clinton to Order Effort to Make Pollution Fairer." *New York Times*, February 10, p. A1.

Cutter, S. 1994. "The Burdens of Toxic Risks: Are They fair?" *Business and Economic Review* 40: 3–37.

_____. 1995. "Race, Class, and Environmental Justice." *Progress in Human Geography* 19: 107–118.

Daniels, G., and S. Friedman. 1999. "Spatial Inequities and the Distribution of Toxic Releases: Evidence from the 1990 TRI." *Social Sciences Quarterly* 80(2): 244–262.

Davies, J. 1972. "The Role of Social Class in Human Pesticide Pollution." *American Journal of Epidemiology* 96: 223–238.

Dellums, R.V. 1992. "A Challenge to Congress: The Need for New Legislation." In U.S. Environmental Protection Agency. "Environmental Protection—Has It Been Fair?" *EPA Journal*. Washington, D.C.: U.S. Government Printing Office.

Dorfman, R. 1979. "Indicence of the Benefits and Costs of Environmental Programs." *Journal of the American Economic Association* 67: 333–340.

Dow Chemical. 1989. *The Morrisville Program: The Morrisville Program Handbook*. Dow Chemical.

Downey, L. 1998. "Race and Income as Predictors of Environmental Justice." *Social Science Quarterly* 79: 766–778.

Downs, A. 1957. *An Economic Theory of Democracy*. New York: Harper-Row.

Doyle, K. 1994. "Environmental Justice: A Growing Movement." *Black Collegian* 24(4): 36–40.

Dubin, J.C. 1993. "From Junkyards to Gentrification: Explicating Right to Protective Zoning in Low-Income Communities of Color." *Minnesota Law Review* 77(4): 739–801.

Dunn, W.N. 1994. *Public Policy Analysis: An Introduction*. 2nd ed. Englewood Cliffs, N.J.: Prentice-Hall.

Dye, T.R. 1995. *Understanding Public Policy*. 8th ed. Englewood Cliffs, N.J.: Prentice-Hall.

Easton, B. 1992. "WHEACT (West Harlem Environmental Action) for Justice." *Environmental Action Magazine* 24(4): 33–36.

Edelman, M. 1964. *The Symbolic Use of Politics*. Urbana: University of Illinois Press.

Edwards, M.D. 1992. "Sustainability and People of Color." *EPA Journal* 18(4): 50–52.

Elazar, D. 1966. *American Federalism: A View from the States*. New York: Thomas Crowell.

_____. 1970. *Cities of the Prairie: The Metropolitan Frontier and American Politics*. New York: Basic Books.

_____. 1972. *American Federalism: A View from the States*. 2nd ed. New York: Thomas Crowell.

Environmental Health Coalition. 1993. *Toxic-Free Neighborhoods Community Planning Guide*. San Diego: Environmental Health Coalition.

Ervin, M. 1992. "The Toxic Doughnut: Toxic Wastes in Minority Neighborhoods." *Progressive* 56(1): 15.

Fitton, L. 1992. *A Study of the Correlation Between the Siting of Hazardous Waste Facilities and Racial and Socioeconomic Characteristics*. M.A. thesis. Department of Political Science, Cornell University.

Foreman, C.H., Jr. 1998. *The Promise and Peril of Environmental Justice*. Washington, D.C.: Brookings Institution.

Freeman, M.A. 1972. "The Distribution of Environmental Quality." In A. Kneese and B.T. Bower, eds. *Environmental Quality Analysis*. Baltimore: Johns Hopkins University Press.

Friedrich, R.J. 1982. "In Defense of Multiplicative Terms in Multiple Regression Equations." *American Journal of Political Science* 26: 797–833.

Fruedenberg, W.R., and S.K. Pastor. 1992. "NIMBYs and LULUs: Stalking the Syndrome." *Journal of Social Issues* 48(4): 39.

Geddicks, A. 1993. *The New Resources Wars: Native and Environmental Struggles Against Multinational Corporations*. Boston: South End Press.

_____. 1994. "Racism and Resource Colonization." *Capitalism, Nature, Socialism* 5(1): 55–76.

Geiser, K., and K. Waneck. 1983. "PCBs and Warren County." *Science for the People* (July/August): 13–17.

Gelobter, M. 1987. *The Distribution of Air Pollution by Income and Race, 1970–1984*. M.A. thesis. University of California–Berkeley.

_____. 1992. "Toward a Model of Environmental Discrimination." In B. Bryant and P. Mohai, eds. *Race and the Incidence of Environmental Hazards: A Time for Discourse*. Boulder: Westview Press.

Gianessi, L., and H. Peskin. 1980. "The Distribution of Federal Water Pollution Control Policy in the United States." *Land Economics* 56: 25–102.

Gianessi, L., H. Peskin, and Edward Wolfe. 1979. "The Distributional Effects of Uniform Air Pollution Policy in the U.S." *Quarterly Journal of Economics*: 281–301.

Glickman, T., and R. Hersh. 1995. *Evaluating Environmental Equity: The Impacts of Industrial Hazards on Selected Social Groups in Allegheny County, Pennsylvania*. Washington, D.C.: Resources for the Future. Discussion Paper 95-13.

Godsil, R.D. 1991. "Remedying Environmental Racism." *Michigan Law Review* 90: 394–427.

Goldman, B.A. 1991. *The Truth about Where You Live: An Atlas for Action on Toxins and Mortality*. New York: Random House.

_____. 1992. " Polluting the Poor." *The Nation*, October 5, pp. 348–349.

Gottlieb, R. 1992. "A Question of Class: The Workplace Experience." *Socialist Review* 22(4): 131–166.

Gould, J.M. 1986. *Quality of Life in American Neighborhoods: Levels of Affluence, Toxic Waste, and Cancer Mortality in Residential Zip Code Areas*. Boulder: Westview Press.

Greenberg, M.R. 1993. "Proving Environmental Equity in Siting Locally Unwanted Land Uses." *Risk: Issues in Health and Safety* 235: 235–252.

_____. 1994. "Separate and Not Equal: Health-Environmental Risk and Economic-Social Impacts in Remediating Hazardous Waste Sites." In S.K. Majumdar, et al. *Environmental Contaminants and Health*. Philadelphia: Pennsylvania Academy of Sciences.

Grossman, K. 1991. "The Impact of Environmental Racism on the Black Community." *The Crisis* 98(4): 14–17.

Hahn-Baker, D. 1994. "Rocky Road to Consensus." *Amicus Journal* 16(1): 41.

Haining, R. 1990. *Spatial Data Analysis in the Social and Environmental Sciences.* New York: Cambridge University Press.

Hair, J.D. 1993. "Providing for Justice as Well as Jobs." *National Wildlife* 31(2): 30.

Hall, B., and M.L. Kerr. 1991. *1991–1992 Green Index.* Washington, D.C.: Island Press.

Hamilton, J.T. 1993. "Policies and Social Cost: Estimating the Impact of Collective Action on Hazardous Waste Facilities." *Rand Journal of Economics* 24: 101–125.

_____. 1995. "Testing for Environmental Racism: Prejudice, Profits, Political Power." *Journal of Policy Analysis and Management* 14(1): 107–132.

Handy, F. 1977. "Income and Air Quality in Hamilton, Ontario." *Alternatives* 6(3): 18–24.

Harding, A.K., and G.R. Holdren, Jr. 1993. "Environmental Equity and the Environmental Profession." *Environmental Science and Technology* 27: 1990–1993.

Harrison, D. 1975. *Who Pays for Clean Air.* Cambridge: Ballinger.

Heclo, Hugh. 1979. "Issue Networks and the Executive Establishment." In Anthony King, ed. *The New American Political System.* Washington, D.C.: American Enterprise Institute.

Helfand, G.E., and L.J. Peyton. 1999. "A Conceptual Model of Environmental Justice." *Social Science Quarterly* 80(1): 68–83.

Hill, K.M. 1996. *Environmental Justice: Getting onto the Agenda.* M.A. thesis. Department of Political Science, Colorado State University, Fort Collins.

Hird, J.A. 1993. "Environmental Policy and Equity: The Case of Superfund." *Journal of Policy Analysis and Management* 12(2): 323–343.

_____. 1994. *Superfund: The Political Economy of Environmental Risk.* Baltimore: Johns Hopkins University Press.

Hird, J.A., and M. Reese. 1998. "The Distribution of Environmental Quality: An Empirical Analysis." *Social Science Quarterly* 79(4): 693–716.

Holm, D.M. 1994. "Environmental Inequities in South Carolina: The Distribution of Hazardous Waste Facilities." M.A. thesis. Department of Geography, University of South Carolina.

Hurley, A. 1988. "The Social Biases of Environmental Change in Gary, Indiana." *Environmental Review* 12(4): 1–19.

Inhaber, H. 1992. "Of LULUs, NIMBYs and NIMTOOs." *Public Interest* 107: 52.

Jennings, E.T., Jr. 1979. "Competition, Constituencies, and Welfare Policies in the American States." *American Political Science Review* 73(2): 414–429.

Jetter, A. 1993. "The Poisoning of a Dream (Environmental Activist Patsy Ruth Oliver)." *Vogue* 183(11): 213–217.

Johnson, C.A. 1976. "Political Culture in the American States: Elazar's Formulation Examined." *American Journal of Political Science* 20: 491–509.

Johnston, B.L., R.C. Williams, and C.M. Harris. 1993. *Proceedings of the 1990 National Minority Health Conference: Focus on Environmental Contamination.* Princeton: Scientific Publishing.

Jones, S.C. 1993a. "EPA Targets Environmental Racism." *National Law Journal* 15(49) (August): 28.

_____. 1993b. "Inequities of Industrial Siting Addressed." *National Law Journal* 15 (August): 20.

Jordan, V. 1980. "Sins of Omission." *Environmental Action* 11: 26–27.

Kamieniecki, S., and J. Steckenrider. 1996. "Two Faces of Equity in Superfund Implementation." In S. Kamieniecki, G.A. Gonzales, and R.O. Vos, eds. *Flashpoints in Environmental Policy Making: Controversies in Achieving Sustainability.* Albany: State University of New York Press.

Kasperson, R.E. 1994. "Global Environmental Hazards: Political Issues in Societal Responses." In G.J. Demko and W.B. Woods, eds. *Reordering the World: Geopolitical Perspectives on the 21ˢᵗ Century.* Boulder: Westview Press.

Kazis, R., and R. Grossman. 1983. *Fear at Work: Job Blackmail, Labor, and the Environment.* New York: Pilgrim Press.

Keeva, S. 1994. "A Breath of Justice: Along with Equal Employment Opportunity and Voting, Living Free from Pollution is Emerging as a New Civil Right." *ABA Journal* 80: 88–92.

Kemp, K. 1981. "Symbolic and Strict Regulation in the American States." *Social Science Quarterly* 62(3): 516–526.

Kim, J., and C.W. Mueller. 1978a. *Introduction to Factor Analysis: What It Is and How to Do It.* Beverly Hills, Calif.: Sage Publications.

_____. 1978b. *Factor Analysis: Statistical Methods and Practical Issues.* Beverly Hills, Calif.: Sage Publications.

Kingdon, J.W. 1984. *Agendas, Alternatives, and Public Policy.* Boston: Little, Brown.

_____. 1995. *Agendas, Alternatives, and Public Policies.* 2nd ed. New York: HarperCollins.

Kmenta, J. 1971. *Elements of Econometrics.* New York: Macmillan.

Kohlhase, J. 1991. "The Impact of Toxic Waste on Housing Values." *Journal of Urban Economics* 30: 1–26.

Kraft, M.E., and D. Scheberle. 1995. "Environmental Justice and the Allocation of Risk." *Policy Studies Journal* 23(1): 113–122.

Krieg, E.J. 1995. "A Socio-Historical Interpretation of Toxic Waste Sites." *American Journal of Economics and Sociology* 54: 191–201.

_____. 1998. "Methodological Considerations in the Study of Toxic Waste Hazards." *Social Science Journal* 35: 191–201.

Kruvant, W.J. 1975. "People, Energy and Pollution." In D.K. Newman and D. Day, eds. *The American Energy Consumer.* Cambridge: Ballinger.

Lampe, D. 1992. "The Politics of Environmental Equity." *National Civic Review* 81(1): 27.

Lavelle, M. 1992a. "Residents Want Justice, the EPA Offers Equity." *National Law Review* (September 21): S12.

_____. 1992b. "Transition Meets with Minorities: Environmental Activists." *National Law Journal* 15(15): 3.

_____. 1993. "Environmental Racism Targeted: Congressional Hearings." *National Law Journal* 15(15): 3.

Lavelle, M., and M. Coyle. 1992. "Unequal Protection: The Racial Divide in Environmental Law." *National Law Journal* (September 21): (Supplement).

Lazarus, R.J. 1993. "Pursuing Environmental Justice: The Distributional Effects of Environmental Protection." *Northwestern University Law Review* 87(3): 787–857.

Lee, C. 1993. "Developing Working Definitions of Urban Environmental Justice." *Earth Island Journal* 8(4): 39–43.

Lester, J.P. 1994. "A New Federalism? Environmental Policy in the States." In N.J. Vig and M.E. Kraft, eds. *Environmental Policy Making in the 1990s.* 2nd ed. Washington, D.C.: Congressional Quarterly Press.

Lester, J.P., and D.W. Allen. 1996. "Prejudice, Profits, and Power: Reassessing the Eco-Racism Thesis at the City Level." Paper prepared for the annual meeting of the Western Political Science Association, San Francisco, March 14–16.

_____. 1999. "Environmental Injustice in the United States: Realities and Myths." Paper prepared for the annual meeting of the Western Political Science Association, Seattle, March 25–27.

Lester, J.P., D.W. Allen, and D.A. Lauer. 1994. "Race, Class, and Environmental Quality: An Examination of Environmental Racism in the American States." Paper prepared for the annual meeting of the Western Political Science Association, Albuquerque, New Mexico, March 10–12.

Lester, J.P., and A. O'M. Bowman, eds. 1983. *The Politics of Hazardous Waste Management.* Durham: Duke University Press.

Lester, J.P., J.L. Franke, A. O'M. Bowman, and K.W. Kramer. 1983. "Hazardous Wastes, Politics, and Public Policy: A Comparative State Analysis." *Western Political Quarterly* 36(2): 301–320.

Lester, J.P., and E.N. Lombard. 1990. "The Comparative Analysis of State Environmental Policy." *Natural Resources Journal* 30(2): 301–319.

Lester, J.P., and J. Stewart, Jr. 2000. *Public Policy: An Evolutionary Approach.* San Francisco, Calif.: Wadsworth/Thompson Learning.

Lewis, S., B. Keating, and D. Russell. 1992. *Inconclusive by Design: Waste, Fraud, and Abuse in Federal Environmental Health Research.* Boston: National Toxics Campaign.

Lewis, V. 1992. "A Message to White Environmentalists." *Earth Island Journal* 7(4): 41.

Lewis-Beck, M. 1979. "The Relative Importance of Socioeconomic and Political Variables for Public Policy." *American Political Science Review* 71(2): 559–566.

Lowi, T. 1979. *The End of Liberalism: The Second Republic of the United States.* New York: W.W. Norton.

Lyskowski, K. 1994. "Environmental Justice: A Research Quide." *Our Earth Matters.* NAACP Legal Defense and Education Fund.

MacLachlan, C. 1992. "Tension Underlies Rapport with Grassroots Groups." *National Law Journal* 15(3): 10.

MacLean, A. 1993. "Bigotry and Poison." *Progressive* 57(1): 14.

Mann, E. 1991. *L.A.'s Lethal Air: New Perspectives for Policy, Organization, and Action.* Los Angeles: Labor/Community Strategy Center.

Maraniss, D., and M. Weisskopf. 1987. "Jobs and Illness in Petrochemical Corridor." *Washington Post,* December 22.

Martinez, E. 1992. "Defending the Earth in '92: A People's Challenge to the EPA." *Social Justice* 19(2): 95.

McCaull, J. 1976. "Discriminatory Air Pollution: If Poor, Don't Breath." *Environment* 18(2): 26–31.

Meyer, E.L. 1992. "Environmental Racism: Why Is It Dumped in Our Backyard? Minority Groups Take a Stand." *Audubon* 94(1): 30–33.

Mitchell, C. 1993. "Environmental Racism: Race as a Primary Factor in the Selection of Hazardous Waste Sites." *National Black Law Journal* 12(3): 176–188.

Mitchell, J.T., D.S.K. Thomas, and S.L. Cutter. 1999. "Dumping in Dixie Revisited: The Evolution of Environmental Injustice in South Carolina." *Social Science Quarterly* 80(2): 229–243.

Mohai, P. 1993. "Commentary: Environmental Equity." *Environment* 35(7): 2–4.

Mohai, P., and B. Bryant. 1992. "Environmental Racism: Reviewing the Evidence." In B. Bryant and P. Mohai, eds. *Race and the Incidence of Environmental Hazards: A Time for Discourse.* Boulder: Westview Press.

Morgenstern, R.D. 1999. "An Historical Perspective on Regulating Decision Making: The Role of Economic Analysis." In K. Sexton, et al., eds. *Better Environmental Decision Making.* Washington, D.C.: Island Press.

Morris, W.T. 1970. "On the Art of Model Building." In R.W. Stogdill, ed. *The Process of Model-Building in the Behavioral Sciences.* New York: W.W. Norton.

Moses, M., et al. 1993. "Environmental Equity and Pesticide Exposure." *Toxicilogy and Industrial Health* 9(5): 913–959.

Multinational Monitor. 1992. "The Politics of Race and Pollution: An Interview with Robert Bullard." *Multinational Monitor* 13(6): 21–26.

Myrdal, G. 1944. *An American Dilemma: The Negro Problem and Modern Democracy.* New York: Harper and Row.

Nagel, S.S. 1984. *Public Policy: Goals, Means, and Methods.* New York: St. Martin's.

Najem, G.R., et al. 1985. "Clusters of Cancer Mortality in New Jersey Municipalities, with Special Reference to Chemical Toxic Waste Disposal Sites and Per Capita Income." *International Journal of Epidemiology* 14(4): 528–537.

National Conference of State Legislatures. 1986. *Legislative Staffing in the Fifty States.* Denver: National Conference of State Legislatures.

_____. 1995. *Environmental Justice: A Matter of Perspective.* Denver: National Conference of State Legislatures.

Nichols, A.L. 1994. "Risk-Based Priorities and Environmental Injustice." In Finkel, A.M., and D. Golding, eds., *Worst Things First? The Debate over Risk-Based National Environmental Priorities.* Washington, D.C.: Resources for the Future.

O'Hare, M., L. Bascow, and D. Sanderson. 1983. *Facility Siting and Public Opposition.* New York: VanNostrand Reinhold.

Ong, P.M., and E. Blumenberg. 1993. "An Unnatural Tradeoff: Latinos and Environmental Justice." In R. Morales and F. Bonilla, eds. *Latinos in a Changing U.S. Economy.* Beverly Hills, Calif.: Sage Publications.

Peck, T., ed. 1989. *Psychological Effects of Hazardous Toxic Waste Disposal on Communities.* Springfield, Ill.: Charles C. Thomas.

Perlin, S.A., R.W. Setzer, J. Creason, and K. Sexton. 1995. "Distribution of Industrial Air Emissions by Income and Race in the United States: An Approach Using the Toxic Release Inventory." *Environmental Science and Technology* 29: 69–80.

Polloch, P.H., and M.E. Vittas. 1995. "Who Bears the Burden of Environmental Pollution? Race, Ethnicity, and Environmental Equity in Florida." *Social Science Quarterly* 76: 294–310.

Portney, K. 1991. *Siting Hazardous Waste Treatment Facilities: The NIMBY Syndrome.* New York: Auburn House.

Posner, R. 1974. "Theories of Economic Regulation." *Bell Journal of Economics and Management Science* 5(3): 337–352.

Ramirez, O. 1992. "The Loss of Native Lands and Economic Blackmail." *Social Justice* 19(2): 78–86.

_____. 1993. "EPA Commissions Civil Rights Allegations." *Environmental Week* 6(40): 1–2.

Rees, M. 1992. "Black and Green: Race and Environmentalism." *New Republic*, March 2, pp. 15–17.

Reich, P.L. 1992. "Greening the Ghetto: A Theory of Environmental Race Discrimination." *Kansas Law Review* 41: 300–331.

Ringquist, E. J. 1993. *Environmental Protection at the State Level: Politics and Progress in Controlling Pollution*. New York: M.E. Sharp.

_____. 1995. "The Sources of Environmental Inequities: Economic Happenstance or Product of the Political System." Paper prepared for the annual meeting of the Western Political Science Association, Portland, Oregon, March 16–18.

_____. 1996. "Searching for Institutional Discrimination: State Facility Siting and Environmental Equity." Paper presented at the annual meeting of the Western Political Science Association, San Francisco, March 14–16.

_____. 1997. "Equity and the Distribution of Environmental Risks: The Case of TRI Facilities." *Social Science Quarterly* 78: 811–819.

_____. 1998. "A Question of Justice: Equity in Environmental Litigation, 1974–1991." *Journal of Politics* 60(4): 1148–1165.

Rios, R., G. Poje, and R. Detels. 1993. "Susceptibility to Environmental Pollutants among Minorities." *Toxicology and Industrial Health* 9(5): 797–820.

Rosenthal, A. 1981. *Legislative Life*. New York: Harper and Row.

Russell, D. 1989. "Environmental Racism." *Amicus Journal* (Spring): 22–32.

Sabatier, P. 1975. "Social Movements and Regulatory Agencies." *Policy Sciences* 17(3): 301–342.

Saffell, D.C. 1990. *State and Local Government: Politics and Public Polic*. 4th ed. New York: McGraw-Hill.

Sanford, T. 1967. *Storm over the States*. New York: McGraw-Hill.

Satchell, M. 1992. "A Whiff of Discrimination? Racism and Environmental Policy." *U.S. News and World Report*, May 4, pp. 34–36.

Schneider, P. 1994. "Respect for Earth: The Environmentalism of Chief Oren Lyons Stems from his Iroquois Heritage." *Audubon* 96(2): 110–115.

Seager, J. 1993. *Earth Follies: Coming to Feminist Terms with the Global Environmental Crisis*. New York: Routledge.

Sexton, K., and Y.B. Anderson. 1993. "Equity in Environmental Health: Research Issues and Needs." *Toxicology and Industrial Health* 9(5) (Special Issue): 89–117.

Sexton, K., Y.B. Anderson, and J.L. Adgate. 1999. "Looking at Environmental Justice from an Environmental Health Perspective." *Journal of Exposure Analysis and Environmental Epilemiology* 9(1): 3–8.

Sexton, K., and R. Zimmerman. 1999. "The Emerging Role of Environmental Justice in Decision Making." In Ken Sexton, et al., eds. *Better Environmental Decisions*. Washington, D.C.: Island Press.

Shaikh, S. 1995. "An Examination of the Presence and Causes of Environmental In-
    equity in Denver, Colorado." M.A. thesis. Department of Economics, Colorado
    State University, Fort Collins.

Shaikh, S., and J.L. Loomis. 1998. "An Investigation into the Presence and Causes of
    Environmental Inequity in Denver, Colorado." *Social Science Journal* 36(1):
    77–92.

Sierra Club. 1993. "A Place at the Table: A Sierra Round Table on Race, Justice, and
    the Environment." *Sierra* 78(3): 51–58, 90–91.

Siler, J.F. 1991. "Environmental Racism? It Could be a Messy Fight." *Business Week*,
    May 20, p. 116.

Small, G. 1994. "War Stories: Environmental Justice in Indian County." *Amicus
    Journal* 16(1): 38–41.

Southwest Organizing Project. 1983. *Intel Inside . . . New Mexico*. Albuquerque,
    New Mexico: SWOP.

Spears, E. 1993. "Freedom Buses Roll Along Cancer Alley." *Southern Changes*
    (Southern Regional Council, Atlanta) 15(1): 55.

Squire, P. 1992. "Legislative Professionalism and Membership Disparity in State
    Legislatures." *Legislative Studies Quarterly* 17: 69–79.

Stretesky, P., and M. Hogan. 1998. "Environmental Justice: An Analysis of Super-
    fund Sites in Florida." *Social Problems* 45: 268–287.

Stretesky, P., and M.J. Lynch. 1999. "Environmental Justice and Predictions of Dis-
    tance to Accidental Chemical Releases in Hillsborough County, Florida." *Social
    Science Quarterly* 80(4): 830–846.

Stigler, George. 1971. "The Theory of Economic Regulation." *Bell Journal of Eco-
    nomics and Management Science* 2(1): 3–21.

Szasz, A. 1994. *EcoPopulism: Toxic Waste and the Movement for Environmental Jus-
    tice*. Minneapolis: University of Minnesota Press.

Szasz, A., H. Meiser, H. Aronson, and H. Fukura. 1992. "The Demographics of
    Proximity to Toxic Releases: The Case of Los Angeles County." Paper presented
    at the meeting of the American Sociological Association, Miami.

Tabachnick, B.G., and L.S. Fiddell. 1998. *Using Multivariate Statistics*. 2nd ed. New
    York: HarperCollins.

Tailman, V. 1994. "Saving Native Lands: One Woman's Crusade Against Environ-
    mental Racism." *Ms. Magazine*, January-February, pp. 28–30.

Taso, N. 1992. "Ameliorating Environmental Racism: A Citizen's Guide to Combat-
    ing the Discriminatory Siting of Toxic Waste Dumps." *New York University Law
    Review* 67(2): 366–418.

Taylor, D. 1989. "Blacks and the Environment: Toward an Explanation of the Con-
    cern and Action Gap Between Blacks and Whites." *Environment and Behavior*
    21: 175–205.

Thomas, J.K., J. Noel, and T. Kodomanchaly. 1999. "An Ecological Study of Demo-
    graphic and Industrial Influences on Cancer Mortality Rates in Texas." *Human
    Ecology Review* 6(2): 32–44.

Truax, H. 1990. "Beyond White Environmentalism: Minorities and the Environ-
    ment." *Environmental Action* 21: 19–21.

United Church of Christ, Commission for Racial Justice. 1987. *Toxic Wastes and
    Race: A National Report on the Racial and Socio-Economic Characteristics of
    Communities with Hazardous Waste Sites*. New York: United Church of Christ.

U.S. Congress. House of Representatives. Subcommittee on Health and the Environment. Committee on Energy and Commerce. 1992. *Impacts of Lead Poisoning on Low-Income and Minority Communities.* 102nd Cong., 2nd Sess. February 25.

_____. House of Representatives. Subcommittee on Transportation and Hazardous Materials. Committee on Energy and Commerce. 1993. H.R. 1924, H.R. 1925, and H.R. 2105: Bills to Amend Solid Waste Disposal Act, The Comprehensive Environmental Response Compensation, and Liability Act, and to establish a program to assure compliance with all environmental health and safety laws, and for other purposes. 103rd Cong., 1st Sess. November 18.

_____. Senate. Committee on Environment and Public Works. 1994a. A Bill to Amend the Comprehensive Environmental Response, Compensation, and Liability Act of 1980, and for other purposes (as reported by the Subcommittee on Superfund, Recycling, and Solid Waste Management). 103rd Cong., 2nd Sess. June 28.

_____. Senate. 1994b. Hearings before the Subcommittee on Superfund, Recycling, and Solid Waste Management of the Senate Committee on Environment and Public Works of the United States Senate. April 12.

U.S. Council on Environmental Quality. 1971. *Annual Report to the President.* Washington, D.C.: U.S. Government Printing Office.

U.S. Department of Commerce, Bureau of the Census. 1981. *U.S. Census.* Washington, D.C.: U.S. Government Printing Office.

_____. 1988. *County and City Data Book, 1988.* Washington, D.C.: U.S. Government Printing Office.

U.S. Environmental Protection Agency. 1987. *Unfinished Business: A Comparative Assessment of Environmental Problems.* Office of Policy, Planning, and Evaluation. Washington, D.C.: U.S. Government Printing Office.

_____. 1992a. *Environmental Equity: Reducing Risk for All Communities.* Washington, D.C.: U.S. Government Printing Office.

_____. 1992b. "Environmental Protection: Has It Been Fair?" *EPA Journal.* Washington, D.C.: U.S. Government Printing Office.

_____. 1993. *Environmental Justice Initiatives.* Washington, D.C.: U.S. Government Printing Office.

_____. 1995. "Relocation of Environmental Justice Office Wins Support from Advocates." *Inside EPA Weekly Report: An Exclusive Report on the U.S. Environmental Protection Agency.* Washington, D.C.: U.S. Government Printing Office, August 4.

_____. Office of Environmental Justice. 1995. *EPA Environmental Justice Monitor—Special Edition.* Washington, D.C.: U.S. Government Printing Office.

_____. 1996. *Waste Programs Environmental Justice Accomplishment Report.* URL: http://www.epa.gov/swerosps/ej/ejaa96/execsum.htm.

_____. 1999. *Brownfields Title VI Case Studies: Summary Report.* URL: http://www.epa.gov/swerosps/ej/html-doc/Report.htm.

U.S. General Accounting Office. 1983. *Siting of Hazardous Waste Landfills and Their Correlations with Racial and Economic Status of Surrounding Communities.* Washington, D.C.: U.S. Government Printing Office.

Ward, B. 1994. "Environmental Racism Becomes Key Clinton EPA Focus." *Safety and Health* 149(3): 183–187.

Waters, Nigel. 1993. "Environmental Discrimination May Merit Study." *GIS World* (May): 74.

Weimer, D.L., and A. R. Vining. 1992. *Policy Analysis: Concepts and Practice.* 2nd ed. Englewood Cliffs, N.J.: Prentice-Hall.

West P.C. 1992. "Invitation to Poison? Detroit Minorities and Toxic Fish Consumption from Detroit Rivers." In P. Mohai and M. Bryant, eds. *Race and the Incidence of Environmental Hazards: A Time for Discourse.* Boulder: Westview Press.

White, H.L. 1992. "Hazardous Waste Incinerators and Minority Communities." In B. Bryant and P. Mohai, eds. *Race and the Incidents of Environmental Hazards: A Time for Discourse.* Boulder: Westview Press.

Wildavsky, A. 1979. *Speaking Truth to Power: The Art and Craft of Policy Analysis.* Boston: Little, Brown.

Wilson, J.Q. 1980. *The Politics of Regulation.* New York: Basic Books.

WIN News. 1992. "The Green Movement for Environmental Justice and Sustainable Economy." *WIN News* 18(4): 20.

Wright, G.C., R.S. Erickson, and J.P. McIver. 1985. "Measuring State Partisanship and Ideology with Survey Data." *Journal of Politics* 47(2): 469–489.

_____. 1987. "Public Opinion and Policy Liberalism in the American States." *American Journal of Political Science* 31(4): 980–1001.

Yandle, T., and D. Burton. 1996. "Reexamining Environmental Justice: A Statistical Analysis of Historical Hazardous Waste Landfill Siting Patterns in Metropolitan Texas." *Social Science Quarterly* 77(3): 477–492.

Zimmerman, R. 1993. "Social Equity and Environmental Risk." *Risk Analysis* 13(6): 649–666.

_____. 1994. "Issues of Classification in Environmental Equity: How We Manage Is How We Measure." *Fordham Urban Law Journal* 21: 633–669.

Zupan, J.M. 1973. *The Distribution of Air Quality in the New York Region.* Baltimore: Johns Hopkins University Press.

About the Authors

James P. Lester, who died in May 2000, was professor of political science at Colorado State University. He received his Ph.D. from George Washington University in 1980 and taught at Texas A&M University, the University of Kentucky, the University of Oklahoma, and Denver University. He lectured extensively on environmental politics and policy at several European universities, including the University of Linkoping (Sweden), Aarhus University (Denmark), the University of Geneva (Switzerland), the Budapest University of Economic Sciences (Hungary), and Humboldt Universitat zu Berlin (Germany). He was a member of the Executive Council of the Public Policy Section of the American Political Science Association (1996–1998), the Executive Council of the Policy Studies Organization (1988–1990), and the Editorial Board of the *Western Political Quarterly* (1990–1993). He coedited *The Politics of Hazardous Waste Management* (Duke University, 1983) and *Dimensions of Hazards Waste Politics and Policy* (Greenwood Press, 1988), edited *Environmental Politics and Policy: Theories and Evidence* (Duke University Press, 1989, 1995), and coauthored *Implementation Theory and Practice: Toward a Third Generation* (HarperCollins, 1990) and *Public Policy: An Evolutionary Approach* (West/Wadsworth Publishing Company, 1996, 2000).

David W. Allen is associate professor of political science at Colorado State University. He received his Ph.D. from the University of Wisconsin–Milwaukee in 1984, has taught at Mercyhurst College in Pennsylvania, and has done postdoctoral work at Amherst College and the University of Houston under both National Endowment for the Humanities and National Science Foundation grants. Prior to his career in academia, he served as a chief aide to statewide government officials in the U.S. Virgin Islands and Puerto Rico, as well as a consultant to federal agencies and major U.S. corporations. He has published research on women in the courts, policy preferences and small group behavior of state supreme court justices, the adoption of everyday life policies in U.S. states, and environmental justice in such journals as *Judicature*, *Justice System Journal*, *Social Science Journal*, and the *Western Political Quarterly*. He also directs internships in conjunction with the British Parliament for American undergraduates and is a published poet.

Kelly M. Hill received her M.A. in political science from Colorado State University in 1996. In 1991, she received her B.S. in journalism from Ohio University. She has served as the public relations coordinator for the Appalachian Ohio Public Interest Campaign and as a legislative aide with the Ohio Legislative Service Commission of the Ohio State Legislature. She served as a policy specialist for the National Conference of State Legislatures. Her issue areas included environmental justice, solid waste management, and energy policy. She is coauthor of *A Legislator's Guide to Muncipal Solid Waste Management* (National Conference of State Legislatures, 1996), *Environmental Justice: A Matter of Perspective* (National Conference of State Legislatures, 1995), and *Tax Implications of Electric Industry Restructuring* (National Conference of State Legislatures, 1998). She is the author of *A Legislator's Guide to Alternative Fuel Policies and Programs* (National Conference of State Legislatures, 1997). Currently, she is working as a freelance writer and teaching in Fairbanks, Alaska.

Index